CULTURAL IDENTITY
AND SOCIAL LIBERATION
IN LATIN AMERICAN THOUGHT

*SUNY SERIES IN LATIN AMERICAN AND IBERIAN
THOUGHT AND CULTURE*

JORGE J. E. GRACIA, EDITOR

CULTURAL IDENTITY
AND SOCIAL LIBERATION
IN LATIN AMERICAN THOUGHT

OFELIA SCHUTTE

STATE UNIVERSITY OF NEW YORK PRESS

Published by
State University of New York Press, Albany

© 1993   State University of New York

For information, address State University of New York
Press, State University Plaza, Albany, NY 12246

Production by M. R. Mulholland
Marketing by Fran Keneston

Library of Congress Cataloging-in-Publication Data

Schutte, Ofelia.
    Cultural identity and social liberation in Latin American thought
/ Ofelia Schutte.
        p.   cm. — (SUNY series in Latin American and Iberian thought
and culture)
    Includes bibliographical references and index.
    ISBN 0–7914–1317–9 (alk. paper). — ISBN 0–7914–1318–7 (pbk. : alk.
paper)
    1. Latin America—History—20th century—Philosophy. 2. Latin
America—Intellectual life—20th century. 3. Identity (Psychology)—
Latin America. 4. Liberation theology. I. Title. II. Series.
F1414.S36   1993
980.03'3—dc20
                                                                91–752
                                                                   CIP

10 9 8 7 6 5 4 3 2 1

For my mother and in memory of my father

CONTENTS

ACKNOWLEDGMENTS

This book is the product of several years' research and a decade-long commitment to developing the study of Latin American philosophy in the United States. The project was supported by a Fulbright Senior Research Fellowship, obtained in 1985 for the purpose of studying the theme of cultural identity in Latin American philosophy at the Universidad Nacional Autónoma de México in Mexico City. Special thanks are owed to the Fulbright Scholar Program and to the Centro Coordinador y Difusor de Estudios Latinoamericanos at UNAM for making the first important stages of this project possible.

A number of individuals have offered their friendship and support during various stages of the project. In particular, I would like to thank my friend and colleague Helen Safa for her generous and persistent enthusiasm for this project over a period of several years. I also owe special thanks to Horacio Cerutti Guldberg, Mary Castro, Amy Oliver, David Crocker, Jorge Gracia, and Andrés Avellaneda for their comments at different stages of the work. The readers of the manuscript for SUNY Press offered valuable criticism and suggestions. I am most grateful to my friend Teresa Jesionowski for her generous and skillful assistance with the manuscript during the copy-editing stage.

Several professional associations have provided an opportunity for the discussion and criticism of ideas related to this study. Principal among them has been the Society for Iberian and Latin American Thought. Other associations where papers related to a number of themes explored in the work have been presented in recent years are the Argentine Association of Women in Philosophy, the Radical Philosophers' Association, the Society for Phenomenology and Existential Philosophy, and the Latin American Studies Association.

The Center for Latin American Studies at the University of Florida and the Latin American Collection at the University of Florida Smathers Libraries have contributed significantly to the success of the project by providing valuable resources and an academic environment where the study could be pursued with efficiency and care.

Lest there be any misunderstanding about the intent of this book, I want to emphasize that it is written in the spirit of a scholarly book and that the philosophical discussion of the theme of liberation pursued herein is offered in the context of a strong personal commitment to peaceful and democratic social change. The responsibility for choosing the themes and sources for discussion has been wholly my own.

I am grateful for permission to use parts of chapter 7, on Latin American feminism, that originally appeared in "Philosophy and Feminism in Latin America: Perspectives on Gender Identity and Culture," *The Philosophical Forum* 20:1–2 (1988–89): 62–84.

Excerpts from *Seven Interpretive Essays on Peruvian Reality* by José Carlos Mariátegui, translated by Marjorie Urquidi, © 1971 are reprinted by the kind permission of the University of Texas Press. Excerpts from Gustavo Gutiérrez, *A Theology of Liberation: History, Politics and Salvation*, translated and edited by Sister Caridad Inda and John Eagleson, © 1973 are reprinted by permission of Orbis Books in Maryknoll, New York, and SMC Press in London, England. The author and publisher are grateful to these publishers for granting permission to reproduce these materials.

INTRODUCTION

The reflections forming part of this study are derived from an effort to understand the relationship between liberation, cultural identity, and Latin American social reality from the standpoint of a historically rooted critical philosophy. Questions of both a personal and an intellectual nature have given rise to this study. Theoretically, I am concerned with exploring the relationships between cultural identity, sociopolitical theory, and social change. In this context, some questions related to the nature of social and political liberation raised by Latin American philosophers have caught my interest. The objective of developing a position of mutual respect and equality in North-South relationships (historically marked by an excess of power in the North and dependence in the South) is one of the goals of these investigations. These theoretical problems are not disconnected from the lives of Hispanics in the United States, who are the most apparent intermediaries between the two cultures. In my own case, as someone bound to reflect on her cultural roots in Cuba, I find it important to analyze some key issues regarding cultural identity and liberation theory in Latin America since these topics provide a bridge from which to gain an understanding of recent Cuban political history. This work, however, will not be about Cuba. It is about the construction of a philosophical perspective on the subject of cultural identity based on concerns expressed by a diversity of political and intellectual movements interested in social liberation within the Latin American continent.

The persistent question, how can one do philosophy from the standpoint of a Latin American interested in liberation from social oppression, has led me to a consideration of three interrelated topics: cultural identity, liberation theory, and feminist thought. The resulting investigation utilizes an individually crafted perspective to analyze small pieces of some rather monumental topics in North-South relations by means of a study of some key issues and texts in Latin American philosophy and social thought.

Methodology

Latin American philosophy tends to be highly self-conscious about the question of methodology. The adoption of a particular methodology can usually be linked to the impact of major schools of European and Anglo-American thought on the continent. For example, the influence of positivism during the latter part of the nineteenth century and reactions against this philosophical school in the early part of the twentieth century have played a large role in the development of Latin American thought.[1] The importance given to methodology as such, however, may be much older—it is very possibly a carryover from the scholastic tradition transplanted into the region during colonial times.

In our own time, the more universally recognized schools of thought rest on accepted and well-defined methodologies. Latin American philosophical Marxism, with its clearly defined subsystems of historical and dialectical materialism, is rigorously methodological. Post-Hegelian historicist perspectives show a strong dialectical orientation, while Christian perspectives on liberation are guided by theological studies for which methodological issues are also of primary importance. The influence of Anglo-American analytic philosophy, with its emphasis on linguistic analysis, clearly stated definitions, and the use of numerous logical distinctions, can be felt in some liberation-minded thinkers. Other schools of thought more explicitly rooted in the Latin American condition show that the use of strictly defined methodologies has often given way to the use of a problem-oriented analysis. For example, some schools of thought pursue an analysis of national identity, while others favor taking, as a point of departure for critical study, a position to which the nineteenth-century Cuban writer José Martí gave the name of *nuestra América* ("our America," as valued by many Hispanics).

From a methodological standpoint, feminist philosophy may follow either a culturally specific or a distinctly feminist-grounded route, depending on whether its object of study is feminist theory as such or the involvement of women in the culturally rooted life of their communities. Feminist academic philosophy, currently at an incipient level in Latin America, is strongly influenced by developments in feminist theory in Spain, Italy, France, and North America. The question of social liberation is much more important to Latin American feminists than that of cultural identity, except for research conducted on the participation of women in social movements, where the specific nature of the participation and the demands put forward are strongly affected by a culture-specific understanding of gender. But there has also been in the past an exclusion of feminist issues from the general philosophical analysis of Latin American cultural identity. (My own use of terms like "man" and "he" responds to the degree to which the theory under discussion retains a masculine-oriented view of reason and history.) One of the aims of this study is to move beyond this limitation. For this shift to occur, however, there must also be a shift of emphasis from an exclusive to an inclusive perspective on the object of study of previously male-dominated genres of philosophical discussion. In particular, the discourse of cultural identity and social liberation needs to be situated within a pluralistic research context. Even the discourse of "alterity" in classical forms of the philosophy of liberation has not been immune from paying insufficient attention to feminism in its analysis of liberation and oppression. Besides calling attention to this omission in Latin American liberation philosophy, the present study seeks to make up for this lack by introducing a research context in which social liberation, feminist theory, and cultural identity perspectives are able to interact freely and thereby influence one another.

Some clarifications are in order so as to avoid misunderstandings of what follows. Not all writers to be examined in this work share the pluralistic theoretical perspective just articulated. It will be seen that, more often than not, grand theories have been constructed to account for an "authentic" interpretation of history or a "correct" version of regional cultural identity. In examining several versions of these theories throughout the twentieth century, my aim is not to provide an even more correct theory that will bring the others under a giant umbrella, as it were, but to note that the concerns for independence, self-determination, and liberation that figure prominently in these accounts from Latin America require legitimate scholarly attention. In other words, while some of the proposed theories may ultimately not be found satisfactory, the problems that generated them are real. Among them are problems related to the search for solutions to the region's economic dependence and for forms of cultural self-understanding felt to be coextensive with autochthonous regional needs. Such problems continue to require a persistent analysis and sustained critical inquiry not only on the part of economists, political scientists, social scientists, and theologians but also on the part of philosophers.

The purpose of this work, then, is not to provide a metanarrative that will address such totalities as "Latin America," "history," "culture," or "liberation" in order to uncover their ultimate meaning. Nor is it to provide a normative analysis of empirically observable cultural formations or social movements according to some rational standard that is supposed to measure the difference between facts and values. Rather, the goal of the investigation is to document and analyze a diversity of intellectual positions and/or movements that, to some extent, have been representative of philosophically significant concerns for "identity" in various parts of the continent since the 1920s. A certain emphasis has been placed on the work of some "classical" interpreters of cultural identity from the standpoint of a variety of debates that have marked the quest for sources of identity during this time period, especially in relation to the issue of social liberation. Thus the work of José Carlos Mariátegui stands out as a classic of Latin American Marxism, the works of Samuel Ramos and the early Leopoldo Zea as classics of the concern for *lo mexicano*, the work of Gustavo Gutiérrez as a classic of liberation theology, and so on. The intent is not to develop the major philosophical characteristics of a particular position—for example, Marxism—from its inception until its current standing but to study a variety of attempts made to give meaning to the complex and, indeed, conflictive nature of Latin America's social reality.

This approach places philosophy—as well as the philosophical study of the Latin American tradition of *pensamiento* (literary, political, and philosophical thought articulated primarily in essay form)—within a distinctly interdisciplinary context. Such an interdisciplinary approach, in turn, serves to provide a certain intellectual "slice" of Latin American social reality, insofar as we encounter a series of diversified cultural formations containing excesses as well as lacunae that fail to fit precisely into the parameters established for disciplinary philosophical thinking. In this sense, a philosophical study situating itself within a certain interdisciplinary space may be able to capture significant elements of the conflictive as well as richly diversified aspects of Latin American social thought. It should be understood that for every perspective selected, many others have been left out and that, as time goes by, new ones yet to be identified will be emerging. The selection of such writers as Mariátegui, Ramos, Zea, Augusto Salazar Bondy, Francisco Miró Quesada, Arturo Roig, and the school of liberation philosophy follows certain canons of Latin American philosophical study. The inclusion of a chapter on feminism is intended to expand the existing paradigms and bring the question of the equality of women to the forefront of the discussion.

The practice of a perspectival critical analysis has been followed throughout the study. The epistemological position embraced herein is closest to Nietzsche's idea of perspectivism—that is to say, this study is interpretive in nature and constitutes one of a number of perspectives that may be given on the subject being addressed. From the standpoint of the process that led to its realization, it was highly motivated by a desire to clarify and distinguish among various theoretical positions on cultural identity bearing a strong component of liberation thinking. There has been a pervasive effort to resist dogmatisms of the Left. What follows is the product of a will to creative inquiry.

A word of warning is in order given the transition period affecting cultural studies today, in particular, the shift from modern to postmodern views of social reality and culture. With only a few exceptions, Latin American philosophy of the sort to be studied in this work tends to be strongly modernist in orientation. This is not surprising, since basic concepts of freedom and justice still requiring implementation in various parts of the continent depend on the notion of an independent, individual subject who is the bearer of various rights and responsibilities in the sociopolitical arena. In the West, the postmodern deconstruction of the subject and of the discourse and logic of identity has often functioned as a critical tool against dominant normative discourses. In particular, postmodernism has helped to open up new conceptual spaces for the introduction of gender and racially diversified perspectives on cultural values in technologically advanced societies. But societies on the way to development cannot dispense so easily with concepts such as those of the subject, consciousness, or identity, for these are needed in order to establish and protect elementary legal and human rights, which cannot always be taken for granted. Postmodern theory is most compatible with the production of art, literature, and film in Latin America, whereas at present the social and political fabric of the various societies in the region is still in need of modern and high modern discourse in order to guarantee certain basic rights and services for variously defined communities and groups as well as individuals.

In this study only a light touch of postmodern influence may be detected. For the most part, this refers to the inclusion of multiple theoretical perspectives throughout the work.[2] One will be able to observe not only similarities but dissonances in the range of perspectives studied. Moreover, the notion of cultural identity that is thematically central to the work is not tied to a metaphysics of identity, as will be made clear in chapter 1, but is to be understood in a process-oriented and transformative sense. Still, the organization of the work is oriented toward bringing ideas together rather than exulting in the power of the fragment. Although I recognize some of the advantages that result from a postmodern critique of identity and its corresponding celebration of differences, in this work I continue to aim at the kind of comprehensive critical analysis that is the legacy of high modern thought.

Challenges to the Study of Latin American Thought in the English-Speaking World

Some comments about the challenges faced by research on Latin American philosophy in the United States are also in order. The study of Latin American philosophy in the United States has so far been conducted by a small group of specialists.[3] Attention has been given to major Latin American philosophers and to problems fitting such established philosophical fields as metaphysics, theory of value, and a humanist anthropology. Many of these valuable studies address issues of cultural identity and liberation from the standpoint of a universally accepted rationality rather than as offspring of Latin American social and political reality. To situate such writings within a culturally specific context, it has been necessary to rely on some empirical studies as well as interdisciplinary work. An interdisciplinary orientation can enrich a philosophical work significantly, especially in cases where the object of study or investigation is a highly complex one, as in the case of social and political philosophy.

The study of Latin American philosophy outside of Latin America responds today to several important concerns, including the increased recognition of and appreciation for the cultural orientations and values involved in philosophical activity, an awareness of the importance of establishing a meaningful North-South dialogue between philosophers in Latin America and the United States, and the desire to recognize the cultural contributions and value of Hispanic individuals and communities within the United States. The recent changes in the world economic and political situation, particularly the creation of the European Community market, will probably lead to the closer integration of economic markets and political alliances between North and South America. For those positions critical of U.S. dominance in the region, a task of primary importance is to establish in North America a base for understanding North-South relations from a standpoint of respect for the cultural traditions of the Latin American and Caribbean region and the right of self-determination of its peoples. In other words, the differences between cultures—as well as the internal diversity to be found within a given culture—need to be respected so that relations between culturally diversified regions and groups will take place on a basis of mutual respect despite the excessive economic power one of the parties may hold over the other(s).

With regard to the study of Latin American philosophy as such, there are numerous challenges and difficulties of an extraphilosophical nature that need to be met and overcome if a research effort of this nature is to be successful. It is important to mention some of them, because the pursuit of philosophy in developed industrial societies is generally free from such exigencies. Economic and political difficulties affecting access to meetings and publications are not uncommon. Knowledge is disseminated differently in developing societies, and a sensitivity to these differences is essential if one is to prepare a study based on the social, economic, and political realities of the region.

For example, researching Latin American thought in terms of its intercontinental dimensions as opposed to its national characteristics (as has more often been done in the past) is a difficult process for which there is no equivalent challenge in the United States or even in Europe. The vastness of the territory and the plurality of nations within the region affect the logistics of communications among scholars, always subject to being adversely influenced by stressful economic conditions that lead to shrinking educational budgets. At the practical level, this means that the publication of manuscripts can be delayed for lack of funds, and books, when printed, may not attain wide circulation. A difficult economic situation often makes it impossible for philosophers to travel to international meetings. Nevertheless, there is a will to keep working and an extraordinary commitment on the part of individuals to advance a life of knowledge even in the midst of adverse or unpredictable circumstances.

Unquestionably, one of the greatest challenges in the construction of a study such as this one has been that of presenting to a North American audience themes, debates, and problems whose original site is deeply embedded in Latin American cultural history. Several issues have had to be confronted. One has to do with the current availability of primary and secondary sources for the North American reader, and to what degree such sources are found in English translation. Fortunately, there is already a corpus of works in translation that makes available to English-language users much of the material addressed in this study. Another challenge pertains to the problem of the selection of potential topics for discussion. Some of the criteria used for selecting certain writers and schools of thought have already been mentioned. Finally, there is the problem of what I would call "transtextuality"—namely, how to transpose (not to be confused with "translate") a given theoretical discussion from one cultural context to another and the degree to which one has to choose between the letter and the spirit of a debate in order to convey its meaning(s) to the contemporary reader in North America.

With respect to this last point, it became clear as I pursued the study that it is not sufficient to reproduce in English a debate that is taking place or has taken place in Spanish. A whole context of references that give meaning to the original may elude the translation. To a certain extent, one needs to approach this problem in the same spirit as one would approach a discussion of Greek or medieval philosophy from a contemporary perspective. There will be both cultural and historical gaps in the discussion, but some concepts can be reactivated and understood in terms of contemporary expectations and values. In the task of applying U.S.-based research to Latin American issues and problems, such disciplines as literature, history, the social sciences, and theology have already elaborated distinctly recognizable genres of scholarly interpretation. My study is oriented toward the goal that the discipline of philosophy will be led to develop further interest in Latin America in the years ahead, a direction it already begins to show at the moment.

SOCIAL LIBERATION, IDENTITY, AND THE RECOVERY OF EARLY MARXIST THOUGHT: PRELIMINARY OBSERVATIONS

Some preliminary considerations regarding the basic theoretical perspectives employed and pursued in this work can help clarify the principal arguments and positions developed in the study. In this chapter I begin by sketching some characteristics of the place occupied by the concept of social liberation within the broader notion of liberation theory as a whole. I then engage in a critical discussion of the notion of identity in order to clarify the way in which the concept of "identity" will be used in this study. The greater part of the chapter deals primarily with some historical considerations that provide a background for the initial set of philosophical themes and problems to be confronted. Of particular interest is the question of the "crisis" of Marxism today and the relevance of reassessing, from a contemporary perspective, some of the thoughts of the first important Latin American Marxist thinker, José Carlos Mariátegui. The chapter is intended to bridge the gap between the current philosophical concerns and interests of an educated North American reading public and the historical beginning point of my study, which is the thought of Mariátegui in the light of the problems facing Peruvian society in the 1920s. This look backward in time and across different cultures as well as differing ideological frameworks is not easy, but also not impossible, to achieve.

Social Liberation

Personal liberation, social liberation, and national liberation are the three major categories within which the topic of liberation arises in Latin American thought. The notion of personal liberation, in the sense of self-development for a life of freedom and creativity, is the outcome of Western humanist thought. This notion may or may not overlap with the sense of personal liberation derived from religious concepts of redemption or salvation. In any case, the accent is on the individual person with his or her freedoms, rights, desires, and hopes. In general, this aspect of liberation theory will not be addressed here, but an exception will be made in the treatment of women's social liberation, which cannot be understood apart from the question of the repression of feminine sexuality and which therefore involves important issues regarding personal liberation. (The absence of an emphasis on personal liberation, however, does not mean that I underestimate its importance.) The focus of my analysis is on the notion of social liberation, understood broadly to include cultural, political, and economic aspects. Social liberation refers to the need to liberate individuals from structures of social oppression, particularly those that create or reproduce inequities due to economic class, sex, race, or national origin. Some of the groups seeking liberation in the context of Latin American social reality are the poor, women, indigenous people, blacks, peasants, and workers.

Social liberation needs to be distinguished from national liberation, which, in the context of leftist politics, is often taken to mean a "second" or "definitive" independence for the Latin American peoples in relation to Western imperialism or neocolonialism. In recent history, the political positions of the Marxist-Leninist government in Cuba, the Sandinista Front of National Liberation (FSLN) in Nicaragua, and the Farabundo Martí National Liberation Front (FMLN) in El Salvador have represented some of the political philosophies of national liberation movements. Such liberation movements are aimed at displacing from political power certain national governments characterized by the liberation groups as governments that for all practical purposes are controlled by U.S. economic and/or military interests. The strategy for implementing these views within a given society may range from the use of armed struggle to the use of peaceful political means. Advocates of leftist national liberation movements argue that true political independence for the Latin American countries cannot be achieved without breaking with the dominance of U.S. economic exploitation of the region. According to their argument, independence must proceed from a popular base that rejects the power of foreign capital over the region. This power has been achieved primarily through the exploitation of people's labor and various other national resources so as to bring profit to foreign capital or select classes within the state. In Latin America, national liberation ideologies have also been found in "national popular" movements and right-wing movements, where the position of "enemy" switches from right to left according to the political entity targeted for destruction. In this study a distinct conceptual line will be drawn between philosophies of social liberation and those of national liberation.

It will be seen from this sketch, though, that in the case of leftist national liberation movements, there is a borderline area between social liberation and national liberation theories where the positions appear complementary, particularly if a democratic path to national liberation is chosen. There are, however, versions of national liberation theories stating that the *only* path to social liberation is through a revolution assuring national liberation, so that the goals of social liberation must take second place to those of national liberation. In contrast to the latter view, I take social and personal liberation as the fundamental goals of liberation, rejecting the argument that *only* a victory at the level of a national liberation movement can guarantee the former. In general, any argument taking the form that "only x can assure the path to liberation" is interpretable as a potentially new form of ideological and political domination. Nevertheless, I regard many specific goals of national liberation movements as not only reasonable but very worthwhile, so long as they are disengaged from an exclusivist claim to truth or justice. When analyzing liberation theory, it is therefore of critical importance to distinguish between the general framework of a theory and its particular claims. Given the overlapping area that in some cases governs the discourse of social and national liberation theories, I want to state clearly that the standpoint taken in this work is one concerned with the theme of social liberation, within the parameters outlined.

As already suggested, the notion of liberation is also used by conservative and right-wing groups to indicate freedom or release from what they take to be oppressive situations and structures. The Far Right also has its theories of national liberation of the people against imperialism. In this case "imperialism" is prefaced by such adjectives as "Western," "Jewish," "Soviet," "Marxist," and so on. Expressions such as "the liberation of the soul before God," "democratic liberation from totalitarian Marxism," and "the liberation of woman for motherhood" are ways of addressing the overcoming of some perceived oppressions in terms of the old-fashioned struggle between Good and Evil. The use of a dualism of good and evil as a basis for liberation theory—whether used by the Right or the Left—will be rejected in this study because of its tendency to result in a dogmatic or authoritarian orientation. The notion of social liberation to be pursued here presupposes "liberation" from such dualistic forms of reasoning.

Included in the types of liberation theory under discussion will be some perspectives on Latin American Marxism, theories of cultural or national identity, the theology of liberation, the so-called philosophy of liberation, and gender theory or feminist thought. Given the limits of time and resources, it is not possible to cover other topics of great interest, particularly the African heritage in Latin American culture. Still, what is said here about indigenous cultures and about the *mestizo* consciousness can be extended to the African heritage, which is an especially important cultural element throughout the Caribbean and in some countries like Brazil.

The "Identity" Issue in Liberation Theory

The "identity" component of liberation theories serves as a definitional factor in the struggle for freedom, self-determination, and social justice. It delineates boundaries between self and other, establishes trails of continuity back to a given origin, and very often creates rational links between the stated origin of the group's values and the goals and actions of its members. Identity can be an "arm" of liberation theory used to reinforce the goals of those struggling against oppression by a hostile or superior force. Yet identity is a powerful concept that can also be used to oppress people. Indeed, it is often used in this negative way. By means of an assigned "identity," people can be manipulated to act in a particular way in conformity with a given role or model. They can be easily rewarded or punished depending on whether they fit or fail to fit the desired role. Given this ambiguity in the use of the concept of identity, which can just as well serve to free up individuals or restrain them in extraordinarily subtle ways, I will explain briefly how one might approach the concept of cultural identity from a critical standpoint.

Cultural identity, like the concepts of ethnic identity or gender identity, can be used to distinguish the positive features uniting a number of individuals around something they hold to be a very valuable part of their selves. In this case, the values upheld refer to a certain cultural heritage to which individuals feel strongly attached by historical and/or affective ties. To speak of a Latin American cultural identity is to define a given system of values intended to preserve and enhance a specific cultural heritage, and to promote, within the international community, an outlook favorable to recognizing the validity and integrity of these values. In the case of the North-South relation holding between the United States and Latin America, to speak of a Latin American cultural identity could also refer to a process aimed at rectifying an imbalance of power between the United States and Latin American countries, which, to a significant extent, puts at risk the cultural production of the latter. In other words, U.S. values "invade" Latin American societies through the media and entertainment industries and through the incessant push to create new markets for North American products. There is no corresponding penetration of U.S. culture by Latin American–oriented values or products. For example, the film industry in both continents is almost entirely controlled by Hollywood.

Some of the paradigms used to defend the integrity of Latin American culture are José Carlos Mariátegui's affirmation of the values of the continent's indigenous pre-Columbian heritage (chapter 2), Samuel Ramos's idea of a Mexican identity rid of resentment and feelings of inferiority toward European culture (chapter 3), Leopoldo Zea's notion of a continental Latin American identity as an affirmation of *mestizaje* (a cultural and/or racial mixture rooted in the region's history), and Arturo Andrés Roig's notion of a cultural legacy (*legado*) subject to critical evaluation and social reform by members of a cultural community (chapter 4). Sources of inspiration for some of these ideas can be found in José Martí's notion of *nuestra América* (our America) and José Vasconcelos's *raza cósmica* (cosmic race).[1] For Martí, "our America" refers to the concept of a Latin America for Latin Americans, a notion charged with important cultural implications whose contemporary political overtones are roughly equivalent to a rejection of U.S. domination in the area. Vasconcelos's metaphysical and rather mystical notion of a universal cosmic race was intended to symbolize the most spiritual evolution of humanity, which the Mexican thinker thought would someday be born from Indo-Hispanic America. The philosophical values attached to notions of cultural identity are very often linked to political movements for self-determination and to *indigenismo* or other expressions of native cultural ties in the arts and literature. The Mexican Revolution of 1910 and the Cuban Revolution of 1959—the latter strongly influenced by the political ideals of Martí—exemplify political struggles that had a significant impact on the arts and literature of the region.

In order to free as much as possible the concept of cultural identity from a dogmatic approach to values, it is important to consider the notion of cultural identity as the result of a freely engaged in, collective interpretive process, always open to modification or transformation on the part of the members of a cultural community. As the Argentine philosopher Arturo Roig has pointed out, there is a cultural legacy into which every individual is born. Having experienced one's personal and social life in terms of this legacy, each individual is also empowered to transform it through the imput of her or his creative work and social praxis. The urgent and critical problem for Latin Americans therefore has to do with salvaging the "weight" of regional cultural formations in view of foreign-imposed conditions for further growth. Various nations in Latin America face a burdensome foreign debt and other economic problems that place significant limits on the development of the cultural vitality of the people. The stunting of regional resources also leads to the "brain drain" of professionals to the North and to the confinement of the popular sectors to the single task of assuring their basic economic survival. All of this exacerbates further the cultural development of the region. It would seem that culture becomes entirely dependent on the movement and accumulation of capital. Just as environmentalists speak of endangered species, so we could speak of endangered cultures.

Thus for liberation theory dealing with the North-South tension there arises the problem of how to assess the weight of European or North American culture vis-à-vis cultures of particular Latin American nations. Advocates of a universal view of reason in history generally hold that the most rational civilization prevails in the end. When their attention turns toward Latin America, they tend to be drawn to the "universal" values found in Latin American philosophy rather than to the philosophical importance of culture-specific values found in Latin American thought. Their respect for a particular cultural formation is only a consequence of the respect for the universality of human reason, with the latter usually defined and understood in exclusively Western terms. Diversity is therefore seen as an offspring of oneness. In contrast, advocates of a cultural pluralism would be more willing to accept the peaceful coexistence of various culturally identified groups without prior appeal to a universal norm that would grant each group its particular legitimacy. According to this view, each group would have access to its own cultural legacy in a relationship of parity and mutual respect toward other groups. If we take the latter approach, it is easier to see that the question of cultural identity cannot be set apart from the question of difference. Difference is a fundamental factor making possible the conditions for identity. "One" is always an abstraction and departure from the rich manifold of experience. Moreover, culture cannot exist without a significant and constant amount of grass-roots activity; it should not be reduced to a definition that is applied normatively from the top down or from the established parts of society to peripheral sectors. If it weren't for the periphery, the center could not exist.

Seen from this context, the question of cultural identity acts as a buffer between models of "liberation" based on the notion of full assimilation of minorities and marginal sectors into the already constituted framework of values of the society at large, and a defense of the particular interests of disadvantaged groups. A favorable weight is given to the knowledge, traditions, and skills possessed by the marginal sectors, in contrast to the tendency of the dominant culture to depreciate or reject their value precisely because they are different or marginal. In short, the standpoint of identity adopted here refers ultimately to a differential reality, not to a centrally controlled regulative force. The "identity" of which I speak here is not derived from a fixed origin, but is a result of multiple configurations always in the process of reorganizing and redefining themselves. In terms of liberation theory, such identities-in-the-making result from a process of selecting endangered or forgotten differences and bringing them to public attention. This involves breaking through the silence imposed on some forms of thought and only subsequently trying to "position" such differences within the general purview of the culture for the enrichment and benefit of all.

One kind of discourse that is breaking out of its imposed silence is that of feminist thought. A feminist perspective belongs within liberation theory but at the same time transforms it. The introduction of this perspective aims at rethinking the nature of the cultural legacy in terms no longer tied to the masculine values characterizing patriarchal thought. Moreover, a feminist perspective guarantees that the needs, desires, and interests of women will be given weight equal to those of men. Until recently, feminism itself has been an underdeveloped area of study in Latin American thought. The prevalent perception is that feminism is alien to Latin American cultural values, which allegedly are tainted hopelessly with machismo: I intend to show, however, that feminist values have strong cultural roots in the region (chapter 7). The major problem in Latin American cultural life is not the absence of great courage, individual creativity, and independence among women, but the public silence that often hovers over women's most intimate vision of the world. Up to the present time the discourses of liberation and cultural identity theory have continued to reproduce for the most part a male view of what it would mean to liberate the region from social oppression. There is a great need to break out of this pattern of cultural interpretation, which assigns the value "cultural identity" to a discourse produced almost exclusively by men, while "gender identity" becomes the specialized province of women's theorizing. Insofar as women are to be considered equal participants in the process of liberation and full participants in the process of the formation of new cultural values, it is essential to incorporate the contribution of feminist perspectives into this branch of Latin American thought.

Historical Roots of Liberation and Cultural Identity

One of the many problems generated by underdevelopment is the lack of an established collective "memory" where the legacy of a society or a people may find its recognizable roots. To compensate for this problem, for example, newly liberated groups shaking off the chains of oppression often make a conscious effort to establish genealogical accounts of their struggles for freedom and justice, showing how these struggles embody a collective meaning and rise above the passing of time. Similarly, in response to skeptics' remarks regarding the so-called nonexistence of Latin American philosophy, scholarly research is careful to point out that more than one generation of thinkers has received recognition in this field both at home and abroad. It should come as no surprise, therefore, that a study such as this one, attempting to encompass a wide spectrum of contributions to the subject of cultural identity and social liberation in Latin America, should also embark on the historically conscious path of theoretical "recollection." Apart from its intrinsic interest, this approach will allow us to refer to a body of knowledge to which we can turn on subsequent occasions as new aspects and implications of this problem are explored.

A loosely structured historical orientation has therefore been used both to aid in the narrative development of the study and to highlight particularly interesting or relevant theories of liberation appearing in the region throughout the last few decades. Following the preliminary observations given in chapter 1, an analysis will be undertaken of José Carlos Mariátegui's socialist anthropology in the 1920s (chapter 2). Chapter 3 will cover selections from the 1930s and subsequent years of Mexican-based studies in cultural identity, as represented primarily by the work of Samuel Ramos and the early Leopoldo Zea. The theme is extended into the second part of the century, especially the decade of the 1960s, which experienced the impact of the Cuban Revolution and the death of Ernesto "Che" Guevara in Bolivia in 1967. During this period we see the debate between Augusto Salazar Bondy and Leopoldo Zea regarding underdevelopment and how underdevelopment affects the existence, productivity, and vitality of a Latin American philosophy.

In the late sixties and early seventies there was a proliferation of liberation-oriented themes among philosophers, Christian activists, and theologians in Latin America. An analysis of some representative works and themes from this broad intellectual movement will be given in chapters 4, 5, and 6. For such philosophers as Leopoldo Zea, the issue of asserting a national identity—which in the early part of the century had a strong impact on cultural identity theory—expanded into that of adopting a continental "Latin American" identity. This perspective is associated primarily with a post-Hegelian approach to the philosophy of history (chapter 4). For others, including the precursors and creators of the theology of liberation (chapter 5), specific issues such as poverty, marginality, and oppression came to represent the point of departure for a contemporary Latin American philosophy. In addition, a "philosophy of liberation" emerged in Argentina in the 1970s, marked by a highly ambiguous and potentially repressive use of the term "liberation." An examination of certain basic arguments offered by "the philosophy of liberation"—as this wing of liberation theory chooses to call itself—shows that some of the positions it advocated carried authoritarian and absolutist elements not wholly incompatible with the use of repressive political force (chapter 6). Finally, the importance of including feminist theory as a component of Latin American perspectives on cultural identity and liberation will be examined. The needs of women in the region for equality and the protection of their basic rights and liberties correspond well with the process of democratization affecting many social and political structures (chapter 7).

The approach outlined is highly selective of the material potentially available to an investigation such as this one. For any one of the major thinkers or issues selected, there is a wealth of related material that could not be covered. The decision to move through different figures and schools of thought, choosing to discuss only a certain fragment of a potentially vast reserve of material, was made so as to emphasize the rich tradition and high degree of interest in liberation thought existing for decades now in the continent. Moreover, it is rare to see a study attempt to incorporate as many different perspectives as are included here. This is due precisely to the richness that each perspective holds on its own and to the internal "loyalties" binding the members of each school to a certain group of intellectual predecessors. Often these loyalties are determined through a form of patrilineal heritage from the "founders" of a certain perspective or school down to the present members. Thus Mariátegui, a journalist and political organizer, has only recently become of interest to mainstream sectors of Latin American philosophy. Past studies of Mariátegui have often linked his thought to that of other early twentieth-century Marxists, to the broader legacy of Latin American Marxism, or to the development of Peruvian thought. A study of Ramos's ideas is usually preceded by an analysis of the work of the Mexican philosophers Antonio Caso, José Vasconcelos, or Alfonso Reyes, rather than by a chapter on Mariátegui's thought. The study of feminism has often been excluded from a discussion of Latin American philosophy and the philosophy of liberation, particularly as these fields are studied in Latin America.[2] The theology of liberation until most recently has not been given a status of paramount importance within the study of Latin American philosophy.[3] Each tradition has followed its own "founders" and discourse in a relationship more or less parallel to other traditions. The different traditions are brought together here because they all speak to basic philosophical queries related to a critical assessment of Latin American social reality. All of them provide special insights on approaches to liberation theory.

The Crisis of Contemporary Marxism and the Relevance of Mariátegui's Work

Of special interest to the study of Latin American cultural identity and liberation is the thought of José Carlos Mariátegui. His thought is often considered to lie at the margins of philosophy, but in some respects this very fact only adds to its interest. Though marginal to philosophy, Mariátegui's thought occupies a central place in the history of Latin American Marxism. He becomes a suitable candidate for inclusion in this study because a study of liberation theory should not do without some analysis of Marxism, and Mariátegui holds one of the most original Marxist positions in the history of the continent. Moreover, his views, while not always completely persuasive, are most interesting for our time. The so-called crisis of Marxism today should not deter us from an appreciation of the works of Mariátegui. If we think of Marxism as being in a crisis today due in large part to its separation from the will of the people and to its pursuit of a dogmatic rather than pragmatic approach to social reality, then there is much to be learned from a thinker such as Mariátegui. Leninist in his day but remarkably unorthodox in his philosophical orientation, Mariátegui showed a strong preference for ideas associated with William James, Bergson, and Nietzsche. His thought symbolizes the openness, creativity, and innovativeness with which Marxist ideas can be applied to an analysis of Latin America's specific problems. He is regarded as someone who had an exceptional understanding of the specific needs of his native land.

Mariátegui's popularity among a wide variety of intellectual and political sectors—including critical Marxists, historians of Peruvian thought, literary critics, and revolutionary Marxists—reached a peak in the 1970s and early 1980s. In *Marxist Thought in Latin America*, Sheldon Liss remarks: "No Latin American Marxist receives more acknowledgment of intellectual indebtedness than José Carlos Mariátegui."[4] Michael Löwy calls him "undoubtedly, the most vigorous and most original [Marxist] thinker from Latin America."[5] Mariátegui's legacy is claimed by both Leninist and critical Marxists. For example, the Argentine writer José Aricó, a sharp critic of Marxist dogmatism, calls Mariátegui's *Seven Essays* "the only theoretical work which is really significant for Latin American Marxism" half a century after its publication.[6] A recently published Cuban anthology, *Marxistas de América*, refers to him as "the first figure of Marxism-Leninism in our continent, both in terms of the sharpness and quality of his expression and the profundity of his thought."[7] Perhaps because of the untimely appropriation of his name by the extremist group Sendero Luminoso of Peru, there is less attention focused on Mariátegui today than there would be otherwise. This circumstantial factor, however, shall not deter or hinder me from engaging in an analysis of his thought.

Mariátegui's Position within Marxist Theory

With the political changes in the world today, Mariátegui's thought acquires new relevance. His thinking, however, was very

much a part of the political realities of his day. In order to understand its theoretical context, a look at some of the conditions out of
which it sprang is necessary.[8]

Born in 1894 in the southern part of Peru, he came from a
modest background. He was raised by his mother, a woman of
partly Indian origin. When he was eight years old, an injury left
him crippled in one leg. As a teenager, Mariátegui began to work
as a linotypist's assistant for a major newspaper in Lima. He
worked his way up in the newspaper business, eventually becoming a well-known journalist and editor. Most of his writing was
done for publication in newspapers and political journals, including the cultural and political review *Amauta* (1926–30), of which
he was founding editor.[9] In 1924 Mariátegui suffered a significant
personal blow when a major illness forced the amputation of his
left leg. Confined to a wheelchair for the remaining years of his
short life, he continued to write, edit, and engage in labor organizing. In 1928 he founded the Socialist party of Peru. He died in
1930, at the age of 35.

Mariátegui's complete works fill several volumes, but during
his lifetime only two of his books appeared in print, *La escena con-
temporánea* (1925) and *Siete ensayos de interpretación de la realidad peruana* (1928).[10] The latter, his masterpiece, is actually a collection of seven essays (as the title indicates) that were published
earlier as journal articles. The study was not intended as a nar-
rowly conceived "objective" account of Peruvian social reality.
"Once again I repeat that I am not an impartial, objective, critic,"
he states in the preface to this work. "My judgments are nourished
by my ideals, my sentiments, my passions. I have an avowed and
resolute ambition: to assist in the creation of Peruvian socialism. I
am far removed from the academic techniques of the university."[11]

Though not a scholar by profession, Mariátegui's learning
was exceptional, particularly in view of the fact that he was self-
taught. He himself attributed his most important "schooling"
(*aprendizaje*) to the circumstances surrounding a three-and-a-half
year tour of Europe from 1920 to 1923. He visited several countries, including France and Germany, but for the most part he
lived in Italy, where he pursued his work as a journalist. It was in
Italy that he made two very important commitments—one personal—he married—and the other political—he became a Marxist.
Contemporary Marxist scholars argue that the most important
theoretical influence on him during his stay in Italy came from the
Gramscian publication *L'ordine nuovo*. (There is much speculation

about the unresolved issue of whether Mariátegui knew Gramsci.)[12] He was also highly influenced by the philosopher Benedetto Croce, whom he knew personally, and who encouraged Mariátegui to study the work of Georges Sorel. Mariátegui associated freely with the European political and literary avant-garde wherever he traveled, establishing a rich network of acquaintances within leftist circles in France, Italy, and Germany. At the time, the Left was reading Nietzsche, Freud, and Unamuno as well as Marx and Engels. Mariátegui imbibed this spirit and brought it back with him to Peru, where his main task, as he put it, was to assist in the creation of an Indo-Hispanic socialism.

Mariátegui's Interpretation of Peruvian Economic Reality

Mariátegui turned to socialism as a solution for Peru's economic and social problems because he judged that capitalism would not be able to help his country develop out of a "feudal" type of backwardness. In particular, he wanted to see different living conditions for Peruvian workers and peasants. Though critical of capitalism, he also modified the existing conception of socialism. First, he argued for the incorporation of peasants, not just workers, into the socialist movement. Second, he observed that the majority of Peruvian peasants were of indigenous origin, which lent a special character to Peru's national reality that was altogether missing from European societies. Mariátegui's appreciation of the Peruvian indigenous heritage led him to place an accent on the respect for the cultural diversity of the region and on political organizing based on grass-roots coalitions rather than on centrally controlled, foreign-dominated political parties.

Mariátegui reasoned that the choice of a capitalist model of development in Peru could not offer any realistic solutions for the indigenous peasants, who constituted the majority of the population. Linking the exploitation of the Indians to Peru's "feudal" agrarian economy, he argues that despite Peru's liberal constitution, the exploitation of the Indians remained intact:

The agrarian problem is first and foremost the problem of eliminating feudalism in Peru, which should have been done by the democratic-bourgeois regime that followed the War of Independence. But, in its one hundred years as a republic, Peru has not had a genuine bourgeois class, a true capitalist class. The old feudal class—camouflaged or disguised as a republican bourgeoisie—has kept its position.... The old land-holding class has not lost its supremacy. The survival of the *latifundistas*, in practice, preserved the latifundium.[13]

His basic argument is that the democratic-liberal path to economic and political development in Peru had never been strong enough to dislodge older patterns of land use and peasant exploitation. Liberalism as such could not solve the nation's problems.

Linked to this analysis, Mariátegui offers a second argument for which he has become renowned: the key to the solution of Peru's problems is tied to the liberation of the Indian peasants, and socialism is the most appropriate contemporary system to meet the Indians' needs. He places the argument in support of socialism side by side with the argument for the liberation of the Peruvian Indians:

> In keeping with my ideological position, I believe that the moment for attempting the liberal, individualist method in Peru has already passed. *Aside from reasons of doctrine* [emphasis added], I consider that our agrarian problem has a special character due to an indisputable and concrete factor: the survival of the Indian "community" and of elements of practical socialism in indigenous agriculture and life.[14]

His capacity to value what is different from the norm ("aside from reasons of doctrine") allows him to note in this case the positive features of the indigenous presence in the land. With this view he stands in sharp contrast to those who view the same presence negatively or project upon the Indians a role alien to the historical and cultural development of the region.

Thus his understanding of socialism was quite different from the normative one in which a Western paradigm of scientific progress is superimposed on a given reality in the name of a higher truth. With its unquestioned concept of "science" derived from a linear interpretation of history, such an approach would merely supplant capitalist with socialist economic policies, without regard for grass-roots-level knowledge gained from centuries of experience. Yet, to Mariátegui, the Indians' relation to the land appeared sufficiently "socialist" that he fought to rescue and preserve its meaning.

At the political level, Mariátegui resisted adopting a one-sided approach to social liberation. He believed in working with a united front.[15] On his return to Peru, he collaborated with Víctor Raúl Haya de la Torre, an important leader of the Alianza Popular Revolucionaria Americana (APRA), a leftist political movement. The Apristas promoted the notion of a nationalist anti-imperialist movement, a cause Mariátegui supported. But, from his standpoint, the Apristas represented primarily the interests of the national bourgeoisie.[16] When they began to change the status of their organization from that of a "movement" to that of a political party, Mariátegui broke with them and founded the Socialist party of Peru (*Partido Socialista Peruano*). Arguing against the Apristas, he charged that there was a link between a nationalistic (capitalist) anti-imperialism and racism. The racism of this nationalist sector consisted in a tendency to value foreign capital over the needs of the majority of the Peruvian people, who were not white. In "Anti-imperialist Point of View," a paper delivered by the Peruvian delegation to the first Latin American conference of the Communist International in 1929, Mariátegui argued that the Peruvian bourgeoisie identified primarily with "white" values and did not feel it shared a common culture and history with the rest of the Peruvian people, whose ancestors were Indian. This meant that the anti-imperialist identity to which the Apristas appealed could only be one of words, not deeds. "They pretend to situate themselves at the level of the economic struggle, yet in reality they appeal particularly to racial and sentimental factors."[17] Noticing that a genuine anti-imperialist movement should not be founded either on nationalistic or racial sentiments, Mariátegui argued that a class analysis was needed to identify the cause of Peru's economic problems. In other words, the national bourgeoisie could not act to resolve the country's problems because it was bound to find the power of foreign capital much more attractive than the needs of Peru's own *mestizo* and Indian population.

Thus, Mariátegui realized that the cultural values tilted in the direction of capitalism were loaded with racial values that underestimated the civilizing potential of indigenous cultures. Yet, one might ask, can socialism understand this problem and situate itself on the side of what is indigenous? It would seem that, politically, socialism cannot do so without breaking with foreign control over regional parties (the type of control exercised by Moscow at the time). Moreover, and most ironically, socialism could not appreciate the contribution of an indigenous heritage of the sort valued by Mariátegui without assimilating a large dose of antipositivist Western thought, often labeled "irrationalist" by traditional

Marxists. Mariátegui's conception of socialism therefore challenged ruling Marxist orthodoxy both politically and ideologically.

Mariátegui's Political Activity

As noted, in 1928, after splitting with Haya de la Torre over the issue of how to constitute the national movement against imperialism, Mariátegui founded the Socialist party of Peru. He sought to have this party affiliated with the Third International. His proposals for the constitution of the Socialist party, however, met with little sympathy from this group.

A study by the Peruvian Marxist Alberto Flores Galindo of the relationship between Mariátegui and the Comintern offers some helpful information. Flores Galindo notes that even in 1927 the International was not aware of Mariátegui's work. When he and some other intellectuals were arrested for a brief period that year, accused by the government of promoting a communist conspiracy (charges denied by Mariátegui), the telegrams sent in solidarity with the group came from distinguished writers and intellectuals like Gabriela Mistral, Alfredo Palacios, José Vasconcelos, Manuel Ugarte, Waldo Frank, and Miguel de Unamuno.[18] After a delegation of Peruvian workers was invited to participate in a workers' congress held in Moscow in May 1928, Mariátegui received an invitation to attend the First Latin American Syndicalist Conference and the first Latin American Communist Conference, held in Uruguay and Argentina, respectively, in 1929. He could not attend either meeting because of his poor health. Yet at the Buenos Aires meeting, two of his papers, "The Problem of the Races in Latin America" and "Anti-imperialist Point of View," were presented by the Peruvian delegation.[19]

Among the discrepancies between the views of Mariátegui and the Third International were issues related to the local autonomy of the Peruvian party and the composition of its membership. Flores Galindo notes that "the positions of the Peruvian representatives were very much criticized by the IC [Communist International]."[20] Flores Galindo refers to three major discrepancies: the desire of the Peruvians to ground their position in a historical appreciation of the social conditions of the Andine region, as opposed to adopting a Eurocentric notion of Marxism; the understanding of the role of intellectuals as organic, rather than officialistic or bureaucratic; and the issue of the constitution of the party. With respect to the latter point, Mariátegui's Socialist party was formed around the idea that a political vanguard would unite and lead a diversity of progressive regional groups, in contrast to the idea of a Communist party with a predefined identity imposed uniformly from abroad on all Latin American countries.

These points raise the question of the meaning of a Latin American political Marxism as conceived by Mariátegui and subscribed to by his Peruvian colleagues. Flores Galindo points out that Mariátegui's position shows a new way for Latin American Marxists.

> Our way was not the European way. This is why Mariátegui situates himself on a radically different plane of analysis and reflection: in contrast to both the Apristas and the orthodox Communists, the problem [for him] was not how to develop capitalism (and therefore repeat the history of Europe in Latin America), but rather how to follow an autonomous way. From this it can be concluded that without the connection with the poets and essayists of the indigenist school and without the rural uprisings, Mariátegui's Marxism would lack a crucial trait: his challenge to [capitalist] progress and his rejection of the linear and Eurocentric image of universal history.[21]

Up to a point Flores Galindo understands Mariátegui's critique of the European ideology of progress, but he forgets to note how indebted Mariátegui was to other forms of European and even North American thought, including Bergson's philosophy of creativity and William James's pragmatism. These influences would make Mariátegui's thought just as controversial among traditional Marxists as his grass-roots orientation and indigenist perspective would scandalize the Stalinist-dominated Comintern.

An insightful perspective on Mariátegui's political Marxism is offered by the Argentine writer José Aricó. From a standpoint critical of orthodox Marxism, Aricó notes that the debate regarding the name of the party Mariátegui insisted on calling "Socialist" rather than "Communist" had important theoretical and political implications.

> The socialist definition of the party was not a simple problem of nomenclature. It was linked to (1) a particular conception of [political] alliances; (2) a decision that diverged from the Comintern in terms of the party's class components, insofar

as it wanted to be the political organ of Peruvian workers, peasants, and intellectuals; (3) a rather heterodox vision of its process of constitution, in that its leadership, rather than being the cause, ought to be the result of grass-roots activity in the different centers of the country. This explains why, until the end of his life, Mariátegui insisted...on the socialist, popular, and autonomous character of the new organization.[22]

Aricó's analysis confirms the point made earlier about the concept of identity to be pursued in my analyis of liberation, which takes identity as a result of a life-oriented process of activity, rather than a fixed origin or point of departure that must be duplicated indefinitely for the identity to hold. If Aricó is right, Mariátegui's concept of a socialist political identity would stand out in sharp contrast to top-down notions of identity imposed by doctrinaire parties on their members.

With his life-oriented concept of socialism, which still merits significant consideration today, Mariátegui was fighting an uphill battle, whose successful conclusion was not to be attained in his lifetime. A month after his death, the Socialist party, led by its newly elected secretary Eudocio Ravines, changed its name to the Communist party. Ironically, Ravines, who did everything in his power to destroy Mariátegui's influence during his term of office, was expelled from the Party in the 1940s. He later became an anti-communist propagandist.[23] In contrast, the brilliance of Mariátegui's work has withstood the years as a testimony to his rich, controversial, and dynamic vision of society.

The European Avant-garde and a New Vision of Peruvian Reality

Mariátegui's claim that a liberal, individualist perspective was one whose "time" had passed for Peru appears to be derived in large part from his political experiences in Europe in the early 1920s. He never subjects his postindividualist perspective, however, to a rigorous, critical examination. Three theoretical-political influences appear to be combined in it—one derived from a Leninist revolutionary orientation in Marxism, another from the rise of the fascist movement in Italy, and yet another from the literary avant-garde. Fascism, which he opposed, was strongly anti-individualistic. Leninism, interpreted by Mariátegui as postindividualistic, has operated historically as an anti-individualist and antiliberal force rather than as a postindividual or liberal force. This leaves one category, that of the literary avant-garde, as the most probable source of inspiration for Mariátegui's open-minded, antinormative Marxism. Let us explore for a moment this aspect of Mariátegui's thought, which is rarely understood in connection with his capacity for producing a truly original interpretation of Latin American social reality. His remarks in the preface to the *Seven Essays* shed some light on this problem.

Highly unusual about the *Seven Essays* are the opening comments in which Mariátegui expresses a very strong affinity with Nietzsche. This Marxist book, celebrated as the most original and profound of its time by fellow Marxists, is headed by a Nietzschean aphorism from the period of *The Wanderer and His Shadow*: "I will never again read an author of whom one can suspect that he *wanted* to make a book, but only those writers whose thoughts unexpectedly became a book."[24] What does this mean? Mariátegui seems to be referring to an intentional and goal-oriented rationality that, as the organizational structure of a text, is displaced by a grouping of thoughts assembled together by virtue of some other principle. The element of spontaneity is mentioned by Mariátegui, but one could equally talk about the creative drives of the unconscious or perhaps even an existential imperative. Mariátegui is more explicit in the body of the preface, where he refers once again to Nietzsche as an author whose spirit of literary creation is interlaced with his own:

> I bring together in this book, organized and annotated in seven essays, the articles that I published in *Mundial* and *Amauta* concerning some essential aspects of Peruvian reality. Like *La escena contemporánea*, therefore, this was not conceived of as a book. Better this way. My work has developed as Nietzsche would have wished, for he did not love authors who strained after the intentional, deliberate production of a book, but rather those whose thoughts formed a book spontaneously and without premeditation. Many projects for books occur to me as I lie awake, but I know beforehand that I shall carry out only those to which I am summoned by an imperious force [sólo realizaré los que un imperioso mandato vital me ordene]. My thought and my life are one process [Mi pensamiento y mi vida constituyen una sola cosa, un único proceso]. And if I hope to have some merit recognized, it is that—following another of Nietzsche's precepts—I have written with my blood [Y si algún mérito espero y reclamo que me

sea reconocido es el de—también conforme un principio de Nietzsche—meter toda mi sangre en mis ideas].[25]

He understands his creativity as an author as a uniquely personal expression of his passion for life—"I have written with my blood." In *Thus Spoke Zarathustra* Nietzsche had stated: "Of all that is written I love only what a man has written with his blood. Write with blood, and you will experience that blood is spirit."[26]

To some extent, the conception that "authentic" writing emerges from the author's life force, without being subjected to an intentional "cut" redirecting the energy to the satisfaction of a self-consciously teleological reason, is analogous to the conception of the relation between the Spanish conquest and pre-Columbian civilization presented in the very first sentence of the *Seven Essays*.

> The degree to which the history of Peru was severed by the conquest can be seen better on an economic than on any other level. Here the conquest most clearly appears to be a break in continuity. Until the conquest, an economy developed in Peru that sprang spontaneously and freely from the Peruvian soil and people. The most interesting aspect of the empire of the Incas, which was a grouping of agricultural and sedentary communities, was its economy.... With abundant food their population increased. The Malthusian problem was completely unknown to the empire.... Collective work and common effort were employed fruitfully for social purposes.[27]

He goes on to say that the Spanish destroyed this carefully built economic system without being able to replace it with anything better. The conquistadors were concerned primarily with what made them wealthy. They plundered the temples and used up the land at will, without any regard for the indigenous society and economy they were dismantling. The disintegration of the indigenous society that resulted from the conquest left the nation fragmented and unable to recover a strong economic system. Mariátegui's vision emerges from a Marxist perspective, but its significance is much broader than that of Marxism. In particular, his view of the conquest as a "cut" into a non-Western self-sustaining economy of material wealth based on attachment to the land as "mother" reveals some affinities Mariátegui has with postmodern feminists and Nietzsche in the treatment of such concepts as continuity, abundance, and violence.

To describe the history of Peru as that of a land-based community of indigenous people whose living continuity was severed by the "cut" of an external conquering force is to situate oneself "before the cut," that is, before what postmodern discourse might call the (violent) entry of Western logocentrism into the cultural economy of the continent. Postmodern feminist writers also situate themselves before a cut, in this case that of phallocentric discourse. Nietzsche, too, claims that his writing responds to impulses existing before a cut; in this case the cut represents the logical restriction of artistic impulses carried out by a "Socratic" conception of existence. The conquest, phallogocentrism, and Socrates respectively symbolize the economic usurpation of a living, material, voluminous wealth conceived without boundaries (e.g., Mariátegui's non-Malthusian indigenous community, Luce Irigaray's notion of a feminine "sex which is not one," and Nietzsche's notion of the Dionysian).[28] If such a position "before the cut" is to be taken as the starting point of a cultural critique, one would assume that the notion of connectedness, continuity, or proximity would have a very strong place in the critic's perspective. The connectedness of the Indians to the land and of the writer to his lived experience are two figural themes found at the outset of Mariátegui's study. The indigenous economy before the conquest—an economy "that sprang spontaneously and freely from the Peruvian soil and people"—is analogous to the author's thoughts that gather themselves spontaneously into a book, following a model highly reminiscent of Nietzsche's notion of free spiritedness.

The conquest therefore does not represent for Mariátegui a higher step in civilization reaching the Americas—as it did to Marx and Engels—but an interruption of the living continuity of pre-Columbian culture by usurpers. He points especially to the subsequent destruction of the Inca culture and the fragmentation of the remaining elements that survived the onslaught and plunder. Mariátegui also emphasizes that the Spaniards were not able to replace what they stole from the people. In his view, the Western logos that has been used to justify the European expansion to the Americas is not entirely valueless, but nevertheless it is not deserving of our unconditional support. The philosophies of creativity and the unconscious, the Jamesian affirmation of the will to believe, the European literary avant-garde, and the Peruvian literary current of *indigenismo* were interconnected, interrelated perspectives for Mariátegui, because he saw in all of them an intellectual or artistic resistance to the plundering effects of the Western rational machine.

With respect to the relation between the people and the land, Mariátegui's alternative to the political organization imposed by the conquest is found in the concept of a new regionalism. Today his concept of regionalism could be updated and expanded to include important ecological concerns. In his discussion of regionalism and centralism, Mariátegui begins by defining a region in a way that resists a bureaucratic or conventional understanding of the term. "A region is not created by a government statute. Its biology is more complicated," and its roots are more ancient than the nation itself.[29] "No intelligent regionalist," he remarks, "would claim that the boundaries of regions coincide with our political organization, that is, that 'regions' are 'departments.'"[30] "Department" is "a political term that does not designate a reality" but primarily "a convention that only satisfies a functional need or criterion of centralism."[31] For this reason, Mariátegui states that he cannot conceive of a regionalism that only condemns centralism and does not proceed further to question the territorial divisions established by the central authority. Municipal autonomy as such cannot be the end of a new concept of regionalism. The region is prior to the municipality and must embrace the particular heritage of a community. For example, in Spain and Italy regions are clearly differentiated by "tradition, character, people, and even language."[32] Peru in turn consists of three regions demarcated by its "physical geography": the coast and the sierra, along which the population is distributed, and another mountain area still lacking a specific social reality. Mariátegui's respect for diversity and for regional "cultural habitats" could be expanded today to include a special concern for the region's corresponding natural habitats. Such natural habitats can easily be described within his theoretical terms as material life-support systems for land-based communities.

Last, Mariátegui, though a regionalist, was in no sense a separatist. "The historical purpose of decentralization is to encourage not secession but union, not to separate and divide regions but to assure and perfect their unity within a more functional and less forced association. Regionalism does not mean separatism."[33] It would seem from this that he holds that a nation is founded on an association of people with interconnected regional traditions acquired after long years of residing in a particular physical or geographical environment. This might explain why for him the indigenous population of Peru forms the core of the country's national identity, in contrast to the "Western," "bourgeois" conception of the same territory, which identifies the nation only with the values and interests of a minority dominant class. Moreover, Mariátegui holds that the land should belong to the Indians and should belong to them communally, for, prior to the conquistadors' "cut," they were the occupants (and, by religious belief, the children) of the land.

Mariátegui's Reconciliation between Artistic Free-Spiritedness and Marxist Commitment

In Mariátegui's use of Marxism one may see a combination of three factors: his conception of Marxism as a science, as a faith, and as an aesthetic impulse stimulating the artistic, creative side of what is otherwise considered a political process. It is not easy to discern these three interactive levels of Mariátegui's Marxism, since he himself never outlined them—their union was probably "spontaneous" for him. Most important, their constitution is difficult to discern because, also probably without intending it, he broke many conventional rules to get there.

Mariátegui's concept of Marxism as a science is highly indebted to the Italian philosopher Benedetto Croce. In *Defensa del marxismo*, a series of articles appearing in *Amauta* in 1928–29, he explicitly borrows from Croce several key notions identified as the core of Marxism.[34] Most important of these is the view that, from a historical standpoint, Marxism is a theory designed exclusively for the critique of society as it exists under capitalism. "Historical materialism is not, precisely, a metaphysical or philosophical materialism, nor is it a philosophy of history, left behind by scientific progress. Marx had no reason to create anything more than a method of historical interpretation for [analyzing] actual society."[35] Marxism should not be seen as a philosophy of history without qualification, but only as a "method of historical interpretation" most relevant for the period in which capitalism is the dominant economic system. It is, in other words, an interpretive method that allows us to understand the root causes of certain major (structural) social problems and to envision the dawn of a transition to a more just social system. Historical materialism is not to be confused with philosophical materialism.[36] From these premises, the conclusion may be drawn that it is possible to use the theory of historical materialism without being a philosophical materialist. The separation of Marxism as a critical theory of the capitalist social order from Marxism as a philosophy of the cosmos allows much space for the kind of coalition work Mariátegui believed in. For example, one could be religious and at the same time accept a Marxist critique of capitalism as an economic system. Indeed, the theology of liberation developed at the end of the 1960s and the actual cooperation of Marxists and Christians in recent political liberation movements demonstrate this well. Most significantly, one could be a Marxist without accepting dialectical materialism as a universal science. In fact, one could be, philosophically, a pragmatist, or a Bergsonian, without this implying a contradiction within Marxist theory or "doctrine." Marx himself was only a Hegelian because of a historical accident:

> Whereas Marx was not able to base his political plan or conception of history in De Vries's biology, Freud's psychology, or Einstein's physics—just as Kant, who, for his philosophical development, had to be content with Newtonian physics and the science of his time—subsequent...Marxist intellectuals [have] not ceased to assimilate the most substantial and active [elements of] post-Hegelian or postrationalist philosophical...speculation.[37]

Thus, for Mariátegui, the contemporary state of the sciences and the arts enhances a philosopher's theory, while in another sense it delimits it, since there can always be a further evolution in human knowledge. It was his view that Marxism should be kept alive by the latest developments in scientific theory and in the world of contemporary culture, and that a shift in philosophical outlook from dialectical materialism to contemporary and even avant-garde conceptual models is not incompatible with Marxism but on the contrary can enliven it. "Vitalism, activism, pragmatism, relativism," he writes, "none of these philosophical currents, in what they could contribute to the Revolution, has remained at the margin of the Marxist intellectual movement.... This ought to give some food for thought to certain...philosophers who are full of rationalist prejudices and superstitions."[38] As mentioned earlier, if alive today Mariátegui would have much to discuss with postmodern writers.

Not having recourse to today's strategic critique of logocentrism, Mariátegui turned to the principal avenues of supplementing (not deconstructing) reason available in his day: art and "faith." He understood well that William James's "will to believe" could have as its object a political commitment rather than a religious faith. Indeed, his own spirit was moved by the belief in the transformation of Peruvian society and the "redemption" of the Indians through a social revolution. This brings us to the second important aspect of Mariátegui's Marxism—his conception of Marxism as a faith. Borrowing this view from Croce and particularly from Sorel, he wrote, "Vain are all attempts to classify [Marxist criticism] as a simple scientific theory, when it works in history as a gospel and a means of mobilizing the masses."[39] From this perspective, Mariátegui takes seriously the contributions of psychoanalysis, James's "will to believe," and various other explanations of the power of belief in human life. This aspect of his Marxism, though, has a negative side, since it is linked to Sorelism and to an overoptimistic assessment of Lenin. When this perspective has the ascendance in his thinking, his writing becomes excessively rhetorical, as in the following typical statement of his views: "Sorel, so influential in the spiritual formation of Lenin [a claim denied by Lenin], elucidated the revolutionary socialist movement...in the light of Bergsonian philosophy, continuing [the work of] Marx who, fifty years earlier, had elucidated it in the light of the philosophy of Hegel, Fichte, and Feuerbach."[40]

Last, the aesthetic dimension of Mariátegui's Marxism relates the art of creating a revolution to the revolutionary power of art. For him, creativity itself contained a revolutionary potential. For example, at a time when moralistic Marxists were condemning Joyce, he praised Joyce for his extraordinary depiction of Stephen Dedalus in *A Portrait of the Artist as a Young Man*. He also referred in passing to the "colossal novel *Ulysses*, persecuted in England by an Inquisitorial puritanism."[41] The *Seven Essays* concludes with a long chapter on Peruvian literature, and *Amauta* contains a literary and artistic (usually indigenist) design that relieves the focus on "doctrine." The "shape" given to the *Seven Essays* is not dissimilar to the one he would have preferred giving to his political organizing: a loose confederation of ideas—or, in politics, a coalition of groups brought together from within the society rather than by means of an external, teleologically directive force (e.g., the Party central command). I think the question that baffles most readers of the *Seven Essays*—namely, why does Mariátegui begin with Nietzsche and not with Marx or Engels as a proper Marxist ought to do?—finds its answer in the type of aesthetic position he held: in short, his passionate, open-ended, life-affirming, creative style.

Mariátegui's work does not lack some important limitations. It is not my intent to depict him as a flawless thinker or, worse yet, a kind of political saint. In the interest of pursuing some of the more philosophically significant positions of this nonphilosopher's thoughts, I shall concentrate my analysis on what could be called his "socialist anthropology." From this perspective we shall enter the Latin American continent in the 1920s. Before us lies the Peruvian and European scene, as described through Mariátegui's prose.

MARIÁTEGUI'S SOCIALIST ANTHROPOLOGY

In this chapter, I will analyze three major aspects of Mariátegui's socialism: its roots in an existential and left-Sorelian view of the universe, its conception of a socialist ethics, and its contribution to the creation of an Indo-Hispanic socialism. The existential, ethical, and sociopolitical dimensions of Mariátegui's Marxism, on the whole, constitute what I would call a "socialist anthropology." The discussion of these themes, meant to be selective rather than all-inclusive in character, is based on an analysis of three important texts: *El alma matinal* (1923–25), from Mariátegui's early Marxist period, and *Defensa del marxismo* (1928–29) and *Seven Interpretive Essays on Peruvian Reality* (1928) from his late period. The chapter concludes with a few observations on the unfinished character of Mariátegui's thought, due to his untimely death in 1930 at the age of thirty-five. A tentative balance is drawn regarding the accomplishments of Mariátegui's vision of socialism in relation to gaps or ambiguities found in his theory, which are of special relevance today.

El alma matinal: Existential Dimensions of Mariátegui's Thought

The existential dimensions of Mariátegui's thought—his perceptions of the place of human beings in the universe and in history—can be found in a series of articles published in the posthumous work *El alma matinal*.[1] These articles, considered part of Mariátegui's "early" work by Marxist supporters who frown on his Bergsonian and Sorelian ideas, were published only three to four years prior to the more definitive *Seven Interpretive Essays* and *Defensa del marxismo*.[2] Significantly, they demonstrate how Mariátegui's thought is grounded on a metaphysical view of human nature, one of whose principal components is the will to believe. This position gives him a rather unique place within Marxism

insofar as he rejects both positivism and a purely atheistic interpretation of existence. He opts instead for a perspective sympathetic to vitalism, pragmatism, and existential thought.

The four brief articles (a few printed pages each) in *El alma
matinal* are entitled: "Two Conceptions of Life" ("Dos concepciones
de la vida"), "Man and Myth" ("El hombre y el mito"), "The Final
Struggle" ("La lucha final"), and "Pessimism of Reality and Optimism of the Ideal" ("Pesimismo de la realidad y optimismo del
ideal"), the last a phrase borrowed from the Mexican philosopher
José Vasconcelos. Within the context of a social critique of the contemporary cultural scene, Mariátegui addresses such existential
themes as the meaning of life and the "will to believe." He also
pursues what he takes to be the contrast between bourgeois and
Marxist conceptions of existence. These four articles appear under
a section entitled "The Emotion of Our Times" ("La emoción de
nuestro tiempo").

The title of the book, *El alma matinal*, refers to the rising
spirit of the times (the first postwar period), a spirit he linked to
the dawn of day. Building on the contrast between decadence and
new life, a common theme of the period, Mariátegui works with
two images (*alma, matinal*). *Alma* refers to the soul or principal
emotion of the age. *Matinal* relates this emotion to a feeling of
activity and vigor, in sharp contrast with the "twilight" spirit of
melancholy and lament for a life-style of the past.[3] Mariátegui
comments on the shift in the European spirit away from the feeling of "twilight" conveyed by Anatole France and Gabriele
D'Annunzio and toward an idealization of the dawn.[4] Mariátegui is
keen on describing the mood behind major political movements of
the period, as evidenced by the use of such metaphors.

In his introduction to this work Mariátegui depicts ironically
the fascists' appropriation and exploitation of the dawn metaphor
in the service of their political objectives:

Mussolini sends Italy to bed at 10:00 P.M.; he closes the
cabarets and bans the Charleston. His ideal is a provincial,
peasant Italy, rising at dawn, free from effeminacy and urban
artifices, with many rustic children on its broad lap. By his
decree, as in the days of Virgil, the poets sing to the country,
the seed-time, the harvest. And the French bourgeoisie, in
love with tradition and work —the laborious bourgeoisie, eco-
nomical, measured, continent (not Malthusian)—also claims
for its household the fascist schedule. It dreams of a dictator

with Roman virtues and Napoleonic genius who would culti-
vate his corn field and vineyard during his free time.[5]

This idyllic picture, however, soon gives way to a discussion of
what becomes the major theme of his articles, namely, the "emotion" that appeared to be moving both fascists and bolsheviks to
action at this time.

As a journalist, Mariátegui's accent is on portraying the
actors in the sociopolitical panorama he liked to call "the contemporary scene." He does not often engage in an extensive analysis of
their ideas. This gives his work a distinct advantage when it comes
to describing the "style" or "image" presented by various thinkers,
writers, and political actors of the age. But it leaves him vulnerable to the thoughts of those whose emotional or stylistic delivery
he finds especially attractive. For this reason, it will be noticed
that at times Mariátegui will show an extraordinary enthusiasm
for certain ideological positions that, from our perspective, appear
to be philosophically unsubstantiated, though as images of the
contemporary scene they are, no doubt, exceptionally compelling.

"Two Conceptions of Life"

Fascism, as Mariátegui came to know it in Italy, was not a
phenomenon alien to Western culture but an aspect of some of its
accepted political expressions. Fascism had an immediate presence
in society and it exerted power over large numbers of people. It is
instructive to observe the kind of appeal this ideology can exert,
especially among those whose feelings are swayed by its soul-grip-
ping, extremist rhetoric. In "Two Conceptions of Life," Mariátegui
positions fascism alongside bolshevism, both displaying the "postwar" emotion of the age—an emotion prone to exult in what is
heroic, daring, and violent, in contrast to what is measured, cautious, and reasonable.[6] In Mussolini's words:

It is not worthwhile to live, as men and as members of the
party, and, above all, it would not be worthwhile to call ourselves fascists, if one did not know that one is in the midst of
a storm. Anyone is capable of sailing in a benign sea, where
the winds inflate the sails, when there are no waves or
cyclones. What is beautiful, what is great, and I would like to
say what is heroic, is sailing when the tempest intensifies. A
German philosopher used to say: live dangerously.[7] I would
like this to be the word of command for the young Italian fas-

cist movement: to live dangerously. This means to be ready for anything, for any sacrifice, for any action, when what is at stake is defending the fatherland [*patria*] and fascism.[8]

This type of rhetoric also excites the spirit of many revolutionaries, although their political aim is different. Bolsheviks and fascists stand out in contrast to the more moderate members of the political Right and Left, whom Mariátegui considers unwilling to take any political risks:

> The program of all these people is condensed in one word only: normalization. Normalization would be the return to a quiet life, the driving away or the burial of all romanticism, of all heroism, of all quixotism of the Right and of the Left. [They wish to know] nothing of returning, with the fascists, to the Middle Ages. Nothing of advancing, with the bolsheviks, toward Utopia.[9]

The combative style of fascists and bolsheviks seems to indicate an important characteristic of the "emotion" of the first postwar age. There is in this emotion something of a reckless and defiant spirit that, to a certain extent, the young Peruvian found attractive. This will help explain the correlative need, at the ethical level, for a morality of self-discipline and collective order, which, as will be seen, he would endorse some years later in *Defense of Marxism*.

Of special interest to a philosophical analysis of Mariátegui's thought is his assessment of how the postwar spirit penetrates into epistemology, destroying all rationalist formulas. In this context, a new formula, "I struggle, therefore I exist," comes to replace the Cartesian intuition of self-certainty.[10] Mariátegui comments:

> The philosophical formula for a rationalistic age had to be "I think, therefore I am." But this romantic, revolutionary, and quixotic age can no longer use the same formula. More than any thought, life today wants to be action, combat. Contemporary man has need of a faith. And the only faith that can occupy his profound self is a combative one. Who knows when the times of living sweetly will return? The sweet prewar life generated only skepticism and nihilism. And from the crisis of this skepticism and this nihilism, there is born the rude, tough, peremptory need for a faith and a myth that will move human beings to live dangerously.[11]

All this implies that Marx, Nietzsche, and Sorel speak the language of the new age, as opposed to modern philosophy from Descartes to positivism.

When reading this article—and Mariátegui's work in general—one should keep in mind that he died in 1930. For example, it would be difficult for anyone today (except for admirers of fascism) to view this movement as heroic. His observations regarding the postwar spirit are better understood if taken as a direct commentary on intellectual and political influences he encountered in France and Italy in the early 1920s, especially among left-wing Sorelians. A recent study by Jack Roth has documented the prevalence among such Sorelians of the view that bolshevism and fascism constituted the new vital forces of the time in contradistinction to the parliamentary forces of social democracy.[12] This left-wing Sorelian view is the one expressed by Mariátegui in "Two Conceptions of Life." Of special interest to Mariátegui's readers is the fact that the journal *Clarté* (whose editor, Henri Barbusse, was one of Mariátegui's European contacts) went through a Sorelian phase from 1922 to 1925 under the editorship of Édouard Berth. Berth typifies the left-Sorelian perspective Mariátegui adopts here. In *Les derniers aspects du socialisme* (Paris, 1923)—a book found in Mariátegui's collection—Berth argued, among other things, that Lenin was a Sorelian and Nietzschean hero.[13] As Roth's study shows, Berth and others who held similar views modified them within a few years as historical developments led them to be critical of fascism and/or Soviet Marxism. Thus the 1920s was a period in which the sharp ideological divisions between East and West characterizing later European developments in the twentieth century had not yet been established. This could also explain Mariátegui's use of the historical categories "prewar" and "postwar" as a reference point for his discussion of new ideological movements.

Although Sorelism is said to have died out gradually after the 1930s, what stands out about the twenties and thirties is the degree to which Sorel, an ideologist of syndicalism, influenced his contemporaries—including two figures as different as Croce and Gramsci. Part of what made Sorel so attractive was the ambiguous way in which he combined an old-fashioned regard for sacrifice and virtue with a critique of capitalist stagnation. To many he seemed to offer the hope that a new era would emerge as a result of a moral struggle for justice carried out by the organized working class. Mariátegui, for example, often appealed to Sorel when he wished to argue on behalf of legitimate new approaches to Marxism. The distinction between Sorelism, fascism, and Marxism was not drawn as sharply as might be expected in this period.[14] The ethical significance Sorel attributed to the workers' struggle was seen by left-wing Sorelians such as Mariátegui as complementary to the political concept of class struggle advocated by revolutionary Marxism. Right-wing Sorelians, on the contrary, used the ethical perspective advocated by Sorel to distance themselves from a Marxist analysis of social change.

Another point of overlap between Sorel's and Mariátegui's views is the critique of positivism. From an epistemological standpoint, Sorel was a strongly antipositivist thinker. Like many of his contemporaries, he found in Bergson's theory of creative evolution an alternative to positivist thought. Yet Sorel's critique of positivism is more rhetorical than it is substantial. Sorel combined the ambiguities of his ethical position with an antirationalist view of knowledge.

> The positivists, who represent, in an eminent degree, mediocrity, pride, and pedantry, had decreed that philosophy was to give way before *their science*; but philosophy is not dead, and it has acquired a new and vigorous lease on life thanks to Bergson, who...has claimed for the philosopher the right to proceed in a manner quite opposed to that employed by the scientist. It might be said that metaphysics has reclaimed the lost ground by demonstrating to man the illusion of so-called scientific solutions[15]

Despite his praise for Bergson, however, Sorel was neither a Bergsonian nor a metaphysician. He was interested primarily in using Bergson's ideas as a tool for his notion of the historical triumph of syndicalism. Sorel's rejection of positivism and his adoption of intuitionism are therefore remarkably superficial.

> Use must be made of a body of images which, *by intuition alone*, and before any considered analyses are made, is capable of evoking as an undivided whole the mass of sentiments which corresponds to the different manifestations of the war undertaken by Socialism against modern society.... The Syndicalists solve this problem perfectly, by concentrating the whole of Socialism in the drama of the general strike;...everything is clearly mapped out, so that only one interpretation of

Socialism is possible. This method has all the advantages which "integral" knowledge has over analysis, according to the doctrine of Bergson.[16]

Thus Sorel uses Bergson to strengthen the case for his own views and render all other conceptions of socialism meaningless.[17] His primary concern is to advocate the need for both capitalists and workers to believe in the catastrophic event of a general strike as a method for renovating what he takes to be the decadent state of Western civilization. Sorel condemned humanist and democratic reforms within capitalism and argued that humanity could only advance if capitalism became more ruthless and syndicalism more violent. As will be shown, Mariátegui, though a great admirer of Sorel, disagreed with this last point as well as with various other aspects of Sorel's extremism.

"Man and Myth"

In view of the crisis of reason diagnosed by philosophers and thinkers widely read in the early part of the century, such as Nietzsche, Sorel, and Bergson, what does Mariátegui propose as an alternative? In "Man and Myth" he comes closest to expressing his synthesis of a socialist perspective on civilization and a metaphysical approach to the human condition. "Neither Reason nor Science can satisfy all the need for the infinite there is in man," he argues. "Reason itself has taken care of showing men that it is not sufficient for them—that only a myth possesses the precious virtue of filling their profound self."[18] Yet—and here he inserts his socialist (Sorelian) argument—"bourgeois civilization suffers from the absence of a myth, a faith, a hope." The hope in reason has resulted in the paradoxical situation that reason cannot offer any hope. Thus rationalism is only capable of deconstructing itself in an ironic reversal of its own premises. "Rationalism has served only to discredit reason."[19] If reason, narrowed down to a positivistic technicality, cannot offer human beings hope, where else can they look for it?

Mariátegui's tendency is to search for meaning in art, metaphysics, and politics. Regardless of the conclusions drawn by positivism, he insists that "man, as philosophy defines him, is a metaphysical animal."[20] One cannot live creatively without a metaphysical conception of life. Moreover, holding a position that was also Nietzsche's, he emphasized that without a myth, human existence lacks a historical meaning. "History is made by men possessed and illumined by a superior belief, by a superhuman hope; the rest are the anonymous chorus of the drama." In spite of the all-pervasive skepticism brought about by bourgeois civilization, contemporary human beings feel an "exasperated and sometimes impotent 'will to believe.'"[21] In the absence of the belief in God as an objective certainty, the will to believe or the quest for meaning itself becomes the ultimate affirmation of life. It did not occur to Mariátegui to consider that the class emotions described by him might be contingent and could be reversed at some future time if, for example, the bourgeoisie regained its self-confidence or the working class ceased to link its hopes to the belief in revolutionary change.

As he saw it, the bourgeois and the revolutionary "spirits" of the epoch coexisted side by side, one skeptical and incredulous, the other fully believing in the possibility of a social change. For example, Ortega y Gasset referred to a "disenchanted soul" (el alma desencantada), while Romain Rolland wrote of "the enchanted soul" (el alma encantada). "Which one of the two is right?" Mariátegui remarks. "The 'disenchanted soul' of Ortega y Gasset is the soul of the decadent bourgeois civilization. The 'enchanted soul' of Romain Rolland is the soul of the creators of the new civilization."[22]

Mariátegui goes on to identify the spirit of the social classes represented by Ortega and Rolland in their respective visions of reality. In one of the most often quoted passages from his work, he states:

What most genuinely and clearly differentiates the bourgeoisie and the proletariat in this epoch is myth. The bourgeoisie no longer has any myths. It has become incredulous, skeptical, nihilistic. The liberal Renaissance myth has grown too old. The proletariat has a myth: the social revolution. Toward this myth it moves with a vehement and active faith. The bourgeoisie denies; the proletariat affirms. The bourgeois intelligence entertains itself with a rationalist critique of the method, the theory, the technique of revolutionaries. What a lack of understanding! The power of revolutionaries is not in their science; it is in their faith, their passion, their will. It is a religious, mystical, spiritual power. It is the power of myth.[23]

Mariátegui does not cite Nietzsche in this article, although he could have. Perhaps the categories Nietzsche employed to set forth an analogous thesis regarding the power of myth and the decadence of contemporary European civilization—such categories as the "Dionysian," "Apollonian," and "Socratic"—were too far removed from political reality to satisfy Mariátegui.[24] Nietzsche's typology was not sufficiently politicized in terms of the juxtaposition between bourgeois and working-class values. Nietzsche himself had been an opponent of socialism, although many socialists of the period interpreted his quest for a new human type as compatible with their values.[25] Although Mariátegui acknowledged his debt to Nietzsche in the preface to the Seven Essays, in the concluding paragraphs of "Man and Myth" he refers only to Sorel, Bergson, Renan, and Marx. The passage he cites from Sorel's Reflections on Violence is especially appropriate for justifying the relation between socialism and the will to believe. He quotes Sorel as saying:

An analogy has been found between religion and revolutionary socialism. It proposes the preparation and even the reconstruction of the individual for a gigantic work. But Bergson has taught us that not only religion can occupy the region of the profound self; revolutionary myths can do likewise.[26]

From an existential and psychological standpoint, Mariátegui considered socialism the bearer of a life-affirming social myth that responded to the human being's intense will to believe in something transcendent. He felt that such a myth was absent from the bourgeois ideology of the period. Thus he developed the notion of a very strong link between historical change and the beliefs generated by a powerful social myth or analogous vision of reality.

Contrary to Sorel but without explicitly criticizing him by name, Mariátegui formulates a different view of the revolutionary social myth as well as of the social sectors that will benefit from it. Sorel's myth, the general strike, was meant to strengthen both workers and capitalists through the sharp separation and violent antagonism developed between the two classes. Mariátegui's myth, the social revolution, was to strengthen the workers, students, progressive intellectuals, and, most notably, the Indian peasants of Peru (the marginal ethnic sectors) by uniting them in the belief that they could create a new, more egalitarian society. In order to understand this important difference between Sorel and Mariátegui one must take a closer look at each thinker's use of the concept of myth.

Sorel uses the idea of the social myth to rule out perspectives rather than to open new options. As noted, he argues that Bergson's principal contribution was to debunk scientific reasoning. This elevates the syndicalist myth of the general strike by giving it the status of an intuition governing rational analysis. Moreover, Sorel himself depicts the illusion of the general strike as "catastrophic." He thinks the middle class will react to this imagined catastrophe by becoming more brutal and shedding its humanistic values. At the same time that the middle class becomes more brutal, it will be clearer to the workers that they must use violence to destroy the capitalist order. By "violence" Sorel simply means the use of force for the benefit of the majority. Violence is directed against the institutional use of force, including the law, whose object in bourgeois society, he claims, is to benefit a minority. In Sorel's account violence is always legitimated not only because it is a necessary means for obtaining benefits for the majority but because it is a morally purgative activity. It renovates the spirit and leads it to act heroically. If one combines these ideas, the result is a position that denounces reformism (both on the side of capitalists and that of workers), announces the compelling belief in the general strike as a strategy for instilling terror in one class and hope for a victory in the other, and promotes the sharpening of oppositions between capitalists and workers, whose purest and most essential form will take place through the use of violence. Epistemologically, reasoning is ruled out as a tool for understanding reality in ways not mediated by the Sorelian intuition. At the same time, on an "ethical" plane, violence is consecrated as the highest manifestation of nobility, while the general strike and steps leading to it are regarded as the highest expressions of violence.

Mariátegui's conception of the social myth differs from Sorel's in various respects. Although the Peruvian author speaks of the working-class struggle as heroic, he does not merely select certain classical virtues like heroism and apply them to the working class. He does not use the myth of the social revolution as a way to terrify one class or inspire another. His use of the "myth" is linked to the birth of a new type of consciousness. The myth of the social revolution *results* from this new consciousness, a consciousness through which people are united rather than separated, as in Sorel's case. In particular, the myth operates to unite all who wish to contribute to the new society. It transcends rigid class distinctions. Most importantly, it incorporates the forgotten mass of Peruvians, the descendants of the Incas. Finally, in Mariátegui, the concept of nation is not formed prior to the myth of the general strike, as it was in the case of Sorel's France. The nation is something to be forged through the new consciousness and through the myth of the social revolution. Failure to incorporate the Indians into the social revolution would merely duplicate conditions prior to the social transformation in terms of the "national" (white, colonialist) ideology to which the working class is exposed under capitalism.

The contrast between Sorel's and Mariátegui's concepts of the social myth shows that Mariátegui's position is both creative and revolutionary, whereas Sorel's is authoritarian and conducive to right-wing ideologies. Sorel insisted on masculinist, "ethical" justifications of heroism and violence; he sought the myth of the general strike as a tool to induce cruelty on the part of the capitalists and violence on the part of the workers. The end result of Sorel's myth is the revival of European civilization along ideological lines dear to many who embraced fascism. In contrast, the end result of Mariátegui's myth is the creation of a new society that would respect the previously denigrated cultural traditions of Indo-Hispanic, marginal sectors in a developing country. Before undertaking an analysis of this portion of Mariátegui's contribution—which is elaborated in more detail in his later works, such as the *Seven Essays* and *Defensa del marxismo*—some comments will be offered on two other essays from *El alma matinal*.

The Concept of Struggle

The insights developed in "Two Conceptions of Life" and "Man and Myth" are developed in the next two essays of this collection, "The Final Struggle" and "Pessimism of Reality and Optimism of the Ideal." It was mentioned earlier that Mariátegui did not question whether the alleged skepticism of the bourgeoisie or the predisposition for belief in a great social change on the part of the working class referred to a contingent and reversible or to a necessary and irreversible situation. In "The Final Struggle," however, he does object to the view that the phrase *la lucha final* (from the Communist "International" anthem) would have to be taken literally. The final struggle, he explains, is "at the same time, both a reality and an illusion."[27]

We are dealing here with the final struggle of an epoch and of a class. Progress—or the human process—is fulfilled stage by stage. Therefore, humanity always needs to feel itself close to a goal. The goal of today will surely not be the goal of tomorrow; but, for the human theory in action, it is the final goal.

The messianic millennium will never arrive. Man arrives in
order to depart anew. He cannot, however, do away with the
belief that the new journey will be the definitive one. No revolution foresees the revolution which will come after it,
although it bears its seeds within itself. For man, as the subject of history, there is nothing but his own and personal reality. He is not interested in struggle in the abstract but in his
concrete struggle. The revolutionary proletariat, therefore,
lives the reality of a final struggle. Humanity, meanwhile,
from an abstract point of view, lives the illusion of a final
struggle.[28]

Mariátegui argues that if humanity is represented concretely in the
revolutionary working class, for example, then the social revolution
is its final struggle; but, if humanity is considered abstractly, then
there is no final struggle—only a series of struggles, for individuals
and groups, that, at each historical stage, appear to be "final." This
perspective of perpetual creation and self-overcoming is very much
related to Nietzsche's idea of life as will to power (expressed in
Thus Spoke Zarathustra), as well as to Bergson's view of creative
evolution. Perspectivism is introduced into a Marxist historical
analysis through the suggestion that "the final struggle" to which
the "International" refers is an illusion in which human beings
believe in order to give meaning to their political action.

Mariátegui's existential, antipositivist perspective at times
reminds us vividly of Nietzsche's critique of the Socratic type in
The Birth of Tragedy. In the concluding paragraph to "The Final
Struggle," Mariátegui argues that the impulse to live precedes the
impulse to think. Life (and with it, its necessary complement,
myth) comes before philosophy. Thinking means doubting, a pause
before the necessary action. In contrast to the philosopher and the
literary man, the nonliterary man of the multitudes lives by
instinct, not concerned about the relativity of his myth. "Since he
must act, he acts. Since he must believe, he believes. Since he
must fight, he fights.... His instinct does not lead him astray into a
sterile doubting."[29]

Thus, epistemologically, Mariátegui comes very close to an
existential critique of the inability of reason to reach an absolute
truth, while he also affirms the will to believe in a myth one can live
and die for, in order to give life a fundamental purpose and meaning.
These existential themes—which, as we shall see, also connected
him to the ancient Inca myths of his native land—do not lock him

either into an exclusive preoccupation with individual salvation or liberation, as one finds in much of the Western religious tradition, or into a life of retreat from the world (an ascetic perspective on existence), as one finds in Eastern mysticism. While Mariátegui held that one does not find the ground of Being by knowledge but by faith, this faith is one that inspires action in the social sphere. Not finding strength in philosophy as epistemology, he turns to find strength in ethics, specifically, in theories and practices that focus on the strengthening of the will. In "Pessimism of Reality and Optimism of the Ideal," he concludes: "In the new generation, there burns the desire for overcoming the skeptical philosophy. In the midst of the contemporary chaos, the materials for a new mysticism are elaborated.... 'Those who are strong are determined and fight'— says Vasconcelos—'with the goal of anticipating to some extent the work of heaven.' The new generation wants to be strong."[30] From a theoretical perspective, Mariátegui sees the special strengths of the new generation as incorporating the existential, intuitive strengths of a Bergson or a Nietzsche with the revolutionary, dialectical strengths of a Marx, within a tradition of culture and a field of action that is specifically Latin American.

Before moving on to the Indian question, it is important to review Mariátegui's conception of "Ethics and Socialism" in *Defense of Marxism*. The political application of his existential notion of strength is best seen through his development of the theory of the morality of producers in this work and the specific study of the agrarian Indian question in the *Seven Essays*.

Ethics and Socialism

If not founded on a theory of the rational agent, ethics in Mariátegui's theoretical framework is founded on a socialist anthropology. Such a socialist anthropology has two dimensions— the human being, conceived as a thinking and acting (feeling, struggling) being, and the human project of creative production, conceived in its widest sense as the project of creating a new society. Here we find again the two components of "man and myth"— the human being and the creation of the new society that is the concrete objective result of the social revolution. One must make clear, however, that the *understanding* of such a human being and society is mediated through a new consciousness for which the meanings of "human being" and "society" inherited from the past no longer apply.

From the previous examination of Mariátegui's existential perspective in *El alma matinal,* we know that the human being on which Mariátegui founds his socialist anthropology is not one divided between thought and action, or between thinking and feeling, or between living (existing) and struggling for a more *human* world (in the sense of "human" just noted). One might begin to unravel the relevance of Mariátegui's perspective by raising the question of why it is preferable to understand the human being as a unity of thought and feeling rather than as a composite or combination of both. Why is it that all of these functions—thinking, acting, feeling, struggling—should be equally descriptive of what it means to be human? Wouldn't it be preferable, for example, to have a division of labor and a hierarchical control of more and less valuable functions within the human self in the manner proposed by Plato in the *Republic?* There is a resistance to change this model of what it means to be human, just as there is a resistance to give value to the unconscious. It has been an important part of the Western legacy to distinguish the human species in terms of its rationality and to raise or lower the value of all other human faculties and activities precisely in relation to their proximity or distance from reason.

The principal exception to the preceding model in mainstream Western thought has been that proposed by religion, which views faith as higher than reason.[31] In this case, however, the body and the passions are often considered evil, if not of relatively less value than the soul, and the believer who takes on commitments in the secular world has also been considered less perfect than the contemplative or ascetic type. Religion and philosophy have produced a divided (if not dualistic) view of the self and thus have contributed to the fragmentation of human consciousness. There is one place for faith, another for reason, another for imagination, perception, feeling, passion, action and struggle, and so on, in our ordinary philosophical conception of the human being. Like Plato, Aristotle, Aquinas, and Descartes, we still tend to favor the belief in a specialization of functions and a hierarchy of values according to which the highest value is given to those human faculties, such as thinking, which are (or are thought to be) most distant from other forms of life and from the material universe. Human beings give themselves value by means of that which makes them most distinct from their own bodies and their environments. From the time we are very young we learn to disengage thinking from action, willing from feeling, and reasoning from imagination.

These habits are reinforced especially if we are destined to move into such higher echelons of cultural activity as education, government, or the arts. Moreover, in industrialized Western societies, we gradually learn to dislike speaking in a united voice (with others), just as we learn to take pleasure in speaking as individuals.

Mariátegui's spirit symbolizes the opposite impulse, that is, he represents an impulse toward unity. It is remarkable that even after he was confined to a wheelchair Mariátegui continued working on major intellectual and political collaborative projects, such as the journal *Amauta* and the formation of the Socialist party of Peru. This type of activity represents his anthropological vision of the human being whose thought cannot be divorced from action. The types of project he generated were also meant to unite the voices and efforts of a wide range of individuals from different social and economic classes. Most importantly, he was deeply concerned about the project of creating one nation—Peru—out of the fragmented ethnic elements and cultural traditions that in his day kept the population segregated into privileged and marginal sectors according to race and class.

Mariátegui's vision of the human being raises the question of whether the classless society which is the goal of Marxism does not influence significantly the image of the type of human being who would create and inhabit such a social environment.[32] In both Western and Eastern traditions, cosmological worldviews and visions of what constitutes social harmony have had some impact on what is thought to constitute a stable and harmonious state of being in the self. This type of theoretical problem does not fit exactly under the category of ethics in the narrow sense but in a space positioned somewhere between religion, ethics, and social psychology. Nevertheless, this space must be given a name if we are to discuss the ideas for social evolution developed in and through its perspective. It is not altogether inappropriate to situate the concern for a new consciousness of the relationship between human beings and social world under the title of ethics. From this special standpoint derived from a broader meaning of ethics, Mariátegui's conception of the relationship between socialism and ethics will be analyzed.

Ethics in *Defense of Marxism*

Some ethical dimensions of Mariátegui's socialist anthropology are developed in chapters 6–8 of *Defense of Marxism* under the headings "Ethics and Socialism," "Marxist Determinism," and "The Heroic and Creative Sense of Socialism." In this doctrine-conscious text, he tries to apply his ethical conception of the active human being engaged in creative production to the class-specific notion of a socialist workers' ethics. This more applied aspect of Mariátegui's ethical perspective is not as interesting as the moral outlook derived from his anthropological and metaphysical views. The notion of ethics tends to be subordinated here to that of class struggle, while the notion of struggle is no longer defined in the relative sense outlined in *El alma matinal*. Even in this politically oriented work, however, Mariátegui begins his discussion of a socialist ethics with a set of references to Croce's idealist interpretation of *Capital*. Alternative metaphysical frameworks to materialism are explored as he elaborates an ideology of class struggle.

In his discussion of ethics and Marxism, Mariátegui appeals repeatedly to Croce's insights, first noting that the Italian philosopher is "one of the most authoritative representatives of philosophical idealism."[33] As reported by Mariátegui, Croce argues that although Marxism does not develop a philosophical ethics as such, it is not devoid of moral principles. Some of the reasons offered by Croce as to why ethics does not assume a more prominent status in Marx's thought are the following: according to Marx's materialism, social problems cannot be resolved by "moral" means; bourgeois morality is characterized by class prejudice and hypocrisy; and, not insignificantly, Marx inherited from Hegel a dialectical method focused on problems other than those of moral philosophy. Nevertheless, Marx's conception of socialism and his critique of capitalism are based on inherent moral assumptions. In Croce's words:

> It is evident that the ideality and absoluteness of morality, in the philosophical sense of these words, are necessary conditions for socialism. Isn't it perhaps a moral or social interest—however one wishes to call it—that moves us to construct the concept of surplus value? In pure economics, can one speak of surplus value? Doesn't the proletariat sell its labor power for what it is worth, given its situation in the present society? Without this moral assumption, how could one explain, next to Marx's political action, the tone of violent indignation or bitter satire observed on each page of *Capital*?[34]

Mariátegui also points to Croce's view that the absence of a developed ethical theory in a political philosopher such as Marx is theoretically irrelevant: "It would be the same as to reproach someone who does research in chemistry for not going back to basic research in metaphysics."[35] But Mariátegui moves quickly from theoretical to political issues, arguing that ethics is a basic component of socialist practice. As he develops this last point—which remains unstated in his exposition—it becomes clear that, as he sees it, one of the most important places where ethics and socialist practice converge is in the workers' movement.

In this context, the influence on Mariátegui of Sorel's idea of the morality of producers becomes evident. For example, Mariátegui states that "the ethical function of socialism...should not be sought in grandiloquent decalogues or in philosophical speculations...but in the creation of a morality of producers formed in the very process of the struggle against capitalism."[36] In particular, he endorses Kautsky's view that "the ethic of the proletariat emanates from its revolutionary aspirations."[37] This type of position may be read at face value as a complete subordination of ethics to political activity (of a certain type). Nevertheless, there is another reading, from an anthropological standpoint, that may be given simultaneously, especially in view of the concept of the unity between thought and practice to which Mariátegui subscribed. In this broader sense, the basic idea put forward by Mariátegui here is that a socialist morality is not composed of socialism plus morality, just as the human being is not composed of body plus mind, but that there is a living unity in the morality of socialism, with a strong interrelationship occurring between a moral perspective and socialist practice.

Despite the broader meaning that may be given to this text, however, it is ethically troublesome that in ordinary life Mariátegui's broad view of the human being in action may end up justifying narrow party politics. Mariátegui did not see that in addition to a class critique of morality there needs to be a sharp moral critique of party dogmatism (which he failed to undertake in Defense of Marxism). Otherwise, the process of social liberation easily becomes stagnated, and new forms of alienation come to replace the old. For example, if bourgeois morality is hypocritical, so-called socialist moralities may suffer from the same or similar problems, that is, certain patterns of behavior may be required in socialist systems for a person to be accepted socially. This may easily lead to equally hypocritical behavior. Any time a "politically correct" or "socially accepted" standard of behavior is strongly reinforced with sanctions, one risks losing the margin of freedom necessary for conditions favoring social liberation.

With respect to the notion of a socialist morality, as well as to that of a socialist work ethic, Mariátegui was overly optimistic, as perhaps is the case with his vision of socialism in general. In another instance, for example, he follows Pietro Gobetti, a left-Sorelian contributor to the Marxist publication *L'ordine nuovo*, in thinking that the capitalist factory environment will so act on the worker's psyche as to strengthen his socialist morality. According to Gobetti:

> The factory offers the precise vision of the coexistence of social interests: the solidarity of work. The individual gets used to feeling [that he is] part of a productive process.... Here is the most perfect school of pride and humility.... A rhythm of life based...on the sense of tolerance and interdependence leads workers to acquire habits of punctuality, rigor, and continuity. These capitalist virtues make themselves felt in an almost arid asceticism; but the repressed suffering and exasperation of the workers, in turn, give impulse to the courage for struggle and the instinct for [their] political defense.... The rigid will to carry on the political struggle with dignity is born from this novitiate, which points to the greatest revolution occurring since Christianity.[38]

The socialist work ethic is represented here as a superior (and almost necessary) outgrowth of previously established capitalist "virtues" required to make production effective. Mariátegui therefore thinks of socialism as a system that takes up the more valuable aspects of capitalism while at the same time going beyond them. His views on this subject raise the question, to be considered shortly, as to the extent to which an economically dependent capitalist nation in Latin America can be said to be a suitable candidate for a socialist transformation or revolution.

If this question is to be answered in the affirmative, as Mariátegui would like to do, other factors besides the industrial advances of capitalism and the level of class-consciousness of the workers need to be taken into consideration. In this context, the expansion of Mariátegui's socialist anthropology to include the concerns for the spiritual as well as the material well-being of Peru's indigenous population becomes highly significant. Moreover, his analysis of U.S. economic "imperialism" in the region is also pivotal. In this case, the ethics of class struggle is not only focused on the conflict between labor and capital, as in the Marxist

European model; it must also address the conflict between Peru's national economy and international capitalist investment as well as the internal conflict of interests between the economically well-off national ruling classes, mostly of Hispanic origin, and Peru's economically and racially marginalized indigenous sectors. Mariátegui did not enter into a discussion of these topics in *Defense of Marxism*, possibly because he had already delved into them at length in the *Seven Essays* and other articles, where he dealt specifically with Peruvian social reality as opposed to European debates on the nature of Marxism.

Two other points remain to be noted with respect to the type of ethical values Mariátegui associated with socialism. In chapter 7 of *Defense of Marxism*, he criticizes the view that Marxism implies a social determinism. In chapter 8 he comments on what he takes to be the "heroic and creative" sense of socialism. Both points address the issue of the function of human beings' consciousness and will in the process of creating a new society. In this context he offers—though not without some contradiction—a critique of economic determinism at the same time that he appears to endorse a version of historical determinism.

Chapter 7 of *Defense of Marxism* deals briefly with the question of determinism within Marxism. Mariátegui argues that critics of Marxism often exaggerate the connection between Marxism and determinism so as to portray Marxism as "a product of the nineteenth-century mechanistic mentality" and thus incompatible with the postwar voluntaristic conception of life.[39] He notes that "when Marxism has proved itself to be revolutionary—that is to say, when it has been [a genuine] Marxism—it has never obeyed a passive and rigid determinism."[40] A genuine Marxism is always on the border of being considered too utopian by its critics. A deterministic approach to Marxism, he thinks, is one that tones down its revolutionary qualities. He distinguishes between economic determinism and political realism, attributing only the latter perspective to Marx. It is because he was a realist, not a determinist, Mariátegui thinks, that Marx placed a great deal of importance on showing that the very process of the development and perfection of capitalism leads toward socialism. Apparently he was not familiar with certain writings of Marx where a different assessment of the transition to socialism is suggested.[41] For Mariátegui, the historical link between capitalism and a Marxist socialism is indisputable since the latter emerges in Western culture as a critique of the former.

The notion that Marx valued capitalism and its contribution to the progress of civilization is expanded upon in chapter 8. "Marx discovered and taught that one must begin by understanding the fatality of the capitalist stage and, above all, its value."[42] Mariátegui takes this position in order to situate his option for socialism on a ground beyond resentment and a mere dualism of good and evil.

> Socialism, after Marx, appears as the conception of a new class, as a doctrine and a movement having nothing in common with the romanticism of those who repudiate—as an abomination—the work of capitalism. The proletariat was to succeed the bourgeoisie in the civilizing enterprise. It would assume this task, conscious of its responsibility and its capability—acquired in revolutionary action and in the capitalist factory—when the bourgeoisie, having fulfilled its destiny, ceased to be a progressive and cultural force.[43]

One of the most fundamental qualities of Mariátegui's Marxism is the ability to offer a positive outlook on a wide range of non-Marxist phenomena, always confident that in the end what is valuable in these phenomena can be used as a contribution to the building of socialism. Thus he argues that the capitalist system is to be opposed through the class struggle but not in a romantic, utopian, or simplistic fashion. Capitalism is the type of opponent that, to be mastered, calls for the highest discipline and creativity on the part of the working class. It is not a question of good versus evil, but of creating a higher social order—something akin to Nietzsche's notion of a "higher culture," except, of course, that in this case the working class, not the individual artist, would be given the role of protagonist in the process.

Mariátegui attempted to reject the reactive values of a "slave morality" while still keeping open the possibility for a genuine form of Christianity to exist. (In Nietzsche's view, the Christian ideology of redemption from sin was coextensive with the notion of a slave morality.) He reserves the term "ethical socialism" (*socialismo ético*) to refer to a "pseudo-Christian" perspective, and speaks instead of the "ethics of socialism," the "ethical function of socialism," and a "socialist ethics" (*ética socialista*). His aim is to distinguish his position clearly from a position he regards as excessively romantic. The latter, he claims, finds socialism attractive for sentimental reasons, as an outlet for a false concept of charity:

By the route of "moral" socialism and its antimaterialistic preaching, one falls back only on the most sterile and tearful humanitarian romanticism, on the most decadent apologetic of the "pariah," on the most sentimental and inept plagiarism of the biblical phrase "the poor in spirit." And this is equivalent to taking socialism back to its romantic, utopian stage.[44]

It is important to note that Mariátegui refers to such an attitude, among other things, as "pseudo-Christian." Unlike Marx and Engels, he had a positive conception of Christianity. He saw the nineteenth-century Marxists as living in an age that had not yet been exposed to such theories as William James's will to believe, which gave a rather different meaning and value to a religious spirituality.

Mariátegui's chapter on religion in the *Seven Essays* ("The Religious Factor") is credited by many today as a point of departure for a new understanding between Marxists and Christians, such as the one attained by the proponents of a theology of liberation.[45] He considers faith to be an important aspect of a person's life.

Nineteenth-century rationalist thought sought to explain religion in terms of philosophy. More realistically, pragmatism has accorded to religion the place from which rationalism conceitedly thought to dislodge it.[46]

He tries to rescue the spiritual meaning of religious belief from the socioeconomic structures that influence its ideological content. In addition, he argues on behalf of accepting a methodology of historical materialism while disengaging it from a metaphysical theory of materialism. His position is succinctly stated in these terms:

Socialism, according to the conclusions of historical materialism, not to be confused with philosophical materialism, considers that ecclesiastical forms and religious doctrines are produced and sustained by the socioeconomic structure. Therefore, it is concerned with changing the latter and not the former. Socialism regards mere anti-clerical activity as a liberal bourgeois pastime.[47]

Here it is also clear that Mariátegui conceives of bourgeois ideology as taking a nihilistic attitude toward religious belief in contrast with socialist principles. As a follower of Sorel, he thinks the latter should be able to rise above this kind of bias.

Mariátegui, then, is tolerant of religious faith as an expression of deeply felt spiritual needs but distrustful of ethical theories that justify socialism from the standpoint of what Nietzsche called a "slave morality." In particular, he opposes theories that take a reactive outlook toward both oppressors and oppressed. This serves to distinguish his high regard for spirituality from any Christian position—which he would call "pseudo-Christian"—that employed a slave morality perspective.

> The ethical, pseudo-Christian, humanitarian socialism that one attempts to oppose anachronously to a Marxist socialism may be a more or less lyrical and innocuous exercise of a tired and decadent bourgeoisie, but not the theory of a class that has come of age, surpassing the highest objectives of the capitalist class. Marxism is totally alien and contrary to these mediocre altruistic and philanthropic speculations. We Marxists do not believe that the enterprise of creating a new social order—superior to the capitalist order—falls on an amorphous mass of pariahs and oppressed who are guided by evangelical preachers of the good. The revolutionary energy of socialism is not nourished by compassion or envy. In the class struggle, where all the sublime and heroic elements of the proletariat's ascent reside, the latter must raise itself to a "morality of producers" very distant and distinct from the "slave morality" which these gratuitous professors of morality officiously insist on providing for it, horrified by its materialism. A new civilization cannot arise from a sad and humiliated world of slaves and miserable people who have no more claim or aptitude than their slavery and misery. The proletariat does not enter history politically except as a social class, at the instant when it discovers its mission of constructing—with elements derived from human effort, whether moral or immoral, just or unjust—a superior social order. And this capacity has not been reached by a miracle. The proletariat has acquired it by situating itself solidly on economic ground, on the ground of production. Its class morality depends on the energy and heroism with which it operates on this ground and on the extent to which it can know and master bourgeois economy.[48]

In other words, the test of the working class's coming of age is performative. Its character must be tested by endurance, discipline, and struggle. Its consciousness must be focused on creating a new order superior to the one preceding it. The socialist ethics must operate beyond resentment, envy, and compassion.

This is to not say, however, that socialism should not view itself as antithetical to capitalist class interests. Mariátegui ends his remarks on ethics and socialism by quoting the following passage from another Italian, Adriano Tilgher:

> [From a historical standpoint] Marx appears as the discoverer and I would almost say the *creator* [*inventor*] of the proletariat. In effect, he has not only given the proletarian movement the consciousness of its nature, legitimacy and historical necessity...and thus infused it with that consciousness that it previously lacked; he has created, one might say, the very notion, and after the notion, the reality of the proletariat, as a class essentially antithetical to the bourgeoisie.[49]

Correspondingly, the challenge to Mariátegui as a Peruvian Marxist was to develop another kind of "new" consciousness, one that would create "an Indo-Hispanic socialism." This would imply expanding Marxism's analysis of class struggle in the direction of an anti-imperialist and proindigenous conception of a Peruvian national identity.

Mariátegui's Indo-Hispanic Socialism

One of the most persistent charges Mariátegui had to face as he tried to forge this new consciousness of his nation's social reality was the accusation of being an *europeizante*, or someone who wants to make everything European. It was not understood that when he spoke of Europe and when he referred to European writers and events, he was not speaking as a European but from the standpoint of what he identified as an Indo-Hispanic consciousness. "I have served my best apprenticeship in Europe, and I believe there is no salvation for Indo-America without Western or European science and thought," he remarks, in defense of his perspective.[50] Indeed, it was in Europe that he became fully conscious of his South American identity, a realization that he made in conjunction with his conversion to Marxism.

Mariátegui's *Europeismo*—as his critics charged—is easily misunderstood precisely because of the strong dependence on Europe characteristic of South American intellectuals. It was not clear to many of his compatriots that someone who embraced with such passion the "latest ideas" from Europe could indeed be an "authentic" Peruvian. The test of time has shown the contrary to have been Mariátegui's case, but the problem still persists: how does one distinguish what is Peruvian from what is European if European ideas come to flood Peruvian intellectual and cultural life? Mariátegui found one answer that was unique: making visible as part of Peru's national life the forgotten masses of Indians who were considered entirely marginal to the nation's cultural identity. In large part, this was the task of the *Seven Interpretive Essays on Peruvian Reality*, his most important work. Before moving on to this text, a few words about the context in which he introduced the discussion of the problems of indigenous people are appropriate.

By all reports, the first major thinker in Peru who turned his attention to the situation of the country's indigenous people was Manuel González Prada (1848–1918). González Prada, an anticlerical thinker of anarchist tendencies, launched the first radical critique of the position of the Indians in Peruvian society in the 1880s. Indians then constituted about four-fifths of Peru's population; they were considered marginal to the white and *mestizo* society, and they lived in destitution and poverty. Since colonial times, various uprisings—the most famous of which had been led by Tupac Amaru in the eighteenth century—had given some visibility to the cause of the self-determination of indigenous peoples.[51] But it is generally acknowledged that González Prada placed the Indian theme at the forefront of national issues in late-nineteenth-century Peru. In "Discurso en el Politeama" (1888), he mentioned the servile attitude of Peruvian rulers and citizens and the position of serfdom in which the Indians were placed in Peruvian society as factors contributing to the defeat of Peru by Chile in the War of the Pacific (1879–83): "If we made a serf of the Indian, what fatherland [*patria*] will he defend? Like the serf of the Middle Ages, he will only fight for a feudal lord."[52] González Prada is known for blaming the debilitated situation of Peru as well as the oppression of the Indians on corrupt government officials, the Catholic clergy, and the wealthy landowners (known as *gamonales*).[53]

At the end of the 1880s, a literary movement known as *indigenismo* was also arising. In 1889 a novel by Clorinda Matto de Turner, *Aves sin nido* (*Birds without a Nest*), helped to bring widespread attention to the Indians' plight. Still, Matto's novel expressed a romantic outlook, while González Prada's arguments combined aristocratic and anarchic elements in his condemnation of the state. Although González Prada had stated in his 1904 essay "Nuestros Indios" that "the question of the Indian is an economic and social more than a pedagogical [question]," an observation anticipating Mariátegui's approach to this issue, it was Mariátegui's analysis of the Indian problem in the *Seven Essays* that definitively put aside the romantic, individualistic condemnation of the Indians' servitude in favor of a systematic economic and social study of the question.[54] In addition to his socioeconomic focus on the question, however, Mariátegui continued to support the literary movement of *indigenismo* both in the journal *Amauta* and in the chapter devoted to Peruvian literature in the *Seven Essays*.

In his lucid treatment of the subject, Mariátegui tied the problem of the exploitation of the Indians to that of their relationship with the land. He offered a structural analysis of the problem, as I will point out. The problematic relationship between the Indians and the land, moreover, was twofold. First, Mariátegui insisted on the economic aspect—the exploitation of the Indians' labor power by the system of *gamonalismo* (a type of feudalism), which had complete control over rural life. Second, he noted the Indians' cultural attachment to the land due to traditional beliefs they had inherited from their Inca ancestors. For socialism (or any other approach) to solve "the problem of the Indian," Mariátegui went on to argue, it must speak both to the Indians' economic (material) and cultural (spiritual) needs. Mariátegui tried to demonstrate through the use of highly structural (system-oriented) arguments that capitalism could not solve the problems of the indigenous communities and that only socialism could "redeem the Indian." In doing this, whether intentionally or not, he also transformed the meaning of socialism and gave it a decidedly ethnic-national character. In and through a socialist indigenism he found the only route to articulate a national identity for Peru: "The redemption of the Indian is the cause and the goal of the renovation of Peru."[55]

"Mariátegui's historical merit," claims Antonio Melis, "consists in linking the problem of the Indian with the theory of agrarian reform."[56] This is indeed true, but it is only one important aspect of his contribution. The other aspect consists in his tying together the solution to the problem of the Indian and the question of a Peruvian national identity. In order to grasp this, we need to understand the nature of Mariátegui's socialist anthropology. The redeemed Indian in a socialist restructured society comes to symbolize for him, in a concrete manner and in his own country of

Peru, the abstract socialist vision of the new society and the new human being. Thus his socialist anthropology has a cultural base that neither Marx nor Engels could have envisioned—human beings who are not white, who are not European, whose ethnic traditions are firmly rooted in the American continent as descendants of the Incas, and whose pre-Columbian origins also place them symbolically at the height of the civilizations existing in this continent before the conquest. Mariátegui did not try to idealize the past, nor did he view the Indians in an atemporal framework. His concern was only to understand the importance of their heritage from the standpoint of a new historical epoch. In many respects, the artwork of some of the Mexican mural painters such as Diego Rivera, whose vision of Indo-Hispanic America was awakened by the Mexican Revolution of 1910 (and in Rivera's case, also by his own Marxist beliefs), comes close to the type of regeneration of the American continent and its people articulated by Mariátegui's socialist anthropology.

Let us now take a closer look at the two-tiered components— economic and cultural—of Mariátegui's analysis of the problem of the Indian. Mariátegui's argument is structural. He locates the cause of the misery of the Indians in an economic system that exploits them. "The problem of the Indian is rooted in the land tenure system of our economy," he states. "Any attempt to solve it with administrative or police measures, through education or by a road building program, is superficial and secondary as long as the feudalism of the *gamonales* continues to exist."[57] Morever, he emphasizes the structural nature of the backward and dependent aspects of the Peruvian economy in terms of the international capitalist control of markets and division of labor. "Why has this problem of our economy not been solved?" he asks, referring to Peru's dependence on importing such basic foodstuffs as wheat and grain. "The obstacle to a solution is in the very structure of the Peruvian economy, which can only move or develop in response to the interests and needs of markets in London and New York."[58]

In Mariátegui's original text, the above sentence actually reads: "El obstáculo, la resistencia a una solución, se encuentra en la estructura misma de la economía peruana."[59] The word *resistencia* (resistance) has been left out of the English translation. Perhaps his use of it in this context is not immediately clear. But if one also looks at *Defense of Marxism*, one will notice Mariátegui arguing that just as Freud discovered the phenomenon of resistance to psychoanalysis in the patient who wishes to avoid the psychoanalytic cure, there also exist economic interests that function in resistance to socialism and therefore create an obstacle to a global solution of socioeconomic problems.[60] Mariátegui seeks a structural solution to the phenomenon of economic dependence just as psychoanalysis seeks a structural solution to the patient's cure. The obstacle *and* resistance to a solution of the problem of dependence, he wants to say, lie in the very structure of the economy. And *gamonalismo* is the internal structure this system takes inside Peru. But the power of *gamonalismo* is not confined to the economic sphere; it affects Peru's national life as a whole. In particular, he notes in the *Seven Essays* that the term refers not only to the social and economic system run by the large landowners (in its impersonal aspects) but to a wide social network of people profiting from this system, from bureaucrats and middlemen to those Indians who end up in certain positions of privilege over other members of their group. "The central factor" of this larger phenomenon, he states, "is the hegemony of the semi-feudal estate in the policy and mechanism of the government."[61] The question then arises as to whether a liberal government would be able to free itself from the web of influences established by this system. He is not optimistic on this point.

Mariátegui perceived the problem of the Indian to be so deeply rooted in the class structure of the country that only a socialist transformation could actually solve it by dislodging this socioeconomic system from power. From a theoretical political standpoint, he observes, the bourgeois revolution should have released the Indians from servitude. But in Peru, the bourgeoisie was weak, remaining partly dependent on the feudal-style estate system as well as on foreign capital. With a weak and not sufficiently innovative bourgeoisie, *gamonalismo* maintained its power within the capitalist period of the republic, making the Indians' position even more destitute. Since, historically, liberal principles of economic and political reform "were sabotaged by the very class charged with applying them,"[62] liberalism ceased being a practical or effective option:

Revolutionary and even reformist thought can no longer be liberal; they must be Socialist. Socialism appears in our history not because of chance, imitation, or fashion, as some superficial minds would believe, but because it was historically inevitable. On the one hand, we who profess socialism struggle logically and consistently for the reorganization of our country on

Socialist bases; proving that the economic and political
regime that we oppose has turned into an instrument for col-
onizing the country on behalf of foreign imperialist capitalism, we declare that this is a moment in our history when it
is impossible to be really nationalist or revolutionary without
being Socialist. On the other hand, there does not exist and
never has existed in Peru a progressive bourgeoisie, endowed
with national feelings, that claims to be liberal and democratic and that derives its policy from the postulates of its doctrine.[63]

The inevitability that Mariátegui attributes to the appearance of
socialism in Peru is not presented here as a purely determined
matter but as the product of an intelligent choice to be made in the
face of a dire situation that calls for a solution. He argues that a
progressive liberal position has never been able to gain a material
base in Peru; therefore, classic liberalism is impotent before the
problem. Later, in "Anti-imperialist Point of View," he states (from
the standpoint of a Marxist international politics) that it is no
longer possible for a Peruvian (or a Latin American) to be genuinely nationalist or revolutionary without being socialist, a statement
he directed especially at leaders of the APRA political party.
    In the *Seven Essays,* Mariátegui does consider alternatives
other than a socialist transformation to the problem of the Indian,
such as reforms in education and the law, and appeals to religious
and moral humanitarian sentiments. But, as in the case of liberalism, he discounts them on the grounds that Peru's historical development shows them to have been ineffective. For example, he
notes that during the colonial era, at a time when the Catholic
church wielded a great deal of power, the Dominican friar Bartolomé de las Casas tried to ensure that the Indians would be
treated humanely. Despite the power of the church and the "Laws
of the Indies," passed in Spain as a result of Las Casas's efforts,
the Indians remained in a condition of practical slavery. "In practice, the Indians remained at the mercy of a pitiless feudal system
that destroyed the Inca society and economy without replacing
them with an [economic] order capable of organizing production
progressively."[64] Later historical developments did not deal with
this problem. "The revolution of Independence, as is known, did
not constitute an indigenous movement."[65] In addition to the fact
that the Indians remained marginalized and exploited in the
decades following independence, there was a failure to relate the

solution of the problem of indigenous people to an appreciation of the special relationship existing between them and the land.

In a section added to the second edition of the *Seven Essays,* not included in the English translation of this work, Mariátegui states:

> It was the task of the Republic to raise the condition of the Indian. But acting against this duty, the Republic has impoverished the Indian, worsened his depression, and exacerbated his misery. The Republic has meant, for the Indians, the ascent of a new dominant class that has systematically appropriated their lands. For a race of agrarian customs and spirit such as the indigenous race, this despoilment has constituted a cause of moral and material dissolution. The land has always been the whole joy of the Indian. The Indian has been married to the land. He feels that "life comes from the land" and returns to the land. Therefore, the Indian can be indifferent to everything except to the possession of land that he cultivates and fertilizes religiously with his hands and with his spirit.[66]

In chapter 3 of the *Seven Essays,* he also observes that the relationship of the Indian to the land transcends a purely economic analysis:

> The subordination of the Indian problem to the problem of land is even more absolute, for special reasons. The indigenous race is a race of farmers. The Inca people were peasants, normally engaged in agriculture and shepherding. Their industries and arts were typically domestic and rural. The principle that life springs from the soil was truer in the Peru of the Incas than in any other country.... [Luis E.] Valcárcel, in his study of the economic life of Tawantinsuyo, writes that "the land, in native tradition, is the common mother; from her womb come not only food but man himself. The cult of Mama Pacha is on a par with the worship of the sun and, like the sun, Mother Earth represents no one in particular. Joined in the aboriginal ideology, these two concepts gave birth to agrarianism, which combines communal ownership of the land and the universal religion of the sun."[67]

The Inca system that antedated the Spanish conquest was an agrarian communism. The latter, Mariátegui thinks, "cannot be negated or disparaged for having developed under the autocratic regime of the Incas," since it "assured the subsistence and growth of a population that came to ten million when the conquistadors arrived in Peru"—a population that was reduced to one million after three centuries of Spanish rule.[68] During this time the Indians who survived were "reduced to servitude and peonage," but they retained a communistic spirit of work and cooperation through the system of the community of families known as the *ayllu*.[69]

In addition to arguing that the solution to the Indian problem must be not only economic but cultural, and that socialism is the economic and ideological system best suited to solve the Indian problem, Mariátegui claims that the descendants of the Inca are culturally predisposed toward socialism and communism because of the communal habits of work and cooperation they have inherited. The spirit of individualism fostered by a society of free competition is alien to the Indian, he notes, not only because he has not had to live in such a society but because in order to survive under *gamonalismo* the Indians have had to depend for support on their ancient forms of community, the *ayllus*. The Indians' ancient heritage and the nature of their struggle for survival have therefore made them communist in spirit. "And the Indian has never felt less free than when he has felt alone."[70]

Mariátegui's views of the predisposition of the Indians toward communism may be questioned either by those who think he projects too much of a contemporary idea of communism onto the distant past (the Inca civilization) or by those who think he fails to give present-day Indians sufficient latitude to choose a way of life other than communism or socialism.[71] Yet (with respect to the first objection) in a note whose length constitutes almost an additional section of the chapter, Mariátegui distinguishes between "Inca communism" and "modern communism":

> The two communisms are products of different human experiences. They belong to different historical epochs. They were evolved by dissimilar civilizations. The Inca civilization was agrarian; the civilization of Marx and Sorel is industrial.[72] In the former, man submitted to nature; in the latter, nature sometimes submits to man. It is therefore absurd to compare the forms and institutions of the two communisms.[73]

Mariátegui also expresses some of his views on the political character of modern socialism:

Although autocracy and communism are now incompatible, they were not so in primitive societies. Today, a new order cannot abjure any of the moral gains of modern society. Contemporary socialism—other historical periods have had other kinds of socialism under different names—is the antithesis of liberalism; but it is born from its womb and is nourished on its experiences. It does not disdain the intellectual achievements of liberalism, only its limitations. It appreciates and understands everything that is positive in the liberal ideal; it condemns and attacks what is negative and selfish in it.[74]

Despite the brevity of Mariátegui's style and his periodic use of a socialist rhetoric, at his best he is a writer who does not fail to make as many distinctions as are needed for the sake of clarity and precision. One may disagree with Mariátegui's views on the Inca empire or on modern socialism, but he himself did not confound the two, nor did he take either one to be an earlier or later stage of the other.

The second objection, whether Mariátegui attributed an undue degree of communist spirit to Peru's indigenous culture in its contemporary expressions, is debatable. On the one hand, he based his views on the fact that the *ayllus,* or Indian communities, still formed the nucleus of the Indians' sociocultural heritage. He did not argue that the Indians were incapable of adapting to a capitalist economy; he only claimed that, given their socioeconomic conditions and their cultural legacy, they would much more likely adapt to a socialist agrarian reform and a socialist society that respected their ethnic traditions. On the other hand, Mariátegui's perception of the Indian spirit should not be disconnected from his perception of the human spirit (regardless of ethnicity) engaged in creating a better society in a better world. Because he already saw human beings and their social interactions through the perspective that I have tried to describe as a new socialist anthropology, it is clear that he saw not only Indians but all human beings as inclined to a great deal of solidarity and cooperation with their fellows and peers, in a manner that simply cannot be attributed to individualistic philosophies. His assessment of "the problem of the Indian," I think, was quite genuine and did not entail an attempt to manipulate the indigenous population to accept a socialist ideology. Mariátegui himself refers to this new consciousness when he states:

Today, with the appearance of a new ideology that expresses the interests and aspirations of the masses, who gradually

have acquired a class consciousness, a national movement
has arisen that sympathizes with the lot of the Indian and
makes the solution of his problem basic to a program for the
reform and reconstruction of Peru.[75]

Clearly his perspective is that socialism should embrace the cause
of the Indian. As to the converse, whether persons of indigenous origin should embrace the cause of socialism is not really Mariátegui's
(or the Western middle-class critic's) place to say, for this choice,
properly speaking, belongs only to the group in question and to the
individuals who form this group. What Mariátegui has done is to
offer a vision of society in which the Indian population is seen as an
essentially creative and dynamic participant in the productive
process, on a par with everyone else. In addition, he has tied the
cultural identity of the nation to the identity of the redeemed or
regenerated Indian, thus reversing and surpassing to the fullest
extent the social and economic effects of the Spanish conquest.

The Unfinished Character of Mariátegui's Thought

Mariátegui's work has been a source of inspiration and
debate for many contemporary Latin Americans, Marxists and
non-Marxists alike. The fact that Mariátegui died at the age of
thirty-five and in the year 1930, with much of his thinking still
undeveloped, raises much speculation about what his position
might have been regarding the political nature of the contemporary world. The discussion will conclude by sketching three problems left ambiguous in his work—problems that have a bearing on
the general themes of cultural identity and liberation theory
addressed in this study.

The first issue deals with the question of the transition to
socialism in underdeveloped societies. Mariátegui holds two separate theses whose implications appear to be empirically incompatible. In the *Seven Essays* he argues, on structural grounds, that
the nature of capitalism (particularly in its imperialist phase)
makes it impossible for countries with backward or capitalist-
dependent economies to pull themselves out of this position; thus
the only hope or salvation for a country like Peru would be to
embrace a socialist economic system based as much as possible on
a self-sustaining economy. Such an economy would presumably
include both an industrial sector, with elements borrowed from
advanced Western technologies, and a conservationist rural sector,

oriented toward the preservation of ecological and communal values. He does not indicate how an economic system that is inherently flawed can gain enough impetus or momentum to switch over to a self-sustaining socialist economy.

Moreover, the transition to socialism he advocates is further complicated by the fact that in *Defense of Marxism* he appears to argue an incompatible thesis, namely, that a successful change from capitalism to socialism cannot take place unless the working class (under capitalism) is able to achieve mastery over the bourgeois system of production and acquire a socialist consciousness in the process. This would imply that the working class is capable of creating a genuine socialist system only after having mastered the bourgeois system of economics. Yet if Mariátegui were to wait for the latter conditions to take effect in Peru—whose economy he acknowledged to be structurally backward due to the very structure of dependent capitalism itself—it would follow that the working class could never obtain the required conditions for mastering capitalism. In such circumstances, the transition to socialism would have to be postponed indefinitely. A developing country like Peru would be doomed to exist in a "no exit" situation: too backward to reap the benefits of advanced capitalism, yet too weak to take the plunge into the construction of a socialist economy. Clearly, Mariátegui did not wish to reach this conclusion.

Perhaps this explains why in the *Seven Essays* he appeals to other reasons for justifying the transition to socialism in Peru, such as the restoration of the land to the Indians in a way that would preserve their centuries-old communistic practices. The larger argument then would have to be that the Spanish conquest initiated a period of exploitation of labor and wealth in South America that only a socialist revolution can redress or reverse historically. In fact, this argument is present in the *Seven Essays*. But it has several gaps, especially insofar as no explicit model of socialist development is proposed. For example, Mariátegui does not explain how the socialist system, which he takes to be a further development of capitalism and not its radical (double) negation, can reverse the economic situation of the country.

To help resolve some of these gaps and discrepancies—at least conceptually—I would suggest that by "socialism" Mariátegui meant both an economic and a political system. He sees the socialist economic system as an outgrowth (a superior outgrowth) of capitalist production, and the socialist political system as a movement reversing the conquest's—and later, imperialism's—fragmentation

and internal debilitation of the American territories (now constituted as separate nations or republics). This latter aspect explains
why Mariátegui's Marxism took such a strongly cultural and
nationally oriented turn, aimed at the strengthening of the formation of a Peruvian national identity. Socialism is seen as a means
of achieving the political rehabilitation of a previously colonized
and economically backward country. This vision of socialism is still
very much alive among many Latin Americans today, given the
failure of capitalism to deliver strong and healthy economies to the
region. Hence the renewed and continuing interest in Mariátegui's
ideas and in socialist alternatives to capitalist-dependent economics in general. From our perspective today, we could say that socialism, as it presents itself to Latin Americans and their specific social
reality, is better undertood as a political choice carrying certain
economic implications than as an economic necessity carrying certain political implications.

Another problem left ambiguous by Mariátegui is the extent
to which his affirmation of the will to believe and his rejection of
rationalism and positivism affect the critical power of Marxist philosophy. Of special concern are the implications of his views on the
relation between Marxist intellectuals and Marxist party dogma.
It would appear from his unorthodox, if not eclectic, perspective
that Mariátegui is a highly antidogmatic Marxist. Yet *Defense of
Marxism* concludes with a defense of dogma. Mariátegui argues
that "in order to think freely, the first condition is to abandon the
concern for absolute freedom."[76]

> Dogma is understood here as the doctrine proceeding from a
> historical change. And, as such, as long as the change is tak-
> ing place, that is, as long as the dogma is not transformed
> into an archive or a code of the past ideology, nothing guaran-
> tees creative freedom, [or] the original function of thought,
> more than dogma. The intellectual, in his speculative activi-
> ty, needs to find support in a belief, in a principle, that makes
> of him a factor in history and progress.... A dogmatist like
> Marx or Engels is able to influence events and ideas more
> than any great heretic or any great nihilist. This fact alone
> should override every [feeling of] apprehension, every fear
> regarding the limitations of what is dogmatic.[77]

This argument, however, is too contrived. In particular, it leaves
untouched the question of what kind or kinds of influence on social

reality are thought to be desirable. Against Mariátegui, it could be observed that a dogma, insofar as it is an unquestioned belief, accepted without a critical framework of reference, is probably one of the most dangerous weapons to be placed in the hands of individuals and peoples. If intellectuals, particularly Marxist intellectuals, cannot put in question the dogmas issued by the party or parties claiming to represent them politically, what sort of future does this evoke for socialism? Moreover, what sort of prospect does it evoke for philosophy?

For his part, Mariátegui seems to take refuge in the view, stated elsewhere in *Defense of Marxism*, that Marxism is part of the modern age—a time, he thinks, in which "no social and political doctrine could appear in contradiction with history and science."[78] But this view, which basically implies that, due to their appearance at a certain stage in history, some political doctrines are necessarily supported by reason and science, is itself a dogma. To avoid this problem one needs to be able to make a distinction between what Mariátegui calls "absolute truth" (on one side), what he calls "dogma" (on the other), and those theoretical perspectives supported by critical reasoning, which fall into yet a third category (not mentioned by him). If this distinction makes sense, this means that the Marxist method of historical materialism cannot be so neatly disconnected from other ways of doing philosophy (in particular, from critical philosophy), as Croce seemed to think and as Mariátegui was persuaded to argue, following Croce.[79] A Marxist philosophy in the full sense of the term is always a critical philosophy, and as such its task is precisely to unmask various uncritical illusions and dogmas. This does not mean the will to believe is nonexistent, but that within some measure it ought to be subject to critical analysis. Failure to reach this standpoint in which one finds strength in Marx's legacy as a critical thinker (e.g., by depicting Marx as a "dogmatist") can easily lead to the limiting practice of placing Marxism on the side of repression rather than on that of self-determination and democracy.

Given Mariátegui's deep love for a healthy, dynamic cultural community as well as his own deviations from Marxist dogma, including his public disagreement with positions advanced by the Third International, one can only infer that in this inopportune defense of dogma he is trying to compromise with party hard-liners by celebrating dogma in the abstract while refusing to follow it in practice. Yet this is a weak position for a Marxist leader to take, in addition to being one that leaves a negative precedent in the

history of Latin American Marxism. The best that can be said for
Mariátegui in this respect is that he failed to find the right words
or the appropriate formula to express how someone with as heterodox views as he had could be a genuine and, in fact, prominent
representative of Marxism.

Finally, there is the question, left unresolved by Mariátegui,
of his own position vis-à-vis the relation between European and
Latin American thought. He left behind a number of statements
saying there was no salvation for Latin America apart from
Europe, or even this: "The new civilization is being forged in
Europe. America has a secondary role in this stage of human history."[80] Moreover, in the often quoted essay "La unidad de la
América indo-española" (1924), Mariátegui states that Hispanic-
American thought is only in the process of formation and has not
as yet achieved a cultural standing in its own right (a claim that
would seem to place him on the fringe if not outside a Latin Americanist perspective on thought and culture).

> It is absurd and presumptuous to speak of an autochthonous
> and genuine [Latin] American culture [una cultura propia y
> genuinamente americana] in the process of being formed or
> elaborated. The only evident thing is that a vigorous literature
> already reflects a Hispanic American outlook and humor. This
> literature—[which includes] poetry, the novel, criticism, soci-
> ology, history, philosophy—still does not tie [Latin American]
> peoples together; but it does forge ties within intellectual cate-
> gories, even if only partially and in a weak manner.[81]

In spite of this moderate assessment of the status of Latin American thought at the time, Mariátegui fully recognizes the legitimacy
of Latin American thought and culture as such. In the paragraph
preceding the just-quoted statement, he notes:

> The identity of the Hispanic-American man finds an expres-
> sion in intellectual life. The same ideas, the same feelings are
> circulating throughout all of Indo-Hispanic America. Every
> single figure of intellectual vigor has an influence over the
> continent's culture. Sarmiento, Martí, and Montalvo do not
> belong exclusively to their respective fatherlands [patrias];
> they belong to Hispanic America. The same may be said of
> poets such as Darío, Lugones..., and others.... At present, the
> [philosophical] thought of Vasconcelos and Ingenieros has

continental repercussions. Vasconcelos and Ingenieros are the masters of an entire generation of our America [de una entera generación de nuestra América].[82]

In keeping with his political perspectives, Mariátegui wished to link this type of intellectual and cultural development to a socialist practice. His thinking is therefore misunderstood if one fails to take into account either his socialist commitment or his reserved but nevertheless explicit comments regarding the legitimacy of a culture proper to Latin America as such ("una cultura propia" "de nuestra América").

It is inaccurate, then, to portray Mariátegui as an *europeizante* or as a thinker whose role lies outside of the development of Latin American thought. The whole thrust of his political and intellectual activity in Peru after returning there in 1923 from his three-year tour of Europe was to help his own country advance, particularly on a political and cultural front. His attraction to European avant-garde theories of the time led him to take an interest in European thought, though not to the total neglect or exclusion of that of his own country and Latin America in general. In particular, he pursued and supported avant-garde intellectual currents in both his country and the region; an example is the literary movement of *indigenismo*, behind which he put the weight of his socialist journal *Amauta*. He was especially interested in following the latest ideas and trends in a wide diversity of intellectual, artistic, and political movements. Had he been alive today, it is reasonable to think that he would have pursued the latest ideas in Europe's more recent movements of poststructuralism and postmodernism, just as in his own day he was fascinated by the work of Unamuno, Nietzsche, and Freud. Despite any formal defense Mariátegui may have made of dogma over "free thinking," he remains an outsider to any rigid dogmatic tradition. And, despite his celebration of European thought over that of his native Latin America, he remains one of Latin America's most original and provocative thinkers of the century, an outstanding contributor to the project of building a new nation and a new society based on a combination of socialist principles, avant-garde European thought, and an Indo-Hispanic cultural legacy. Like so many other outstanding figures of Latin American thought, he remains a representative of the region's mixed cultural legacy, or *mestizaje*.

PHILOSOPHY AND THE PROBLEM OF CULTURAL IDENTITY: FROM RAMOS TO SALAZAR BONDY

The theme of cultural identity gained impetus in Mexican philosophy in the 1930s and has continued to be one of the central topics of a Latin American philosophy up to the present time. This chapter will cover its development in the work of the Mexican philosopher Samuel Ramos, its treatment in the early work of another Mexican, Leopoldo Zea, and its climax in the late 1960s and early 1970s in the debate between the Peruvian philosopher Augusto Salazar Bondy and Zea regarding the authenticity of Latin American philosophy. The discussion will focus on the evolution of the concept of cultural identity in Latin American philosophy. There are two principal stages to the discussion. The first stage evolves from the concept of a national identity. The second addresses a broader concept of cultural identity, one that encompasses the whole continent—the Latin American and Caribbean region—and even embraces what has been known in the latter part of this century as the "Third World." It is not difficult to extrapolate from the nation to the region and from the region to a sector of the world still bearing the effects of colonialism, whether in more pronounced or latent forms. But it is also important not to fall into too broad generalizations, which, if pursued uncritically, will lose the specificity of the problems under discussion. This discussion will therefore center on some very specific points arising out of the work of, primarily, Samuel Ramos, Leopoldo Zea, and Augusto Salazar Bondy, all of whom have made important contributions to the study of this problem from the standpoint of the discipline of philosophy.

Cultural identity is a central theme in nineteenth- and twentieth-century Latin American social thought. The contributions of Ramos, Zea, and Salazar Bondy touch on key aspects of the concern for cultural integrity and authenticity. Three principal topics are

explored: the relation between cultural identity and self-knowledge, a project largely mediated by existentialism and psychoanalysis; the relation between cultural identity and nationalism, out of
which a philosophy of history will develop; and the relation between
cultural identity and liberation from underdevelopment, a perspective leading to a philosophy of liberation. The first approach insists
on looking at subjective reality, at the state of mind of the Latin
American men and women who are the subjects (makers) of culture. The second concentrates on developing a view of cultural identity consonant with external reality (the nation, history, and so on).
The third approach questions the efficacy of the other two models in
the light of the crisis affecting today's societies. Yet these three perspectives, as we shall see, are interrelated.

The positions of Ramos, Zea, and Salazar Bondy represent
important perspectives within the humanist tradition developed
by distinguished intellectuals from the middle and upper classes.
We are no longer dealing with the notion of an Indo-Hispanic
socialism developed by an intellectual from a working-class background such as Mariátegui. Yet Mariátegui's influence will be felt
in the perspective of the Peruvian philosopher Augusto Salazar
Bondy. My discussion begins with the issue of how to make sense
of the relation between Europe and Latin America (or a particular
Latin American nation such as Mexico). Historically, the middle-
class intellectual has spent a great deal of effort trying to give a
meaning to the conquest and to the hybrid culture that arose as its
historical effect: a culture that is neither fully European, since it
was transmitted to America, nor fully American, since it was domi-
nated by Europe. Unlike the Marxist analysts, who take the view
that any adverse effects of the conquest and colonialism are fundamentally due to economic causes and must be resolved by economic
means, Ramos and Zea will offer idealistic interpretations of the
problem of Latin Americans' sense of subordination to European
culture. An outlook more conscious of materialism will be offered
by Salazar Bondy, who will tie the problems of the region not to a
people's sense of inferiority or to a short-lived national heritage
but to the economic condition of underdevelopment.

The problem of a Latin American cultural identity dates back
at least to the nineteenth-century struggles for political independence from Spain and other colonial powers in the region. At that
time, there was a need to give a political meaning and unity to the
newly constituted American republics.[1] The concern with identity
has also been evident in the repeated attempts to define the differ-

ences between North and South America, or between the United States and Latin America.[2] My discussion of the problem begins in the 1930s, during the first European postwar period, when Europe was facing a major crisis with the increased impetus of fascism. In Mexico, the political situation called for a rethinking of the country's national identity in the light of the Mexican Revolution of 1910 and the gradual institutionalization of political power taking place in the decades following the Revolution. The increased emphasis on the development of a Mexican national identity coincided with the decreased status of a previously venerated European culture, now apparently besieged by insurmountable problems. Moreover, Spain was undergoing a deep political crisis. The Spanish Civil War at the end of the 1930s caused a number of Spanish philosophers to emigrate to Mexico. They were to be highly influential in calling for a serious reconsideration of the meaning of a Latin American cultural identity. This conjunction of political events, involving the European crisis, the search for a definition of the ideals of the Mexican revolution, and the impact of the Spanish *transterrados* in Mexican universities, seemed especially propitious for the development of a philosophy of culture (and later a philosophy of history) in the region.

These philosophical developments did not emerge without important cultural precedents. The work of the "Ateneo de la Juventud" (founded in 1908), whose task had been to renovate and extend Mexican culture, had included the writings of José Vasconcelos, Antonio Caso, and Alfonso Reyes, among others.[3] In *Profile of Man and Culture in Mexico* (1934), Ramos likened these men to the soul of Mexico, although a soul without a body.[4] There was still lacking a social milieu that would allow their ideas to be disseminated throughout the society. With the publication of Ramos's book and the migration of the Spanish *transterrados* to Mexico in the years following, a favorable climate developed for further examination of the question of the authenticity of Mexican culture. Attention was placed on analyzing the reasons that led Mexicans to live outside their "being."[5] By this, Ramos meant that Mexicans were living with a view of the world alien to their own cultural reality.

The Problem of Cultural Authenticity

The issue of authenticity in discussions of a Latin American cultural identity responds to several recurrent concerns. One type of concern is whether the region's cultural formations reflect

native or alien values, that is, to what extent they represent a
Latin American reality or an alien reality superimposed on the
societies of the region. In the context of Ramos's analysis, the issue
is whether culture in Mexico can emerge from an excessive dependence on European or North American values. The problem of imitation, of being a copy rather than an original, belongs to this specific concern. A second issue is whether Mexican culture has a
solid sociohistorical base or whether it reflects an illusion about
the nature of Mexican reality. Is the cultural life of the country in
touch with the very reality it tries to represent? This is the problem of whether one is living a lie, not because one imitates what is
alien to one, but because one fails to know or appreciate what most
properly belongs to oneself. These dimensions of the problem suggest that inauthenticity results from a confusion or the lack of a
clear definition about one's identity and one's own reality. It also
appears that both aspects of the problem are interrelated and
mutually reinforcing. One imitates other cultures because one cannot locate the values proper to one's own, and one fails to identify
these values because of a false type of admiration for other cultures. Yet another concern related to authenticity assumes a characteristic importance. This is whether a particular culture is able
to sustain a set of enduring autonomous values over a period of
time. In the present case, does Mexican culture have a recognizable past and a recognizable future that it can call its own? Or are
its past and future subject to change according to whatever is fash-
ionable or worthwhile in the eyes of foreign cultures? These three
dimensions of the problem of authenticity are present in Ramos's
discussion of Mexican culture, although he does not distinguish
explicitly among them. It is important to keep these distinctions in
mind, however, not only as we look at his position but as we examine the perspectives of Zea and Salazar Bondy on this subject.

When addressing Ramos's contribution, it is helpful to reclas-
sify these three aspects of the problem according to the categories
and terms used by the Mexican philosopher. His approach to the
problem of inauthenticity is predominantly psychological. He
emphasizes three principal aspects: the problem of inferiority—the
perceived inferiority of Mexico to Europe, which, in Ramos's view,
leads Mexicans to a blind imitation of Europe; the problem of self-
knowledge (or a corresponding flight from reality)—the idea that
lack of awareness of their own reality leads Mexicans to live fake
lives, with deep splits between reality and illusion; and the lack of
any substantive moral values, which leads them to think of life

only in terms of survival. One lives only for the day, it is argued, without regard for the past or future. Depending on where a philosopher locates the major problem of inauthenticity, a correlative assessment will be given regarding the causes of and/or solutions to the problem. For Ramos, the major problem lies in the second category, that is, in the split between reality and illusion or the failure to be in touch with what is real. The major cause of this split, he argues, is a pervasive (though ultimately unjustified) feeling of inferiority. He suggests that neither the sense of inferiority nor the deeper split in the self of which it is a sign can be healed without a properly trained and strengthened moral character. In the end, therefore, the foundation of a truly authentic Mexican culture will rest on the moral character of its citizens. This moral character should be strengthened through the development and adoption of a new humanism. Now let us see in more detail how Ramos constructs his argument.

The Problem of Inferiority

The first thing Ramos must do in order to justify his psychological approach to the analysis of the limitations of and possible options for a genuinely Mexican culture is to explain the relation between psychology and the philosophy of culture. In the opening sections of *Profile of Man and Culture in Mexico,* he argues that the psychological focus of his study properly belongs to the philosophy of culture, inasmuch as culture has both an objective and a subjective side. The latter relates to the human being who contributes to the making of culture, the human being who is actually the subject of cultural values. Without the human being, culture would not exist. In the absence of a strong national cultural legacy, Ramos notes, one must look at the subjective potential from which such a culture will emerge, if it is to do so successfully in the future. In trying to decipher the "soul" of the Mexican, he scrutinizes the human potential out of which an authentic culture will develop. In this he resembles Nietzsche, whose views on self-knowledge and cultural values are periodically mentioned in this discussion. But Ramos notices a major impediment keeping Mexican men from creating an adequate culture: their escapism, or the inability to see the world in a realistic light. The cure that will be proposed to heal the Mexican soul is the pursuit of the Socratic maxim of self-knowledge. Ramos agrees with Nietzsche that we are not transparent to ourselves because, in a sense, we are afraid to reach self-awareness. Invoking Nietzsche's challenge, "How much truth can a spirit endure?" Ramos begins his most critical journey into the alienated nature of the Mexican mind.[6] The courage of becoming acquainted with the most difficult truths about oneself is thus contrasted with the false bravery (*valentía*) associated with chauvinistic and macho attitudes.

Ramos's Adlerian psychological analysis begins with a reference to the problem of insecurity. In general, he notes, insecurity is related to a lack of power. The subject feels weak and incapable of obtaining the results he desires. There are various ways of dealing with this problem. One is by lowering one's expectations and restricting one's goals to a more modest sphere of activities.[7] This is the healthy way to overcome a predominantly psychological type of insecurity. But there are some individuals who will not accept or take this option. In particular, there is the psychological type who wants his ego to prevail under any circumstance. He is willing to admit anything except that there is a discrepancy between his personal "worth" and his self-image. Ramos attributes the source of this falsely superior self-image to a feeling of inferiority. In order to escape this feeling, the individual "abandons the realm of reality to take refuge in a fiction."[8] The emerging portrait bears some similarities to what Sartre would call "bad faith." In other words, one is incapable of facing one's situation, so one begins to "live" in a substitute world—an illusory or fictional construct. This will only add to the sense of insecurity, however, since the fact that one is living an illusion (in compensation for the reality one does not want to face) will make one doubly insecure. The subject becomes defensive, aggressive, hostile, sometimes violent, and extremely irritable toward anything that might call into question his illusory world.

This psychological portrait of the person affected by an inferiority complex is transferred to the Mexican situation as Ramos tries to unravel what he takes to be traits of immaturity in some aspects of the Mexican character. "I maintain that some expressions of the Mexican character are ways of compensating for an unconscious feeling of inferiority," he argues.[9] Ramos also insists that by this he does not mean that individuals who show these character traits are less capable than others, only that they *feel* inferior. "The Mexican has devalued himself, committing an injustice against his own person."[10] Thus he seems to think that the problem lies not so much in the objective situation as in the state of mind of the alienated person. By constantly asking his compatriots to become more concerned about their immediate reality,

Ramos is actually trying to create a formula that will help lift their spirits. One must keep in mind that Ramos is not addressing the social reality of a truly destitute person or sector of the population. He is concerned only with the psychological problems of those who needlessly develop a sense of inferiority because they use illusory or excessively idealized standards as a basis for measuring their own worth as persons.

It is also important to specify the type of inferiority under analysis by Ramos, since this feeling may be caused by a wide range of subjective and objective factors. Ramos is concerned in particular with the weak self-image adopted by a Mexican man when he compares himself unfavorably with his European counterpart. What is at stake here is that this is not a comparison of one man to another or even of one "type" to another. The sense of inferiority and frustration experienced by the alienated Mexican is actually a function of something much larger than himself. It results from the unequal status between two different cultures. This condition leaves its mark on the collective consciousness of the citizens of the less powerful country. Unless they learn how to cope with this problem, Ramos argues, it will leave an adverse effect both on their lives and on their own developing culture.

In trying to understand the reasons for the feeling of inferiority attributed to Mexican men, Ramos looks at both remote and more proximate causes. He turns to history and to the concept of nationalism so as to provide some objective foundations for the psychological problem under discussion. In particular, he suggests that, while the origin of the feeling of inferiority may be found in events dating back to the conquest and colonization periods, it was not until after independence from Spain in the nineteenth century that the problem of unrealistic comparisons between Mexico and the European nations became evident. Although Mexico was a newly constituted nation, it tried to place itself at the height of European civilization, "causing a conflict between what is wanted and what is possible."[11] There was thus a lack of cultural experience, as well as a lack of perspective on reality. "So far the Mexicans have only known how to die; but now it is necessary to acquire the wisdom of living," he cautions.[12] These observations show a synthesis of the three problems mentioned: the problem of imitating Europe, the problem of a lack of perspective on reality, and the absence of a culture that can withstand the test of time.

Ramos offers suggestions for solving these major problems. On the issue of imitation, he suggests the alternative of "assimilation." (This point will be developed at length by Leopoldo Zea.) The practice of imitating European culture must be replaced by the assimilation of such a culture. "Between the process of imitation and that of assimilation there lies the same difference," he notes, "as there is between what is mechanical and what is organic."[13] On the issue of the absence of a perspective that lasts through time, Ramos suggests the need for a new humanism, a theme explored in *Hacia un nuevo humanismo*.[14] The new humanism contains a cultural as well as a moral component. On the cultural side, Ramos refers to Nietzsche's call for returning to the "meaning of the earth," which he understands as a return to "the living spirit of perennial actuality found in the classics."[15] Unlike Greek and Roman culture, however, the new humanism must oppose all forms of slavery:

> While classical humanism was a movement from the top to the bottom, the new humanism must make its appearance as a movement precisely in the opposite direction, from the bottom up. This is what our times demand. In our modern civilization there are a multitude of factors that have pushed man to the bottom, toward an infrahuman level.[16]

Ramos worries about the developing conflict between a civilization that considers itself "humanist" and the political regimes of the time, which try to turn man into a herd animal. The new humanism therefore involves an ethical renewal that would lead Mexicans to shed the "survival morality" of living just for the day and the narrow individualism accompanying it. There must also be a broadening of perspective regarding the value of all races and their contributions to culture. "We obviously do not believe in the theory of inferior races that could be sustained when the value of European culture was considered absolute."[17] In particular, he opposes Hegel's opinion of the inferiority of Americans to Europeans. The limitations of nineteeth-century Mexico, he adds, were not caused by racial factors but by the excessive ambition of the ruling minorities, who "disregarded the true problems of the Mexican people."[18]

Although the proper assimilation of foreign influences and the creation of a new humanist perspective are important ways of counterbalancing the weight of inauthenticity, Ramos holds that the main problem to be faced is the lack of authenticity at the level of self-knowledge. This refers to the failure of the Mexican individual to engage in a full recognition of his being. His is a divided and incomplete being since the time of the colony. "A historic destiny placed those men in the midst of two worlds neither one of which is fully theirs. He is no longer European, because he lives in America, nor is he American because he preserves a European sense of life atavistically."[19] For self-healing to occur, he must shed his resentment against what is foreign at the same time that he must acknowledge that the root of his problem lies in having lived outside his own being, or, more precisely, outside "our [Mexican] reality."[20] Well, then, what is this reality?

Ramos explains that the alienation suffered by the Mexican as Mexican is due to his living within an empty reality. His self-image is based on an illusion disconnected from the real world. His ego has a high stake in denying the real world because this is the only way it will preserve its fragile existence. Except for the Indians—whose situation Ramos does not analyze, claiming that their view of time does not allow them to become assimilated into the Western conception of becoming and change—Ramos attributes to all Mexican males, from the popular outcast to the middle-class intellectual, the same problem of suffering from a severe disjunction between a real and a fictive self.[21] About the bourgeois type, for example, he states that each individual lives enclosed within himself and is indifferent to the collective interests of the society.[22] Of the urban type he states that "the principal trait of the Mexican character one can see at first sight is his distrustfulness [*desconfianza*]."[23] He suffers from a nihilistic individualism; he "negates anything at all for no reason," and his lack of orientation toward the future invalidates any long-term goals.[24] Like his bourgeois-intellectual countertype, he resorts to illusion, but in a different form. Rather than hiding his sense of weakness and lack of self-esteem in a subtle way, he shows off his "bravery and power" (*valentía y poder*).[25] He is overexcited and sometimes resorts to violence. Interestingly, Ramos himself appears to engage in an excessive amount of negation toward his fellow Mexicans, although his intention is ultimately constructive.

Ramos's most incisive criticism is targeted at a popular type that to him exemplifies the problem of insecurity, immaturity, and resentment in its most pronounced form. This is the *pelado*, who shows off his false valor by a mixture of machismo and chauvinism. This type "associates the concept of manhood with that of nationality, creating the error that valor is the peculiar characteristic of the Mexican."[26] He also suffers from a phallic obsession:

Since he is, in effect, a being without a substantive content, he tries to fill his void with the only value that is at his reach: that of the macho. This popular concept of man has turned into a dreadful prejudice for every Mexican. When this type compares himself to the foreign civilized man and his nullity stands out, he comforts himself in the following way: "A European, he says, has science, art, technology, etc., etc.; here we have none of this but...we are very much men." Men in the zoological understanding of the word, that is, a male who enjoys all of his animal potency.... If he only knew that this bravery [*valentía*] is nothing but a smokescreen![27]

Ramos's portrayal of the psychological alienation he thought he observed in his male compatriots (Mexican women remain invisible in his analysis of culture) combines the critique of the structural character deficiencies mentioned so far with the optimistic note that if Mexicans were to pay more attention to their own sociocultural reality, a more stable sense of self would develop, out of which a worthwhile national culture could be built. The time is ripe for this, he argues, since it is just at this time that Europe is going through one of its worst crises. "European man" can no longer serve as the standard for the people of the New World. Mexicans are therefore urged to look within themselves—to their own spirit and legacy—in search of a more inmediate and vital source of cultural values. "It is indispensable that each person practice with honesty and courage the Socratic counsel of 'Know thyself.'"[28] The most urgent virtue for society is sincerity. Ramos's idealist solutions include a moral commitment to fight the effects of individualism on the human personality and the appreciation of religion for what it has contributed to curbing egoism.[29]

On the issue of the type of culture that should emerge out of this psychological and moral renovation of the Mexican character, Ramos argues, as Zea will do after him, for a universal culture adapted to Mexican problems and needs. "By Mexican culture," he states, "we understand universal culture made *ours*."[30] He does not conceive of Mexican culture as an original culture distinct and separate from other cultures. He also strongly condemns a narrow and self-centered nationalism. Ramos argues for a synthesis of what is universally understood as culture and Mexican life. The relation of Mexico to Europe—and more recently to the United States—must be assured of being legitimated from a Mexican standpoint. One must be able to look at Europe from a Mexican perspective, as opposed to looking at Mexico from a European perspective.[31] Of course, this solution only brings us back to the dominant question of the debate on the formation of a national identity: What is our reality? What is a genuine Mexican perspective from which people in Mexico can understand and solve their own problems? Perhaps the major lesson derived from Ramos's work is that this question must be posed again by each thinker and each generation of Mexicans in their endeavor to contribute to the development of basic priorities in their cultural expression. Despite his stated objective of renovating Mexican culture, Ramos's approach has significant limitations in that the critical tone he uses to diagnose the country's deficiencies only seems to exacerbate the problem. In his exposition, little sympathy is shown toward his peers or the Mexican people at large. Moreover, the public exposure of people's alleged limitations in a style that does not concern itself with an empirical verification of the charges made is ineffective if the ultimate objective is to enhance the Mexican people's perception of themselves and their culture.

Indeed, Ramos's psychological approach to the question of Mexican cultural reality must be both radicalized and supplemented if it is to pursue the path of self-knowledge that he advocated so vigorously. It is important to extend the notion of assimilation of other cultural heritages not only to the dominant European culture but to the marginalized Indian culture constituting Mexico's historical legacy. Despite its explicit rejection of racial inequality, Ramos's profile of Mexican man and culture does not question the marginal sociocultural role he assigns to indigenous Mexicans. In fact, he justifies such marginality, arguing that Indians value only what is immutable and are therefore unable to adapt to Western culture. But notice that the idea that European or Western culture must predominate is never questioned. It would seem, however, that the *mestizo* who is part European and part American must not only learn to assimilate his European heritage but also his American pre-Columbian heritage. As long as the indigenous elements of the culture remain marginal or largely unacknowledged, the process of self-knowledge recommended by Ramos remains incomplete. The mechanism for revering what is European over what is native also remains intact, even if partially reformed.[32] The same point can be made with respect to the Afro-Latin cultures of the continent and the Caribbean. Until those elements that were most discriminated against at the time of the conquest and the colony are restored to a position of dignity and equality in the cultural legacy of a postcolonial nation, such a nation necessarily remains tied to the colonizer's prejudices and therefore cannot redeem itself fully from colonialism's negative weight.

Ramos's work is only one of several important attempts to address the issue of Hispanic-American cultural identity in the earlier part of this century. I have focused on it because of the influence played by existentialism and social psychology on his notion of the authentic self and because of the connection between some of his ideas and important themes developed later by Zea. At this time there was also a wave of migration of Spanish citizens (including many intellectuals) to Mexico. In philosophy, the idea of exploring the meaning of Mexican reality received a substantial impetus from José Gaos and several other philosophers who made Mexico their permanent home during the 1940s.[33] It was a time not only for Europeans to come to the New World under circumstances very different from those of the conquest, but for Mexicans to ponder on the meaning of this migration, in which about twenty-five thousand people took part. The influence of the Spanish philosopher José Ortega y Gasset became more pronounced, while the search for "Mexican reality" was viewed with strong favor from an Ortegan perspective. In the preface to the *Meditaciones del Quijote*, Ortega had affirmed, "I am myself plus my circumstance, and if I do not redeem it I shall not redeem myself."[34] This theme could be easily applied to the quest for identity in Mexico, whether this identity is sought for by Mexicans or by their close associates, the Spanish *transterrados*.

Despite the importance of Ramos's critique, then, it was only a beginning, to be supplemented shortly thereafter by other perspectives. A more critical view of the historic relationship of dependence between Latin America and Europe was also needed. This shift in emphasis can be seen in the work of Leopoldo Zea, a student of Ramos and Gaos. Zea's perspective—which in its final form becomes a full-fledged philosophy of Latin American history—was part of a lively intellectual environment. I now turn to his early analysis of the issue of Mexican cultural identity, and then to the highlights of the debate on the existence of a Latin American philosophy, in which I examine the repercussions of the issue of cultural identity on the discipline of philosophy.

Zea's Critique of Mexican Positivism

Leopoldo Zea's contribution to the Mexican study of cultural identity begins with his analysis of the role of positivism in nineteenth-century Mexico. He does not abandon altogether Ramos's psychological approach to the question but shifts the method of analysis from the depths of the unconscious to the more visible traces of the Mexican mind as expressed in selected aspects of the country's intellectual history and politics. From an idealist post-Hegelian perspective he employs categories such as "the Mexican consciousness [*conciencia*]" or "the Latin American consciousness" to refer to a historically oriented and positioned consciousness serving the region's political will to independence and freedom. Strongly influenced by Ortega y Gasset's view that "I am myself plus my circumstance," Zea works with two sets of characteristics that determine the human being—human nature (the universal), and nationality (the circumstantial). He links the two through the view that the human being is in essence a historical being. In Zea's view of knowledge, the concept of humanity functions as a universal regulative concept, while the concept of a national (Mexican) or continental (Latin American, Hispanic American) identity functions as the most significant circumstantial factor grounding a person's identity within a particular perspective.

Someone might question what makes the "Mexican" circumstance most important in Zea's analysis of the human condition—as opposed, for example, to a number of other "circumstances" such as class, race, sex, and so on. Zea's position does not deny the existence of other variables but finds in the national factor a more important perspective. The key to understanding Zea's position is found, as we shall see, in his association of historicity with self-consciousness. His argument is in part descriptive but also normative. It is descriptive because in modern times one generally attains consciousness of oneself as a historical agent through the mediation of the notion of nationality. It is normative, however, because it implies that this is precisely the perspective one should adopt in order to reach a historical form of self-awareness, at least in the present age. Zea views a person's historical identity in modern times as the synthesis of the person's cultural and national identities. This means that his definition of a Mexican cultural identity is channeled in large part through the concept of a national identity, while the national identity is largely defined in terms of the cultural dimensions of Mexican life and society.

Within these general parameters, Zea's major contribution is to bring the project of autognosis, or self-knowledge, to the area of the history of ideas. Within this area, his specific interest is the politics of the history of ideas. He does not see the history of ideas in a linear fashion but as the manifestation of a dialectical logic in which there is always a struggle for power and recognition between at least two contenders. In Western culture these contenders struggle for the claim to be considered the legitimate interlocutors of the logos (or reason). This becomes a transcultural problem when Westerners come in contact with non-Western peoples. Zea addresses the problem of colonialism by questioning the political use of the notion of rationality. The marginalization of non-European peoples with respect to Europeans, he thinks, is related to a Eurocentric view of reason, which leads to the perception that non-Western people are inferior to Europeans in their capacity to reason, hence, in their status as human beings. Political questions of autonomy and the right of self-governance hang in the balance. According to Zea, therefore, the problem of inferiority is more complex than the explanation of it given by Ramos. It is a problem located in the public sector—in the public conception of reason and in the use of power. Nevertheless, Ramos's mandate for self-knowledge is on the right track. What it needs is expansion and application to the more public aspects of Mexican reality. Not the soul of the Mexican but the history of ideas in Mexico becomes the target of Zea's analysis. Ultimately, he shares with his predecessor and teacher the intent to engage philosophy in a critical but also positive evaluation of the Latin American and Mexican experience.[35]

Looking back at Zea's productive activity over the past several decades, one can say with some degree of perspective that it was to be his mission to complete, for the discipline of philosophy, the reevaluation of the Hispanic American experience from the status of an "in itself" to that of a "for itself." The intellectual heritage of Hispanic Americans is no longer there for the foreign intellectual to interpret or ignore according to Eurocentric or Anglocentric criteria. It has acquired a voice that can speak on its own behalf, interpret its accomplishments from its own perspective, and make this perspective known at international forums in the relevant disciplines or arenas of public service. Nevertheless, a controversy has emerged regarding the status of Zea's work. Some would argue that his work should not be considered philosophy as such but perhaps belongs to the history of ideas. This view forms part of a larger debate on whether there is to date a genuine Latin American philosophy and, if so, what type of standards such a philosophy should represent. Some of the highlights of this debate will be analyzed shortly. In a sense, however, it is not very important whether one classifies Zea as a philosopher or as a historian of ideas. In the final analysis, what is at stake in Zea's work is the study of Mexican and Latin American history as seen through the lens of the intellectual formation of major contributors to the region's history of ideas. Since the 1940s, Zea has engaged in a critique of the rationality of domination, or, more precisely, of the way in which various sectors of the Mexican ruling class have used pseudophilosophical doctrines to justify their particular ends.[36] The project of self-critique recommended by Ramos is thus applied to the practice of the discipline of philosophy and to the role of the history of ideas in the region.

Zea's early works center on a critique of positivism in Mexico and on the analysis of a Mexican cultural identity. He also begins to develop the theme of a Latin American historical identity in works such as *América como conciencia* (1953). His studies focus on the interrelationship between philosophical ideas, Mexican (or Latin American) history, and political power. In his early works he argues that a Mexican cultural identity must be based on a national identity that represents the people's collective interests, not just the interests of an affluent class. "When the bourgeoisie demanded the rights of society," he notes in *Positivism in Mexico*, writing about the Porfirian era, "it demanded its own rights. Once this class triumphed, it forgot that other classes in society also had rights."[37] Zea agrees with the views of Antonio Caso, Alfonso Reyes, and other members of the "Ateneo de la Juventud" that Mexican positivism functioned as "a political doctrine that served a political faction," protecting their interests, rather than as a philosophical doctrine in its own right.[38] The middle class of the Porfirian era spoke in terms of the universal precepts of law, order, peace, and progress, but actually it adapted the discourse of positivism to fit its political and economic aims.[39]

In *Apogeo y decadencia del positivismo en México*, a sequel to *Positivism in Mexico*, Zea includes an interesting section on how the ruling bourgeoisie of the late 1870s and early 1880s appealed to positivist doctrines to stop a movement for Indian peasants' rights in the state of Hidalgo. For example, one article in the positivist-oriented political newspaper *La Libertad* defends the property rights of wealthy landowners against the Indians' view that the property owners have usurped their land. The author of the article states that the Indians have no ideals except to take "by theft or massacre the property of those whom they erroneously consider the usurpers of their land."[40] Here, Zea comments, one sees that what is vital for the Indians is considered mere violence, theft, and injustice by the landowners. He notes that the landowners appeal to progress, to the idea that the land must be in the hands of those who make it produce the most wealth. Progress is therefore identified with the law of the strongest. Moreover, the property owners argue that if the Indians cannot understand their reasoning, violence (not persuasion) should be used to attain the landowners' ends. The newspaper article concludes: "...in order to avoid greater evils, one must appeal to the only recourse civilization has against barbarism: violence."[41]

The defenders of the bourgeoisie, Zea argues, associate the interests of this class with what they call the *national interest*. As a result, any disruption of the interests of this class is considered a disruption of the nation itself. Moreover, the so-called national interest can be racially biased, working in favor of the white and *mestizo* population and excluding the indigenous sector.

> These men are well aware of the division between the white person or *mestizo* who robs another and the Indian who is robbed [*despojado*], between the *latifundista* and the peasant, between the possessors and the dispossessed. However, in spite of their being conscious of this division, they attempt nothing other than the use of force to assist in its resolution.[42]

He points to the contradictions in their discourse:

> They demand a rational order, but as soon as they cannot convince someone...that they are the sole possessors of all rights, they resort to force in order to prove the justice of their pretensions.... Ultimately they do not doubt that justice, seen from other perspectives, benefits the Indians; but they think that acceding to this will strengthen the forces of a future revolution.... They are progressive, they believe in progress, but only if and when progress doesn't get out of their hands. Thus we find these lovers of progress attempting to stop progress. Instead of guiding the forces that are just taking form in the new social phase, they repress [these forces]...more and more.... But they [have] achieved nothing other than to make them explode in a new revolution.[43]

Zea's description of the dialectic between the possessors of the land and the dispossessed sounds familiar to us because this type of conflict of interests has not been limited historically to the Porfirian era in Mexican politics. It is a conflict that takes on universal traits. Zea wants to ask, Does the law of reason or merely the law of the strongest prevail in history? He distinguishes between the universal claims of reason and the particular perspectives through which such claims are interpreted and made. Philosophy should be on the side of reason, but how often is it used to legitimate a sociopolitical order that benefits only the exclusive interests of some men? In Western culture, philosophy has also been used to promote the ends of "civilization" against "barbarism." But can we be so sure that when we appeal to philosophy in this context we are not falling into a false view of civilization, and, as a result, into a false view of those human beings we imagine are not fully human because they differ from ourselves? The process of self-critique initiated by Samuel Ramos thus turned on a problem seldom criticized by established philosophy: the uses that have been made of philosophy and reason not to enlighten and liberate human beings but to repress them and disenfranchise them from the exercise of their basic rights. Zea approaches this important issue by highlighting the interplay between the universal and the circumstantial elements of philosophizing. One must learn to distinguish well between what is universal and what is circumstantial in human reasoning, so as to avoid the contradictions—not to mention the injustice—implicit in using universal concepts of reason to justify the exploitation of man by man, or of one people or nation by another.

In *Conciencia y posibilidad del mexicano* (1952), Zea explores the origins of what may be called a humanistic *conciencia de mestizaje* or *mestizo* consciousness. In Zea's discourse the Hispanic American *mestizo* consciousness supersedes class consciousness. Such a *conciencia de mestizaje* comes to represent the national and cultural consciousness of the Latin American people.[44] Zea's perspective represents a progressive middle-class position. The *conciencia* of the Mexican person referred to in the title of this work condemns the irrational aspects of the ideology justifying the Spanish conquest and colonization of Mexico:

The European men who participated in the discovery, conquest, and colonization of America were equipped with a conception of the world and of life in which there was no place for the indigenous conception [of the same].... This world, instead of being understood, was condemned and negated in honor of the alleged universality the Europeans had granted

their own culture.... Nevertheless, a world as real as the one
that had been discovered could not simply be denied. Despite
all the efforts of European man to deny this reality, replacing
it with his own, it remained alive and thriving.... [The Latin]
American man, a product of this encounter, gradually
becomes aware of this, his double reality. At the same time,
as an expression of his humanity, he becomes aware of his
undeniable right to universality.[45]

Thus the humanist *mestizo* consciousness arises out of a double
vision that the Mexican individual is able to acquire because of his
special place in history. It was Zea's belief that historical events
from the conquest to the Mexican Revolution had given the Mexican person a privileged place in the Americas for developing this
type of consciousness.[46]

Another point of departure, however, for the development of a
consciousness of *mestizaje* is the analysis of contemporary events
in world history. In *América como conciencia* (1953), Zea observes,
referring to the series of crises in Europe that led to the Second
World War and its aftermath:

[Latin] America has lived as an echo and shadow of Europe.
But once the culture of this continent, European culture, has
reached the crossroads and threatens to collapse, what can
America do? Also collapse [with it]?[47]

What collapses in America, argues Zea, is not culture itself but the
need to imitate Europe, together with the "echo" and "shadow"
that had been the products of such imitative efforts. In other
words, we could say that Latin American culture is no longer ruled
exclusively by the European gaze. Once this gaze—or its effective
power on the Latin American consciousness—is dissolved, a new
universe with other possibilities and horizons emerges. This new
universe, Zea claims, is one where both Europeans and Latin
Americans face surprisingly similar challenges.

[Latin] Americans as well as Europeans find themselves
without a *ground* that supports them. In a fully problematical situation, both have a need to continue developing a culture. But, at this time, the [Latin] American [individual] cannot continue taking shelter in [a] European culture...because
such a shelter no longer exists.... From this it follows that the

[Latin] American [individual]...will have to find new solutions, new foundations, and he will have to do this on his own [por sí mismo]. [Latin] America, until yesterday an echo and shadow of Europe, will have to find a steady ground [tierra firme] for itself. It will have to resolve, on its own account, the problems of its particular situation [circumstancia]. Well, then, this attaining of a steady ground [tierra firme], this search for solutions to particular problems [problemas circumstanciales], gives birth to a discipline that is natural for man in every problematical situation: philosophy. [Latin] America needs a philosophy; it needs an original [practice of] meditation on and solution to its problems.[48]

Thus Zea presents the argument that historical circumstances have created a need for a solid base on which to build a Latin American cultural project and that this foundation must indeed be associated with the development of an original Latin American philosophy.

Zea's Conception of Philosophy

According to Zea, philosophy represents both the foundation and the highest expression of culture. In this role philosophy's special task is to help human beings give an enduring meaning to the changing circumstances of their lives. Drawing on Ortega y Gasset's concept of culture, Zea notes that "the history of culture is the history of the human being in struggle with his circumstance."[49] But if all the various expressions of culture are an attempt to give meaning to the human condition in a given social situation, philosophy represents the highest level of this attempt because it tries to offer not only an enduring but a universal representation of the meaning of human existence. Through philosophy a culture acquires a type of self-consciousness, that is to say, philosophy is the most significant cultural instrument through which an individual or a people can acquire self-knowledge. Agreeing with Ortega y Gasset, Zea views the self as a historical, changing self.[50] Philosophy is able to give a relatively lasting form to the spatio-temporal, circumstantial, dimensions of human life. Thus the history of philosophy and/or the history of ideas may be said to constitute a record of the human spirit, represented in the collective voices of all the philosophers who, throughout time, have been able to express what they have perceived as the ultimate principles forming the complex aspects and truths of human existence. Philosophy is always something that rises above the here and now. Zea may be interpreted to mean that where there is a lack of ideals that give meaning to life beyond the mere "living for the day," the conditions for culture (as well as for philosophy) are lacking.[51]

In addition to its foundational and discursive cultural role, philosophy is viewed by Zea as always tending toward a practical end. Metaphysics, he claims, generally exists in view of the need to support some "social practice."[52] Intellectuals, facing the task of interpreting cultural events in ways that are meaningful to a contemporary audience, need to be able to relate and adapt "ideas" to "reality."

> The diverse crises suffered by Western culture have had their origin in the lack of coordination between the world of ideas and that of reality. When ideas fail to justify reality, the latter loses its human sense and it is necessary, then, to search for new ideas, new values, that will justify reality once again.... This should be the task of the intellectual.... Otherwise, yesterday's living ideas turn into artifacts, into something dead or useless, without sense for the common man. The intellectual who continues toying with such ideas without trying to give them a new meaning is like a maniac, the possessor of a useless instrument.[53]

Every crisis in cultural values, Zea observes, generates new philosophies and new values. For example, the medieval man in transition to modernity had no way of imagining that reason would replace revelation as the ground of values. Today reason finds itself in crisis. But one should not despair. New values will replace those that are now collapsing. The creation of a Latin American philosophy represents to Zea one of these emerging values.

We have seen that Zea views philosophy as serving the practical purpose of providing a foundation for cultural values. Its practicality, however, does not stop here. Philosophy also helps to resolve problems faced by individuals in concrete situations. But regardless of whether philosophy deals with abstract or concrete problems, philosophical inquiry, according to Zea, cannot avoid carrying the mark of the particular. He does not discard philosophy's claim to universality. But he insists that the standpoint of reason (or universality) is associated in more than a superficial way with the historic/cultural circumstances informing its discourse. Western reason, however, has tried to affirm itself in abstraction from this cultural mark. In contrast, Zea wants to inscribe the Latin American circumstance into the philosophical statement born out of it. His reasoning is in some respects analogous to that of feminist writers who have tried to inscribe gender into philosophical discourse. Yet this attempt by Zea and others (women and blacks, for example) to insert their gendered or racial "circumstance" in philosophical discourse is often met with resistance in Western philosophy because—I would note—this approach to philosophy makes the discipline more vulnerable, less godlike, less "scientific" in a traditional sense, therefore less "final" in an authoritative sense. When one can trace a concept back to the human being who thought it and root this human being in a contingent situation, it is clear that the power attributed to such discourse will be limited in relation to the traditional claim that only reason can condition itself. Yet it would seem that Zea is only insisting on the obvious, namely, that one's philosophical discourse is always marked by one's gender, race, culture, economic class, and so on, and that it is not possible for a person to disengage herself or himself from these circumstances, even by an effort of will or the rules of logic. His argument would seem to be of relevance only as a counterweight to the view that one can do philosophy while eluding the mark of circumstantiality. For Zea, all perspectives are culturally rooted and, furthermore, no particular culture is ethically entitled to impose its standards of rationality and value on other cultures. Universality is an ideal that can only be reached historically in a totality arrived at collectively, having taken into account all particular perspectives.

The ultimate conclusion of this type of reasoning, ironically, is that the adjective "Latin American" in "Latin American philosophy" (as well as "European" in "European philosophy") is discardable. Such an adjective is needed only at an initial stage of awareness so as to identify the limiting or conditioning cultural factor in a philosophical work. In the end, however, the Latin American person, like the Greek or the European before him or her, does philosophy because there is a need to solve a theoretical or practical problem. What is essential to philosophy is the existence of such problems and of human beings for whom finding solutions for them is one of the greatest challenges. "Philosophy ultimately tries to resolve the problems of the circumstance called humanity," notes Zea.[54] Universality is therefore understood as the collection of all the particular (human) perspectives making up the history of philosophy. Zea argues against understanding universality to mean that the rational conclusions derived by one person or group of persons in a particular context should be applied to others in different contexts:

> The solutions that a man, a generation, a people or a culture have given to their problems cannot always be the solutions for the problems of another man, generation, people or culture. This has been one of the errors of our America [Latin America]. We have seen how [Latin] America has done nothing until our times except to wish to adapt itself to solutions given by European culture. This has made of [Latin] Americans maladapted beings: the ideas of European culture are not altogether adaptable to [Latin] American circumstances.[55]

What everyone does have in common is that each one must find the best solutions proper to his or her own circumstance. Philosophy reaches universality when reciprocal recognition of one's humanity can be put in practice among individuals or peoples of diverse or even contrary perspectives.

While it is possible to argue for other conceptions of philosophy than the one offered by Zea, I think it is important to note the coherence of his position. Zea's view of philosophy promotes tolerance of different positions and perspectives by historicizing the philosophical search for knowledge and by relativizing the Hegelian march of reason in history. The latter is no longer seen as the primordial legacy of the European *Geist*. Zea does privilege the relation between philosophy and history, esteeming highly those philosophical perspectives that self-consciously assert their historical origins. I take it that this view does not necessarily imply that the best philosophical productions (in a technical sense) are those that adopt historicist methodologies, but that the most self-conscious philosophical productions are those that fully take into account their historical bearings and that also show a profound respect for the humanity of all peoples. The mission of philosophy is to bring individuals (as well as historically constituted peoples) to a state of self-consciousness about their own values and destiny. But this mission is incomplete if it fails to consider the fact that this type of attempt is always limited, since there are other individuals, peoples, and ages that will also aspire to self-knowledge and in this way are our equals.

Zea's position on philosophy incorporates the three components of authenticity mentioned at the beginning of this chapter.

He tries to show that neither Latin American philosophy nor Latin American culture will ever get off the ground as long as their aim is to imitate foreign models. He believes the inauthenticity of the Mexican individual lies in being a "bad copy" (*mala copia*) of the European, and that this problem has been central to Mexican reality. He does not take refuge in escapism. But precisely in this so-called bad copy he finds a differential positive value, namely, the difference that marks the historicity of Latin American individuals, distinguishing them from North Americans and Europeans.

In the very mark of negation Zea grounds the roots of Latin American creativity. This process is also one that persists through time, giving a special character to Latin American cultural expressions. A revaluation of values takes place, however, so that what was once understood and assimilated as a "bad copy" turns out to be neither "bad" nor a "copy." Authenticity is precisely the process of identifying what is ours (even if it is not judged to be what is optimal). It involves the assimilation of one's own reality (*la propia realidad*), while the meaning given to the past and present is transformed by switching from a passive to an active and dynamic perspective. While Samuel Ramos ultimately faced the problem of cultural identity and inauthenticity by promoting the regeneration of a humanist moral perspective on existence, Leopoldo Zea addresses this problem through a new image of artistic, intellectual, and cultural creativity. A different position on some of these matters, to be examined next, is argued by the Peruvian philosopher Augusto Salazar Bondy in his thought-provoking 1968 monograph *¿Existe una filosofía de nuestra América?*

The Mission of Philosophy According to Salazar Bondy

A significant shift in the interpretation of authenticity is found in the work of the Peruvian philosopher Augusto Salazar Bondy (1927–74). He addresses the issue of whether it is possible to speak of an authentic philosophy or even of an authentic culture in Latin America.[56] Salazar Bondy offers a more contemporary version of the quest for a cultural identity among Latin American philosophers. While Zea's perspective has been characterized as exemplifying a kind of *conciencia de mestizaje*, in Salazar Bondy's case one could refer to a type of *conciencia de subdesarrollo* (consciousness of underdevelopment). His perspective formed part of a debate that took place in the 1960s and early 1970s regarding the existence and characteristics of an autochthonous Latin American philosophy. Implicit in his approach there appears to be a much greater admiration for the products of European and Anglo-American philosophy than one finds in Zea, but also—and possibly as a consequence of this—a much more militant desire for achieving Third World independence from imperialism.[57] Salazar Bondy's position emerged in a historical period that saw the reconstruction of Europe after the Second World War, the greater expansion of U.S. military and economic power in the world, the Cuban Revolution, the hard economic plight of Third World countries, and the rising escalation of the Vietnam conflict.

Theoretically, Salazar Bondy's perspective is linked to the rise of dependence theory in the southern continent. The dominant question is not so much whether the Latin American individual feels inferior to the European, but how the Latin American people can defend their own cultural heritage in a situation of economic dependence and underdevelopment. His point of departure for an analysis of the formation of a regional cultural identity is found in the empirically verifiable structural similarities typifying the various countries of the region. He diverges from Zea's idealist philosophy of history by drawing a tight connection between the issue of the conditions for cultural authenticity and the level of economic development of the region.

There is also a shift in perspective between Ramos, Zea, and Salazar Bondy with respect to the question of what counts as philosophy. Salazar Bondy is strongly influenced by the professional (and especially Anglo-American) model of philosophy prevalent in our times, namely, the expert's view of what constitutes a philosophical work. His methodology and style are largely indebted to analytic philosophy. In his works one finds a special emphasis on conceptual analysis, and on at least one important occasion he identifies the study of philosophy with the use of this method.[58] The result is a narrowing of scope of the issues to be addressed and (through the use of stipulative definitions) a delimitation of meaning of key terms of this discussion, such as "philosophy," "culture," "authenticity," and so on. The analytically trained reader will find his arguments much easier to follow than those of Zea and other post-Hegelian philosophers.[59]

The apparent simplicity of Salazar Bondy's arguments, however, is deceptive. The full implications of his theses are both controversial and complex. He argues not only for a stricter conception of philosophy in the technical, analytic sense, but for the necessity of a radical revolutionary change in all Third World

countries if there is to be any genuine philosophy in such countries. His argument is composed of two essential and interrelated
parts: a negative response to the question of whether there exists a
genuine Latin American philosophy and an explanation of what he
takes to be the cause of this deficiency. One could interpret this
bipartite structure as an attempt by Salazar Bondy to reach a compromise between his philosophical and his political identities.
Ramos and Zea were able to combine their theoretical methodologies (existential psychoanalysis, post-Kantian idealism) with a
positive regard for the possibility of a Latin American philosophical tradition. In this respect, their identities as philosophers and
as members of a Latin American cultural community worked in
unison. In Salazar Bondy's case, however, there is a noticeable disjunction. As a philosopher, he rejects the view that the region has
produced an appreciable philosophical legacy; yet as a Latin American, he blames imperialism for this deficiency. Neither position, if
pushed to the limit, appears to be foundational for the other. I will
argue, however, that the nature of his critique of underdevelopment would seem to lead to a more flexible position on the nature
of philosophy than he is willing to concede in his publications on
this matter.

In *¿Existe una filosofía de nuestra América?* Salazar Bondy
argues that philosophy is characterized, on the one hand, by a
rational, systematic form of reasoning and, on the other, by a need
to be rooted in the life of the community. "Philosophy as such is a
[cultural] product that expresses the life of the community," he
observes.[60] He adds, "Philosophy has to do with truth, but with the
whole truth of existence, clarified by reason."[61] In another context
he explains this concept further. Speaking in Argentina in 1973 at
a symposium on Latin American philosophy, he stated, in response
to another participant's query:

> Your question raises the well-known problem of whether
> "philosophy" is a certain activity of thought that is circum-
> scribed by certain canons, or whether it refers to all elabora-
> tion of thought: philosophy as *Weltanschauung*, a conception
> of the world, etc. When I have spoken here about philosophy,
> I have assumed what all of us think of when we speak of it as
> a systematic body of conceptual elaborations that in one way
> or another are found at the level of a certain type of "techni-
> cal" thinking, made by a certain type of person who is a "spe-
> cialist." This is what philosophy is.[62]

He defends the view that philosophy should not be confused with literature or poetry. Nor should it be confused with popular culture, although it should be in touch with it and, where relevant, analyze both its positive and negative aspects. He observes, with good reason, that it would be useless to debate the issue of whether or not there is a Latin American philosophy unless one takes the meaning of "philosophy" in a limited sense.

The sense in which "philosophy" is understood, then, is that of a cultural product expressing the life of the community in a rational form. Culture also acquires a very specific meaning in this discussion. It is defined as "the organic articulation of the original differential characteristics of a community."[63] Salazar Bondy distinguishes between culture and history by suggesting that the concept of culture is closely related to the concept of community while the concept of history is linked to that of a people or an age.[64] The concept of culture should also be distinguished from other related concepts, such as "ways of acting, ways of proceeding, ways of reacting, peculiarities, or characteristic traits." These concepts, he notes, are closely associated with, but not identical to, the concept of culture. Therefore, he takes the foundation of a cultural identity to lie in the original ways in which a community is organized in relation to other communities, not in special habits of dress, diet, or the like present in each community. This allows him to establish dissimilarities between developed and underdeveloped countries as well as similarities among countries within each group that on the face of it would appear to be dissimilar, for example, the relation between a Latin American and an Asian country.

A culture can also be either fully itself (*plena*) or defective. Salazar appears to hold that an underdeveloped country suffers from a defective culture because its culture does not fully correspond to the needs of the community (or communities) making it up. A culture where the needs of the community are fulfilled would be a culture of liberation (*de liberación*), whereas one that fails to express community needs is a culture of domination (*de dominación*).[65] The cultures of countries or groups that dominate other less advantaged countries (or groups within their own territories) are also cultures of domination, although they benefit from domination rather than suffer from it. Thus, for domination to end, a change must occur both in the underdeveloped and in the developed countries.[66] This view fits in with the theory that underdevelopment constitutes the other side of the phenomenon of development, a perspective elaborated in the 1960s by such social scientists as Fernando Cardoso and André Gunder Frank. These views about a culture of domination or of liberation appear in Salazar Bondy's treatise, although he is not as careful to define these terms as he is when he tries to explain what he means by philosophy as a cultural product.

Salazar Bondy indicates most clearly that one of the signs of a defective culture is the mistaking of inauthentic works for authentic philosophical works—or as he calls them, "products." He clarifies what he means by authenticity by distinguishing among (1) originality (*originalidad*), (2) authenticity (*genuinidad, autenticidad*), and (3) peculiarity (*peculiaridad*). The key to his evaluation of the status of Latin American philosophy revolves around his understanding of these categories in relation to his concept of philosophy. According to him, "originality" refers to "the contribution of new ideas and arguments [*planteos*]." "An original philosophy," he comments, "will be identifiable by its new [*inéditas*] conceptual constructions of recognized value."[67] Originality is therefore basically associated with novelty and value. Implicit in this assumption—and, as we have seen, in his subscription to a technical view of philosophy as defined above—there is the view that originality would be judged by experts.

According to this model, authenticity is synonymous with what is genuine, in the sense of not being fake. "A philosophical product," he states, is authentic or genuine "just as any cultural product...[is genuine insofar as it] is given simply as such and not as something fake [*falseado*], mistaken or weakened [*desvirtuado*]."[68] Thus Kant's philosophy, he notes, is authentic, whereas a spiritualist discourse is not. Finally, there is the trait of "peculiarity," a characteristic he contrasts to both authenticity and originality. "Peculiarity" refers to "the presence of historico-cultural differential traits that give a different character to a spiritual product, in this case a philosophical one.... ["Peculiarity" refers to] a *local* or *personal* tone, something that does not imply innovations of a substantive content."[69] He also observes that the most frequent trait of ideological products is "peculiarity." In this way he distinguishes ideological products from *genuine* philosophical products.

Having discarded repetitive, imitative, and "peculiar" works as inauthentic, Salazar Bondy applies these criteria to the history of philosophical production in Latin America. He judges that all of Latin American philosophy so far has been "defective" either because individual works exemplify some or all of these traits to a greater or lesser degree or—as I take it he is arguing—because, on the average, the totality of Latin America's philosophical output lacks definition beyond these traits. A summary of his argument may be found in *Sentido y problema del pensamiento filosófico hispanoamericano*, a lecture given at the University of Kansas in 1969 which is available in English translation.[70] But this part of his argument has met with objection both in the United States and in Latin America.[71] Critics argue—and I think correctly—that there is indeed a tradition of philosophy in Latin America that includes not just important individual works but a set of coherent themes developed over time and in various countries of the region. Salazar Bondy was not unaware of the facts on which these views have rested. As early as 1954 he published a historical study of Peruvian philosophy, and a two-volume edition of his *Historia de las ideas en el Perú contemporáneo* appeared in 1965.[72] This study covers the philosophical history of positivism, spiritualism, and materialism in Peru from the 1880s to the present, reviewing the contribution of major Peruvian thinkers and intellectuals. Yet in the conclusion to this work Salazar Bondy declares:

> Our social existence has been and continues to be alienated. This means that the true subject of history, oppressed and laid aside (*relegado*), split and alienated (*mediatizado*), has not found itself yet as a living community and has not been able to construct its own history....

> ...I want to insist on this thesis: the frustration of the historical subject in Peruvian life has been especially serious for [the development of] philosophy until our own times.... [For] an alienated existence cannot overcome the mystification of philosophy; a divided community cannot generate a genuine and productive [type of] reflection.[73]

He argues that the problem is not that Peruvian philosophy has been disengaged from social reality. On the contrary, it has observed a close relation between theory and practice. The problem is that social reality lacks unity and integration, thus leading to a weak culture and in turn to weak forms of philosophical and artistic expression.

In short, although Salazar has documented the existence of a rich philosophical tradition in Peru, he concludes that this tradition is structurally defective. After 1968, he pursued this argument further by becoming a more rigorous advocate of analytic philosophy.

If measured by the same standards of systematic rationality that he tries to apply to Latin American philosophical works, however, much of what is considered Western philosophy as well as Eastern philosophy would fall by the wayside. Salazar therefore has a tendency to fall into dogmatism as a result of his understandable concern for scientific reasoning and clarity. But his position can be viewed, alternatively, as performing a highly critical function. The thesis that so far there is no genuine philosophical tradition in Latin America serves to strengthen his analysis of alienation by referring it to a condition of underdevelopment in capitalist-dependent societies. Let us now look at the other side of his argument, which so far remains largely unknown in the United States.

In the first part of his argument Salazar Bondy tried to show that so far there has been no genuine *philosophy* in Latin America. The second part focuses on the problem of the absence of a genuinely Latin American community out of which such a philosophy could emerge. His reasoning here is that there is no genuine *Latin American* philosophy because so far there is no such thing as a genuine Latin America. Both sides of his argument might seem irrelevant to someone who does not share his conception of philosophy. I am assuming, though, that there is at least some legitimacy to Salazar Bondy's view. Let us recall that, apart from the scientific standing he expects philosophy to enjoy, his other expectation is that philosophy express "the life of the community." But while he is quite precise about what he means by a fake versus a genuine philosophy, he is not as explicit regarding what would constitute an authentic community. I will try to fill in some gaps he left in *¿Existe una filosofía de nuestra América?* by referring to lesser-known publications and to some statements he made at the 1973 Argentine symposium on this topic. In fairness to Salazar Bondy, however, it may be recalled that he was not able to develop and perfect his perspective (as, for example, Leopoldo Zea has been able to do over several decades) since he died unexpectedly in 1974, only a few years after having published his principal contribution on the subject.

It will be recalled that for Samuel Ramos and Leopoldo Zea the notion of authenticity carried the principal connotation of becoming aware of one's own reality and taking responsibility for one's cultural and historical situation as opposed to trying to imitate someone else's. Salazar Bondy takes this idea to a radical conclusion by arguing that, since Hispanic American reality is the reality of underdevelopment, in effect its reality is no reality. It is not possible, he argues, to speak of one's "own reality" when one lives in a Third World country. An underdeveloped society lacks substance. It lacks the capacity to direct its own destiny. It is managed by outside economic interests. It is therefore inherently inauthentic. There can be no authentic Latin American philosophy unless there is first an authentic Latin American culture. And there can be no authentic Latin American culture unless the countries of the region emerge from their status as capitalist-dependent societies, for this is the economic structure that asphyxiates, as it were, the otherwise healthy life of the Hispanic American communities. This consciousness of underdevelopment is the driving force behind Salazar Bondy's analysis.[74]

While Samuel Ramos had explored the structural deficiencies of Mexican alienation and Leopoldo Zea had dwelt on the structural strengths of the *mestizo* consciousness, Augusto Salazar Bondy moves his argument to a socioeconomic plane by considering the structural deficiencies of underdevelopment within capitalism. Becoming conscious of Hispanic American reality in this context involves describing such a reality as one of negation, or at least in terms of the absence of a type of fullness that ought to be there. In arguing (as I take it he does) for the dialectical negation of this negation, for the revolution that will definitely overturn the Latin American conditions of underdevelopment and oppression, Salazar Bondy is constructing a new type of dialectics, where the subject of social change is not the working class and its vanguard but the liberation-minded people of the Third World regardless of class or sector. It is possible to interpret this argument—although the Peruvian philosopher does not mention it—as a twentieth-century Hispanic American response not only to Marx's critique of ideology but to his notion of the "poverty of philosophy." For, ultimately, in spite of Salazar's great admiration for Western philosophy and for linguistic analysis in particular, he challenges the idea that this tradition is the standard for philosophical production as such. Western philosophy is rich in originality and technical mastery, but (with few exceptions) it has served and continues to function as a cultural product expressing the dominant elites' view of the universe.[75] The characteristics that Salazar Bondy attributes to philosophy, such as rationality, systematicity, and so on, have only existed historically (in his view) within societies *of domination*. A philosophy that wishes to separate itself from a culture of domination—a philosophy *of liberation*—can only emerge as part of the emerging struggle of the Third World against domination:

When philosophy proposed to liberate itself historically, it did not even achieve the liberation of the philosopher, because no one can be liberated when he or she dominates someone else. So if we want to look at things truthfully, the only possibility of liberation is opened for the first time in history with the Third World, the world of the oppressed and underdeveloped, who are liberating themselves and at the same time liberating the other, the oppressor. Then, for the first time, there can be a philosophy of liberation. In the concrete struggle of classes, of groups, and of nations, there is another who oppresses me, whom unfortunately I must displace from...the machinery of domination. Philosophy must be involved in this struggle, for otherwise it [only] constructs an abstract thought, and then, on the pretext that we are going to liberate ourselves as philosophers, we do not liberate anyone, not even ourselves.[76]

Thus even the best philosophy in the developed (and underdeveloped) countries will remain "poor" unless philosophers somehow make an effort to connect with the forces seeking an end to domination and begin philosophizing from this perspective.[77] Salazar Bondy also urges his Latin American colleagues to be radically self-critical if they are going to reach an understanding of the relationship between philosophy and liberation. One must not deceive oneself by thinking that if one does philosophy with some care one will have reached "autognosis," or be fully liberated.[78]

Zea's Response to Salazar Bondy

In the 1973 symposium, in which Leopoldo Zea also took part, the Mexican philosopher differed from the Peruvian on several issues.[79] Zea refers to Salazar Bondy's position that so far there has not been any genuine Latin American philosophy as utopian. He also disagrees with what I have characterized as the "double negation" structure of Salazar Bondy's reasoning. Zea suggests that to negate the past because one finds it defective, even on the ground of coming to terms with it (as Salazar Bondy does), might be a way to avoid facing reality. He argues that assimilation of the past, including its actual or perceived deficiencies, rather than negation, is the way to construct a Latin American philosophy, indeed, a philosophy of liberation. Zea's position on this matter, which is also the central position of his philosophy of history, will be examined fully in the next chapter.

Zea's published response to Salazar Bondy's 1968 monograph is contained in another monograph of about the same length entitled *La filosofía latinoamericana como filosofía sin más* (1969). In this work Zea elaborates on his conception of philosophy, some of whose principal themes have already been touched on. For example, he emphasizes the theme of philosophizing as a response to human problems—whether of an individual, a people, or humankind. He defends the importance of accepting different styles of doing philosophy, pointing to the diversity of literary expression in the history of philosophy:

> [Those who question whether there has been any philosophy in Latin America] forget that in the history of philosophy they want to turn into a model [of philosophizing]...[one may find] not only the systems of Plato and Aristotle but the poems of Parmenides, the maxims of Marcus Aurelius, the thoughts of Epicurus, Pascal, and many others. In short, there are forms of philosophizing that are expressed just as much in an ordered system as in a maxim, a poem, an essay, a play, or a novel.[80]

Zea also defends the view that there has been a persistent theme in Latin American philosophy since the nineteenth century, namely, the debate on the meaning of a regional or national cultural identity as part of the search for political independence and freedom. In this view he is joined by other critics who disagree with Salazar's claim that Latin America has not produced any genuine philosophy.[81] This is certainly the more moderate way to interpret the history of Latin American philosophy, and there is no lack of foundation for this view. Salazar Bondy's radical argument, however, has a great deal of appeal because there is a grain of truth in it. While there has been a legacy of Latin American philosophy, it could have been richer and—one would like to think—perhaps in conditions other than underdevelopment it would have been better. And although there have been philosophies siding with liberation against oppression, what is still lacking is a massive, universal, and persistent effort toward this goal. The power of Salazar Bondy's argument therefore lies in provoking one not to become self-complacent, not to sit still, despite one's previous or current academic achievements and/or political commitments. Perhaps the most lasting impact of his contribution to this debate is his unswerving quest to provoke his readers and interlocutors to a dialogue that would move them out of their settled views. His radical negation could then be seen as the other side of a profound affirmation of a goal he knew had not yet been reached.

It would not be appropriate to conclude this discussion without reassessing the claim that Salazar's views are utopian. As critics charge, he could have developed a much more positive attitude toward the past achievements of Latin American philosophy. Salazar Bondy himself was conscious of the fact that both the first and second part of his argument were vulnerable to the charge of oversimplification.[82] The forceful way in which he presented his either/or (*either* there is a genuine Latin American philosophy and such a philosophy will be both technically good and born out of a society that has opted for a revolutionary way out of underdevelopment *or* there is no genuine Latin American philosophy) leaves no option for a space in between. But what about figures like Mariátegui, Ramos, and Zea, for example? Shall we say that their work is unphilosophical, inauthentic, or both? And what about a number of other philosophers in Latin America such as José Vasconcelos, Antonio Caso, Francisco Romero, José Ingenieros, Enrique José Varona, and others whose works are worthy of being studied today? Salazar Bondy was not unaware of their importance. On the occasion of the 1973 symposium in Argentina he referred in particular to those whose works laid a foundation for the theories of liberation of the 1960s and 1970s:

First, I want to be fair to certain precedents.... In the 1920s Mariátegui wrote an article where he brought up the question of whether there exists a Hispanic American thought [*pensamiento*], and he says what many of those who came to discuss this subject years after him are saying: that it is not possible to think of a philosophy that is about to produce liberation as long as there isn't a process that destroys the [structural] elements of colonialism and domination.[83] It is important that we can go back to the 1920s to follow these concerns.

Second, it would be a historical injustice not to remember the magnificent movement that took place in Mexico beginning with the 1930s, [first with Samuel Ramos]..., reinforced later by the arrival of the Spanish emigrants...and...by our common teacher [José] Gaos. Leopoldo Zea has worked along this line, there is no need to remind ourselves.[84]

His argument, however, was that in the light of what was going on in the 1970s, it was not enough to repeat the earlier themes of "thinking one's own reality" or to rest assured that Latin Americans had already produced some philosophical works of high value. These types of position, in the 1970s, were not equivalent to what Mariátegui was doing in the 1920s, what Ramos accomplished in the 1930s, or what Zea has contributed since the 1940s. From this he concludes, "We must find a redefinition of all of this thinking, connecting it with a revolutionary movement, with a movement for change."[85]

Salazar's position, then, is not utopian, although it differs substantially in its treatment of the past from Zea's historicist perspective. If anything, his analysis suffers from a mild case of what Nietzsche called "the revenge of the will against the passing of time,"[86] namely, the sense of frustration at values that crumble with the passing of time or at potential values that could have come into being but never did (in this case, due to social injustice, limited opportunity, alienation, underdevelopment, and so on). On the positive side, Salazar urges his readers and colleagues to keep abreast of change and never settle for past successes and victories when there is still work to be done. His critique of underdevelopment and his warning that philosophical excellence is not easy to achieve are much needed today. His position, however, tends to repeat an "either/or" logical structure that, while containing some degree of truth, is too abstract to represent a much more complex reality. The connection he draws between underdevelopment and a weakened form of culture, for example, is highly questionable.[87] Social reality is not so rigidly constituted that all cultural products in an underdeveloped society turn out defective, or that all philosophical expression in developed societies will have a chance to turn out well. Moreover, alienation and domination are not coextensive with capitalism, although in a capitalist society these phenomena take on specific forms that should not be ignored or dismissed. Finally, the boundaries between a culture of domination and a culture of liberation are not as sharp as Salazar took them to be. It is reasonable to think—although this is subject to critical analysis and empirical research—that elements of domination as well as of liberation exist in every culture. Social reality is not as homogeneous as it might appear, although under politically repressive systems the expression of heterogeneity is indeed suppressed.

With respect to the mission of philosophy, it is perhaps misguided to draw a sharp line between the tasks philosophy should serve in the developed societies and those it should serve in the Third World. Zea's position that philosophers must address the problems that appear before them out of their concrete cultural circumstances, while more ambiguous, overcomes this potential divisiveness in that it does not create ethnic or economic boundaries between various philosophical missions but tries to rise to the universal element inherent in them all. For example, if liberation is an important human problem for Latin Americans, Zea would hold that this will also be recognized as an important problem anywhere else in the world. The point is that if a problem is sufficiently important in one part of the world, it will be of concern wherever human beings confront such problems.[88] Latin American philosophy therefore is not created by specializing exclusively in Latin American problems, or by taking a problem such as liberation as an exclusive problem for Third World people. On the contrary, one philosophizes under the belief that if liberation—whether conceived as personal, communal, or both—is an important problem in Latin America, its importance will not be limited to the underdeveloped areas of the world. A problem that is born out of a Latin American situation, in this case, could achieve recognition beyond the region because human beings are not so dissimilar from each other regardless of where and how they live. It is in this sense that a philosophy (if it is in touch with a real problem and if it is constructed properly) moves from the particular to the universal and from the regional level to the world-historical.

The question emerging from Salazar Bondy's analysis, in my view, should be, not whether and why philosophy is defective in underdeveloped countries, but a much broader question, namely, how philosophers in such countries can assist in creating values that strengthen their cultural heritage, giving meaning to it in the face of contemporary problems and needs. Salazar Bondy's contribution to this discussion plays an important role in defining some of the needs confronted by Latin American philosophy in its struggle with a situation of underdevelopment. His perspective, however, is too specialized to serve as a foundation for this broad cultural project whose quest for authenticity would indeed be shortchanged if one of its logical premises involved the rejection or denial of past accomplishments. After his death, several other perspectives offering a more constructive assessment of the historical role of philosophy in Latin America gained impetus. Among them was a major effort by Zea to develop a Latin American philosophy of history. This philosophical project will be considered in the next chapter.

THE HUMANITY OF MESTIZAJE AND THE SEARCH FOR FREEDOM: ZEA, ROIG, AND MIRÓ QUESADA ON CONSCIOUSNESS, REASON, AND HISTORY

The debate on cultural identity and dependence that took place in the late 1960s and early 1970s led to new insights on the question of cultural identity in the region. In this chapter Leopoldo Zea's understanding of a philosophy of Latin American history will be explored, together with related perspectives on consciousness, reason, and history offered by the Argentine philosopher Arturo Andrés Roig and the Peruvian Francisco Miró Quesada. These perspectives have in common the acceptance of the role of reason in history as an integrating and progressive element of regional development and sociopolitical liberation. I begin by examining Zea's historical perspective in his ambitious work, *Filosofía de la historia americana* (1978).[1] Two interrelated sets of arguments from his work will be considered. The first articulates a philosophy of history based on the idea of the search for freedom; the second addresses the cultural specificity of the Latin American situation through the use and interpretation of the category of *mestizaje*. In the first set of arguments, Zea develops a post-Hegelian position regarding the gradual historical advancement of individuals and peoples toward the actualization of freedom. In the second, he constructs a historically conditioned humanist perspective through the use of the regulative concept of the Latin American person as a subject defined by his cultural/racial mixture or *mestizaje*. In the interaction of these two principles one may find the roots of Zea's philosophical historicism.

In *Filosofía de la historia americana* Zea's task is to place the development of Latin American history within the context of world history. In contrast to Hegel, who had confined America to the

margins of European thought, he highlights the historical importance of the hemisphere.[2] Zea's historicist orientation, an extension of the approach to the history of ideas launched by his teachers Samuel Ramos and José Gaos, is logically distinct from the
religious, ethical, or metaphysical perspectives on cultural identity
and liberation I will consider in chapters 5 and 6. Yet despite the
major role he assigns to history, there is no more important axis
about which his interpretation turns than that of self-consciousness. A dialectical relationship is therefore implied between history and human consciousness. Such a dialectic results in the
application of knowledge and action to the pursuit of freedom.
Zea's perspective includes a strong humanist orientation, two components of which are the humanity attributed to the nonwhite, dis-
criminated-against races and the importance given to a political
project of freedom and equality for all peoples.

Historicity, Self-Consciousness, and Dialectics

For Zea, human reality is both conflictive and historical.
Philosophers should not attempt to step out of this historical condition, although they should try to view it in as encompassing and
objective a manner as possible. Zea's positioning of the subject of
knowledge in relation to world history is one that attempts to reconcile fairness to oneself and one's interests with fairness to the
other, with whom one may be in conflict, but who, in a sense, is
one's double. His view of history is strongly influenced by Hegel's
thesis of the desire of consciousness for a reciprocal recognition in
freedom from another consciousness.[3] For Zea, moreover, man's
being-in-the-world is not merely describable as a spatiotemporal
condition. Space and time take on historical characteristics. Without memory, human life would not be possible. And without history, memory itself would be purely experiential and lack all transcendent value. Human life is therefore ultimately grounded in
history and in the dialectic between self-consciousness and history,
out of which a historical identity is constructed. Such an identity is
not comparable to a stamp received passively from one's environment. It is a creative, actively forged awareness born in the ever-
present human struggle for reciprocal recognition and freedom.

Knowledge and action, for Zea, are equally grounded in freedom. Freedom is both an existential projection of human life, the
what-for of existence, and, most significantly, the ultimate expression of human subjectivity, objectified through the struggle for

freedom in history. But knowledge and action are also determined by circumstances affecting the life of an individual or a community. It is especially important to gain a historical awareness of the circumstances affecting a person's everyday life in a society. Only then can one proceed from a merely experiential perception of the meaning of one's life to a philosophical reflection and analysis of one's lived experience. Knowledge and action are therefore dialectically positioned between a determinate level of experiential and/or social circumstances and the creative horizon of freedom, out of which such circumstances may be transformed by human agency or praxis.

Consciousness of *Mestizaje*: The Symbolism of the Conquest

Leopoldo Zea believes that in order to reach both self-knowledge and a proper understanding of one's present social reality, one must sustain a deep awareness of the past.[4] This awareness must include the memory of events that are especially painful or difficult to recall. One event of this type, in the multiple and varied symbolism it evokes, is that of the conquest. The conquest represented power, expansion, mastery, discovery, and adventure for the European conquerors. For the victims of the conquest, however, it meant vulnerability, humiliation, destruction of a civilization, pain, and death. Throughout his interpretation of history, Zea is careful to consider the "other side" of the historical narrative, as institutionalized in the West. He is aware that the "universal history" of which the West speaks offers only one version of history. He does not wish to ignore or abolish the "universality" of history, which he would view as the sum of all peoples' aspiration toward justice and freedom. Yet he is intent on accentuating the dialectical relationship between conquerors and conquered. In the world of power politics, the conquerors define what is human, honorable, and reasonable, while the conquered—though not necessarily any less human—are confined to silence and marginality. Latin American history has had such marginality in relation to Western European history. Thus, if one is to affirm the legitimacy of a Latin American perspective in world history, one must learn to read world history from the margins, as a countertext to a previously hegemonic discourse.

Zea's construction of a regional or Latin American perspective can be seen as a parallel text, subtext, or countertext to the "master" discourse of "universal" history. He is careful, however, not to reject the claim to universality. Instead of rejecting the notion of universality, he expands its scope. Both the center and the periphery are part of the universality of history. His perspective favors the periphery's capacity to speak out on equal terms with the center.

> The philosophy of history in Latin America comes to be the expression of the philosophy of universal history, in which diverse projects are interwoven. These are the projects of the colonizing peoples as well as of those who have suffered or now suffer this type of domination. They are diverse but interlaced projects, converging toward similar, and, for the same reason, conflicting goals. These are the very own projects of...the peoples of Latin America, in inescapable dialectical relationship of stimulus and response, with those of the so-called Western world.[5]

Zea does not dispute the existence of such universal values as freedom, equality, and justice. But he maintains that all perspectives on such values are regional—therefore, equally relative to one another from a cultural standpoint. He addresses, in a critical tone, the issue of the disparity of power between the established Western powers and the more recently constituted nations of Latin America and the Third World. What is truly universal must encompass all perspectives, not just those of the most powerful. The West is blind if it believes its interpretation of history is the only one having a legitimate claim to universality.

But the Third World is also blind if it rejects its relation to the West entirely. The painful elements of this relation must be faced as part of a historical reality. At the root of any analysis of Latin American history is the interpretation given to the Spanish conquest of vast parts of the American continent five centuries ago. Zea holds that one of the most painful things to remember and assume as part of one's Latin American heritage is the event of the conquest. Why is this so? On the one hand, there were the Aztecs in Mexico, mistaking the Spanish conquerors for gods, and therefore committing cultural suicide.[6] On the other hand, there were the Spanish *conquistadores*, hardly to be admired from an ethical standpoint, insofar as they took advantage of their good fortune to exploit or exterminate America's indigenous peoples. How can one trace one's ancestry to such a past without trying to justify—or condemn—the ignorance and violence involved in its undertaking? Zea attempts to retrace the steps back to the conquest with the ultimate aim of reaching a historical type of self-knowledge. His analysis posits two interrelated concepts, which he explores in relation to the events of the conquest: Latin American dependence on the European metropolises and the phenomenon of *mestizaje* (the mixture of two or more cultures and races).

Dependence refers to an objective state of affairs marking the Latin American experience since the European "discovery" of America. In a similar vein, Zea actually refers to the so-called discovery (*descubrimiento*) as a "covering up" (*encubrimiento*) of America.[7] From 1492 until our time, the region has suffered a prolonged condition of dependence, first in relation to Europe and more recently to the United States. At the beginning of the nineteenth century the greater part of Latin America attained political independence from Spanish colonial domination, while Brazil became independent from Portugal. Because Zea's study ends with the nineteenth century, it does not refer, except indirectly, to the system of economic dependence characterizing the Latin American countries today. By pointing to the limitations and shortcomings of the nineteenth-century independence movement, however, he lays the groundwork for the analysis of a second movement toward independence and social justice developing in its wake. The Mexican Revolution of 1910, for example, may be taken as an early instance of a second wave of Latin American independence movements. The point of departure for Zea's philosophical and political standpoint is a *toma de conciencia* (becoming aware) of the situation of dependence endured by the region in spite of the various nations' achievement of political independence from the original colonizers. This situation of dependence is felt particularly in the economic sphere, in the forms of poverty and underdevelopment, and in the cultural sphere, in the form of dependence on cultural products imported from abroad.

In Latin America, therefore, "the philosophy of history...is forged [*se forja*] beginning with the consciousness of dependence."[8] Zea warns that a false consciousness nourished by the very same conditions of dependence has often prevented Latin Americans from reaching a proper assessment of their own cultural past. He also uses the notion of *mestizaje* to ground the region's historical identity in a mixed racial and cultural heritage. Zea's position represents a critique of the value of racial purity as well as an acceptance of the American indigenous element alongside the region's Spanish or European ancestry. Yet *mestizaje* as such is too broad a term to represent the values expressed by Zea's pro–Latin American notion of historical development. As he himself acknowledges, European culture is also the result of a mixture of races and cultures. I will therefore identify certain features of "stages" or "moments" of *mestizaje* depicted by Zea in his narrative of Latin American history, but neither named nor elaborated conceptually by him. They are: (1) *mestizaje* in the context of dependence; (2) *mestizaje* in relation to the first movement toward independence; and (3) *mestizaje* in relation to a second movement toward independence.

Mestizaje and Dependence

In Zea's narrative, the historical origin of *mestizaje* in America is found in the sexual union between the Spanish conqueror and the Indian woman who is part of a conquered people. The significance of this presumably forced union is highly complex at a symbolic level. It also contains an ambiguity with respect to how Latin Americans may regard this aspect of their cultural heritage and identity.[9] According to Zea, in whose account only a masculine view of the meaning of the conquest is examined, the *mestizo* understands that his paternal ancestors imposed by force an order of domination and conquest on the maternal side of his family. In order to legitimate this use of force, the paternal Spanish side rejected the cultural value of the maternal indigenous element. This devaluation, however, could not help but lower the status of the Latin American individual in relation to the European, since the former would always be considered "less than" the latter, based on these standards. Precisely because his Spanish ancestry is overvalued, he will end up devaluing himself. "The *mestizo*," Zea reminds us, "son of an Indian woman and an Iberian father, will aspire, although uselessly, to become part of the paternal world, feeling ashamed of his maternal origin."[10] His assimilation of the colonizer's values, that is, his rejection of his own indigenous native American heritage, exacerbates his position of dependence vis-à-vis Europe.[11] According to Zea's account, he will be left vulnerable to the imposition of other cultural values that are foreign to his heritage. Neither fully Indian nor fully Spanish, one day he may wish to reject both aspects of his historical legacy. If he does so, he will be especially vulnerable to the intromission of Anglo-American values, which he may adopt tenaciously as a result of his wanting to "begin from zero."[12] If this happens (and history shows the degree to which it has happened), Zea warns that in place of the old dependence on Spain and Europe, Latin Americans will only find a new dependence. This time the United States will be the new "master" and "center" whose values are to be imitated. This new form of dependence is linked to the material interests of the Latin American ruling classes, conservatives as well as liberals. "Neocolonialism...does not require an invading military force or a military occupation" to gain power in the region. It gains support from its internal beneficiaries in Latin America. Neocolonialism "does not need to change the mental order [orden mental], only to provide some training for those who have been the faithful guardians of its interests."[13] Under these circumstances, an internal managerial class, the residue of a colonialist order, continues to cater to the advantage of foreign interests.

How does one reverse this process of cultural devaluation and dependence on something that is not one's own? Zea believes freedom from dependence requires the recognition by both parties—the colonizers and those who have suffered the effects of colonization—of the equal human status of those colonized. He exploits this defense of colonized peoples' capacity to feel and to reason in his historical reading of Latin Americans' struggle for freedom from external domination. In so doing, he argues for the reversal of the subhuman status attributed to the Indians and mestizos under the ideology of colonialism. For example, he refers at length to the ideological battle waged in the colonial period between those who argued that the American Indians were human and those who denied them human status. This debate occurred among the Spanish themselves, particularly in the context of what they perceived to be their ethical duties toward the Indians. Two famous participants in this debate were a Dominican friar, Father Bartolomé de las Casas—known as the defender of the Indians—and Juan Ginés de Sepúlveda, a theologian and apologist for maintaining the Indians in a position of social inferiority.[14]

Zea situates the ideological debate between Las Casas and Sepúlveda along the axis of freedom versus compulsion. In Sepúlveda's view, the Spanish had the right to compel the Indians to adopt their religion and other values because "what is superior ought to command over what is inferior."[15] The distinction between what is superior and inferior, adds Zea, is raised in terms of cultural characteristics and differences. He notes that the indigenous people are placed on the side of the serf or slave because they are deemed culturally inferior.

> There is something about the Indians that differentiates them from the European conquerors. Are they barbarians? They are barbarians, not because they lack the *logos*, reason or the word, of which the Greeks spoke, but because their customs and morality do not coincide with those of the Christians.[16]

The fact that their customs were different was used to exclude them from being regarded as worthy of moral consideration on a level equal to Europeans.

> Right and the law must be imposed on them, for their own good, by those who have knowledge of the same. But what is the natural law? It is the same law of which Aristotle had spoken. According to this law, what is perfect dominates the imperfect. This is the reason why the possessor of perfection must guide those who do not possess it until they are able to reach it.[17]

Such logic, in its redundancy, uses reason as an instrument for the domination of non-European peoples.

Sepúlveda argued that the indigenous people were "serfs by nature," a proof of which was the ease with which a handful of Europeans were able to conquer them on their arrival to America. According to this reasoning, Zea points out, the ones who benefit most from the conquest are those who are conquered. Or, in the words of Sepúlveda: "What more convenient thing could have happened to these barbarians than to be subjugated to the empire of those whose prudence, virtue, and religion would convert them from barbarians...to civilized men, insofar as they can attain this [status]; from stupid and lustful [people] to rightful and honest ones?"[18] And finally, what should the Indians have done to repay the benefits they derived from those who claimed to be saving their souls? By the same logic of domination, it was deduced that they were to work for their masters. In particular, Zea states, they were to perform those chores reserved for "people of inferior rank."[19]

Las Casas differed from Sepúlveda in his conception of the duties required of Europeans toward the Indians. Las Casas argued that salvation cannot be forced on anyone, and that it is up to each person to arrive at an understanding of the Christian faith. He also had a high opinion of the Indians' native intelligence: "All of them are endowed with true creative abilities [*ingenio*]."[20] He condemned the exploitation of the Indians, arguing that their incorporation into the Christian order had to be done in a manner consistent with Christ's example, not out of greed and avarice, and certainly not by force. The debate between Las Casas and Sepúlveda therefore seems to hinge, according to Zea, on whether all human beings, regardless of their different customs, habits, and levels of culture, are treated as beings of reason, or whether cultural differences will be used to justify the imposition of the conquerors' values on the conquered.

Left unstated (as well as unanswered) in Zea's discussion is the more radical question: what possible right do some people have over others, even if the former's tactics are to use persuasion rather than force, to incorporate the latter into a new cultural, political, or religious order that comes into being through an invasion of their territory? Zea's views on reason and culture are marked by an ambiguity that, on the one hand, shows a strong concern for self-determination and cultural pluralism among the world's peoples in contemporary politics, but, on the other, depends on concepts of reason and self-determination formulated by modern European thinkers. This means that the question of cultural identity for "Americans" (both the Indians and the descendants of Europeans) seems to begin only with the conquest, once the category of rationality has been imported to America, and not, as in the analysis given by Mariátegui, with the recognition of the legitimacy of indigenous societies whose material organization guaranteed the well-being of the Indians much more efficiently than the order imposed by the conquest. Zea defends the rights of those marginalized within the political and international order established by the conquest, but he does not show the contingency of modernity vis-à-vis other possible cultural formations that might have evolved on the continent. In this way he supports a world-historical order based on a modern European project of rationality. He argues that all human beings are equal by virtue of their being rational and that therefore they have an equal right to self-government and to the preservation of their cultural heritage. It is from this standpoint, rooted in a modern concept of reason (although conscious of empirical cases of ethnic and racial marginality), that Zea gives meaning to the struggles for freedom and justice in colonial Hispanic America.

First Movement toward Independence

The struggle for independence against the Spanish crown in Latin America in the early part of the nineteenth century was a complex process that depended not only on local conditions and leadership but on the turn of political events in Europe. Often forgotten because of its position as a Caribbean French colony, it was the country of Haiti that first won political independence in the Americas outside of the United States. It did so in 1804, following several years of uprisings by the black population against French rule. It was also at the end of the eighteenth century, as early as 1798, that the Venezuelan Francisco Miranda founded a secret society in London—which had become an important point for reunions among South American leaders—for the purpose of achieving the independence of Spanish America.[21] Miranda, known as a precursor of South American independence, later launched an unsuccessful expedition to Venezuela in 1806, after which he returned to London to continue promoting the cause of Spanish American independence.[22] The invasion of Spain by Napoleonic troops in 1808 and the resulting internal upheaval, followed by a growing British interest in extending their trade to South America, helped to create favorable conditions for Hispanic Americans to fight for and win their independence from Spain in the second and third decades of the century.[23]

It should be noted, however, that Cuba and Puerto Rico remained Spanish colonies until the end of the nineteenth century, despite independence protests in both islands dating from 1868. Toward the end of the nineteenth century, the Cuban José Martí and the Puerto Rican Eugenio María de Hostos represented the movements for self-determination and regional integration in their respective countries, as Bolívar had represented earlier for much of South America. Still, the political process of independence in Cuba and Puerto Rico was hindered by the Spanish-American War of 1898, as a result of which the United States seized Puerto Rico as a territory. It also established a four-year protectorate and additional restrictions over Cuba. This truncated development in both islands' legitimate course toward independence from Spain helps shed light on the political histories of Cuba and Puerto Rico in subsequent decades, especially with respect to the issues of nationalism, cultural identity, and the North-South conflict.

In his analysis of the independence struggle, Zea does not cover the various struggles for independence taking place in different regions of Latin America, or the events that led to the formation of the nations occupying this vast geographical area. He notes only the protests of José Morelos in Mexico in 1813, the attainment of Mexican independence in 1821, the liberation of Argentina in 1816 by the Argentine general José de San Martín and his sub-

sequent crossing of the Andes to liberate Chile, the peaceful secession of Brazil from Portugal in 1822, and the definitive battle of
Ayacucho in 1824, won by Simón Bolívar's lieutenant general, José
Antonio Sucre. Zea quickly moves from the question of the attainment of independence by the former colonies to Bolívar's dream of
promoting a form of South American unity that would bring many
of the newly liberated territories together.[24] In fact, Zea's account
of independence concentrates largely on an examination of Simón
Bolívar's vision of Hispanic American unity and his eventual disil-
lusionment with this vision. Bolívar stands out as a symbol of
Latin America's first movement toward independence.

　　With this double focus on the theme of Latin American unity
and the figure of Bolívar as South America's foremost liberator,
Zea considers Bolívar's hope that a new order based on liberty and
unity would succeed the power of the Spanish crown in the liberated territories. His hopes would not be attained, however, since
internal wars and factions led to what Bolívar called chaos, anarchy, and disunity. The different territories and countries, rather
than forming an empire or federation of all Spanish-speaking
Americans, broke into separate nations, whose internal affairs and
power struggles took precedence over any kind of regional organization. Bolívar gradually grew more disenchanted and bitter. A
meeting of representatives of the various regions and countries
held in Panama in June 1826, which he had called in 1824 in the
hope of consolidating Latin American unity, was poorly attended.
Most notably, it excluded Bolívar himself. After seeing his expectations shattered by developments such as the partition of
Venezuela and Nueva Granada, the divisiveness among various
Latin American factions, and the assassination of José Antonio
Sucre, Bolívar went into exile in despair. The *"death of Sucre,"* he
wrote, *"is the blackest and most indelible mode* [sic] of history in
the New World."[25] A few weeks before his death he reflected on his
project for Latin American unity, declaring it a failure. He stated
that to serve the cause of revolutions is equivalent to "plowing in
the sea" and that "the only thing one can do in America is emigrate."[26] Zea views the defeat of Bolívar's project as a reversal from
freedom to anarchy. With anarchy taking the place of liberty,
Latin America would be ripe for falling into new types of dependence, particularly with respect to England and the United States.

　　Bolívar's project stressed the political and cultural unity of
Latin America, and it had failed. Various interpretations have
been given as to the nature of the failure and the meaning of the

freedom to be achieved in the politically independent countries of the region. Liberals blamed the legacy of an authoritarian Spanish past for Latin America's political backwardness and lack of progress. They looked to the United States, France, and England for new ideas and models to implement in the region. Conservatives offered elitist explanations in which the Spanish past was praised, while the Latin American masses were blamed for their failure to be truly Spanish. The conservatives fought the new "foreign" views associated with "progress." According to Zea, the proposals of both sides eventually led to an impasse.[27] Neither side had worked out a good paradigm for interpreting the relation between the past and the present, or between race and culture.

During the first movement for independence there had been a failure of Latin American leaders to accept the reality of *mestizaje*. The conservatives' ideology was to preserve the Spanish order, only without Spain.[28] This was a feudal, colonial order, the heirs of which were the great landowners. Their pride in Latin America's heritage was based on their veneration of the Spanish race and its noble virtues of courage, integrity, and so on. The vast majority of Latin Americans, those of mixed race or of the races discriminated against—Indian and black, primarily—were excluded from the benefits of the new political independence. Those who held the more liberal or progress-oriented ideology, to which Zea gives the name of *proyecto civilizador* (civilizing project), were also affected by racial prejudice against the Indians, blacks, and *mestizos*. Their prejudice took a different form, in accordance with their political ideas. They believed the predominantly authoritarian Spanish heritage had limited Latin America and had retarded its economic progress.[29] Thus they wanted to supplement the process of political independence with what they called "mental emancipation" (*emancipación mental*), to be achieved through the importation of positivist philosophy and/or immigration of large numbers of Europeans to the region.[30]

Zea contrasts the effects of this "civilizing" project in Mexico and Argentina, in particular.[31] In Mexico, as in most of Latin America, the rise of positivism at the time was linked to a desire for social progress, which was to take place through the adoption or adaptation of Anglo-American and French ideas.[32] In Argentina, a special effort was made to change the nature of the society through projects promoting the influx into the country of European immigrants. "We must mix with the population of countries more advanced than our own," Zea quotes the Argentine educator and statesman Domingo Sarmiento as saying, "so that they will communicate to us their arts, industries, activity, and aptitude for work."[33]

The Argentine statesmen Juan Bautista Alberdi and Domingo Sarmiento, described as "civilizers," envisioned the future development of South America as taking place by means of what Zea calls a "blood transfusion."[34] Their goals for the future rested on an ideology of the superiority of some races over others. They desired an aristocratic *mestizaje*, based on the importation to America of preferred European races. "Let us populate!" exclaims Zea, reflecting the civilizers' ideas. "But let us do it with men who make possible the dreams of civilization. A *mestizaje* like that of the United States would make of this America another United States."[35] In this vein, Sarmiento, in *Argirópolis*, noted that if two thousand immigrants were brought into the country, within a few years Argentina would be transformed into another United States.[36] His compatriot Alberdi stated, "Do not fear...the confusion of races and tongues. From Babel, from chaos, there will come out one day, bright and clear, the South American nationality."[37] How to attract the right foreigners to invest in or migrate to South America seemed to be a very high national priority for the region's recently established republics.

These considerations reveal that despite the independence of the Latin American republics from the former colonial powers, there remained a type of admiration for Europe, England, and the United States that to some extent amounted to a new, less explicit but nevertheless real, dependence. This was coupled with a denigration of the Indian, black, and *mestizo* population of the region. Yet how can individuals or a people be really free if they are so dependent on foreign favor or approval, neglecting or rejecting their own heritage? One remedy is to reverse the pattern of self-depreciation by giving a positive value to the *mestizo* population. Another is to view history from the standpoint of an assumptive project (*proyecto asuntivo*) exemplifying an inclusivist attitude toward the region's *mestizo* heritage. Such a project looks at the past in order to assimilate it into the present, and to do so in view of both its strengths and limitations. From this standpoint, Zea argues, it is possible to enter the next historical stage in the pursuit of freedom—a stage characterized by the vision of an egalitarian and self-affirming *mestizaje*.

Second Movement toward Independence: *Mestizaje* in Equality

A change of attitude regarding the cultural value of *mestizaje* and the human value of the *mestizo* is essential if one is to break out of an attitude of dependence toward Europe and the Anglo-American world. Zea singles out the Cuban patriot and writer José Martí (1853–95) as a major spokesman for this positive view of *mestizaje* in the late nineteenth century. Focusing on Martí's well-known essay "Nuestra América," Zea reveals what he takes to be a truly authentic Latin American consciousness with respect to the problem of cultural identity and *mestizaje*.[38] This new, positive view of *mestizaje* expands the libertarian project of Bolívar to a new, egalitarian base. Martí combines Bolívar's idea of political independence from Spain and the support for Hispanic American unity with a democratic, egalitarian, and anti-imperialistic perspective. On the question of racial difference, Martí held that the human being belongs only to one species, humankind: "There are no races,...[only] the universal identity of man. The soul emanates, equal and eternal, from bodies diverse in form and color."[39] His vision lays the foundation for a new type of *mestizaje*, one determined by the principle of equality. In his 1895 farewell letter to his Mexican friend Manuel Mercado, written on the eve of his death as he battled for Cuba's independence from Spain and a possible U.S. occupation of the island in the absence of Spain's forces, Martí speaks with pride of "the *mestizo* mass...—the intelligent and creative mass of whites and blacks."[40] In "Nuestra América" he had said: "We were a mask, with the pants of England, the Parisian vest, the North American jacket, and the Spanish cap. The silent Indian would turn around us and go to the mountains to baptize his children. The black man, looking at us from the distance, would sing at night the music of his heart.... [T]he peasant, the creator, blind with indignation, revolted against the scornful city, against its creature."[41] Regarding the idea of mental emancipation to be achieved by importing European ideas into the region, Martí suggests that "neither the European book nor the *yanki* book give the key to the Hispanic American enigma."[42] Referring to Sarmiento's polarization of European civilization and Argentinian rural "barbarism," the Cuban poet said, "There is no battle between civilization and barbarism, only between a false erudition and nature.... The autochthonous *mestizo* has conquered the exotic *criollo*."[43] Finally, regarding the denigration of Latin America, he stated, "And let the conquered pedant be silent, for there is no fatherland [*patria*] where a man may be more proud than in our painful [*dolorosas*] American republics."[44]

Martí's assessment of *mestizaje* is egalitarian and self-assertive. *Mestizos*, blacks, whites, and Indians are equal in that they are all human. From a cultural standpoint, however, it is important to give priority to one's own cultural legacy. In this vein Martí suggests that despite the great value of the European classics, it is more important for Latin Americans to know their own culture and history. "Our Greece is more important than the Greece that is not ours."[45] Martí's perspective elevates the notion of *mestizaje* by making all races synonymous with humanity. At the same time he also elevates the culture of "our America"—as Martí referred to Latin America—by placing it on a par with other cultures. From this is born the sense of a philosophy of/for "our America," in the sense of the term understood by Martí. The legitimacy of Latin American philosophy, viewed from this standpoint, would be expressed in the practice of affirming, protecting, and defending Latin American cultural differences vis-à-vis the differences delineating the cultures of other regions of the world.

According to this view of philosophy, Latin Americans owe their most intensive loyalty to the knowledge of their own culture. There is a very strong sense of the "for us" in Martí's sentiments about the region's culture. This view displays a strong pride and faith in the achievements of one's culture even if the nations to which this culture belongs do not have a "superpower" status in history. The humanity of *mestizaje* is all that is necessary for these cultures to have a foundational value in world history. In political terms, this approach is often linked with an anti-imperialist position in which Latin American cultural values are seen as threatened by and therefore in conflict with expansionist projects based in the United States.[46] But Zea's humanist argument also proposes a type of peaceful, egalitarian relation of coexistence with the cultural values of dominant nations as long as the latter do not try to superimpose their values on the less powerful. His perspective is vulnerable to accepting idealistic rather than realistic solutions to the problems of inequality and discrimination affecting the relations among individuals, classes, and cultures. Nevertheless, his position is instrumental in helping to raise awareness of the need to extend the human rights and freedoms previously enjoyed by only some individuals and cultures to the rest of humanity, whose cultural marginality or political subordination is no longer deemed justifiable or acceptable.

The Impact and Limits of Zea's Philosophical Outlook

Over the decades during which Zea has contributed to the study of the history of ideas in Mexico and Latin America, his views have had a strong impact on discussions of Mexican and Latin American identity, the history of ideas, and political ideology. In the field of philosophy, some of the best-known authors who have entered into dialogue and discussion with Zea are the Uruguayan Arturo Ardao, the Peruvian Francisco Miró Quesada, the Argentine Arturo Roig, and the Mexican Abelardo Villegas.[47] An anthology edited by Zea and prepared in 1967 under the auspices of UNESCO (though not published until 1986 in Mexico) contains a representative interdisciplinary contribution to the subject.[48] In *América Latina en sus ideas*, these authors, in addition to several others representing related disciplines such as anthropology, literature, and the sociology of religion, present a variety of perspectives on Latin American cultural identity along the lines laid down by José Martí's idea of "our America." In the introduction to this work, Zea refers to the *proyecto asuntivo* as a methodological approach aimed at answering the historically recurring question of Latin America's cultural identity.

> "What are we?" the civilizer Domingo Sarmiento asked himself.... [We are] a strange peculiarity and, therefore, something difficult to define. But [it is] a definition made urgent by the consciousness of the subordinations suffered, a definition necessary so that such subordinations will not be repeated [in history]. This is the project we call "asuntivo," insofar as it tries to assume [our] own reality [*la propia realidad*], our own inescapable experiences and our own history, framed by [alien] definitions or notions. Shall we assume it in the way Hegel spoke of the spirit, creating a culture "par excellence"? The culture that Europe and the West have imposed, superimposed on, or juxtaposed to that of those peoples having doubts about their own inescapable identity? Or shall we assume it within the framework of a full and free humanity?[49]

Only by developing a fully conscious knowledge and awareness of the past, Zea argues, will the "subordinations" of the past not be repeated. He therefore suggests that Latin Americans are still vulnerable to doubt about their own self-worth as cultural beings and that a "becoming conscious" of their historical situation will help prevent future dependencies.

But isn't Zea's analysis of Latin America's vulnerability too idealistic to handle the threat of the gradual erosion of the culture he attempts to preserve? Are the study of the history of ideas and the dissemination of knowledge regarding the region's history and culture sufficiently powerful means to halt the influx of the latest North American or European fashions, ideas, political programs, or even religious sects? How is it possible for people to adopt the full implications of a historically aware standpoint when there is widespread illiteracy, a short life expectancy, and malnutrition? Are the ideas of the educated sectors likely to affect or transform the lives of the disenfranchised masses? Must we not confront an even larger contradiction than that between dependence and freedom, namely, a contradiction between the power of self-consciousness to posit a freedom "for itself" in a relationship of equality with other "for itselfs" and a recalcitrant economic order that systematically generates lack of freedom, inequality, and an ever-widening gap between the rich and the poor? Doesn't the study of the history of ideas in the region tend to centralize the interpretation(s) of the meaning of history in the hands of a small group of intellectuals and politicians? Or would the concept of *mestizaje* invoked by Zea ultimately lead to the collective defense and interpretation of their cultural identity by large numbers of people, and, therefore, to the concept of a radical, egalitarian democracy? In short, is the philosophy of self-consciousness trapped within an analysis of self-consciousness as such, or does it spill over into a philosophy of democratic power for all sectors of the population, including those vulnerable to prejudice and disempowerment? Does the philosophy of self-consciousness contain sufficient criteria for determining the difference between better and worse conceptions of liberation, or are there still gaps left unaddressed by this theory?

Addressing this problem requires a closer examination of what the philosophy of self-consciousness has to offer to liberation theory. In Zea's account of how one becomes conscious of one's cultural identity, which he takes to represent an authentic rather than a fake positioning of consciousness vis-à-vis its sociohistorical environment, one finds the paradigm of a consciousness "for itself" that understands itself as historically rooted and from this position assumes its task of philosophizing. This paradigm is helpful in the sense that it breaks down the monopoly over the discourse of "freedom," "reason," and "self-determination" exercised by conservative Western interests, and allows the claims of less powerful interests (e.g., those of developing nations) to come forward. But the paradigm is contradictory to the extent that it fails to take into account regional differences and ethnic conflicts within nation-states. At the same time, it privileges those interests that are able to engage in the dominant discourse of a philosophy of self-consciousness, a discourse that is culturally alien to the most marginalized ethnic and racial groups and communities in the region. Zea's *mestizo* is a prevalent Latin American type, but he is not the region's only type. Essentializing his "consciousness" as "the" Latin American consciousness, therefore, erases a number of other perspectives, including those of ethnic and racial minorities as well as those of women from all social sectors. Having said this, however, it should also be noted that Zea does not offer an absolutist or purist paradigm; his notion of *mestizaje* is not intrinsically closed off to reformulation, especially as new groups come forward in the political arena to claim their rights of self-governance and freedom.

In this paradigm of liberation, the position of self-consciousness (as a "for itself" demanding certain rights, recognition, and so on) does not change, but its range is extended to include those previously excluded from its borders. As Zea uses it, this model of liberation is flexible with respect to the number of new subjects that may acquire the language of rights, but inflexible with respect to the models of self-consciousness and rationality used to legitimate such rights. While the structure of the "for itself" does not change, its specificity in terms of its concrete determinations may vary. Thus the "for itself" may stand for an individual or a people, for a Mexican, a Latin American, a European, or a North American, for the oppressor as well as the oppressed. In Zea's theory the failure or limitation on the part of the oppressor always lies in not understanding that the other, the oppressed, is also its own "for itself" and must be recognized as such. The failure on the part of the oppressed, in turn, is to fail to recognize its own "for itself" and therefore to fail to enact its own freedom.

Zea's approach is to make the notion of the "for itself" concrete by giving it attributes other than that of individuality (as in existentialism) or class (as in Marxism). When Zea talks about a "for itself" with national characteristics (the Mexican consciousness) or with racial-geographical characteristics (the *mestizo* consciousness) his use of the notion of the "for itself" appears to some as a kind of transgression—a transgression against the "purity" of a "for itself" abstracted from all such determinations. His paradigm is an inversion of the ideologies of fascism and colonialism, in that the latter use racial or national characteristics not to claim the universality of the basic rights of all human beings, but to justify restrictions on such rights and other forms of prejudice and discrimination. His inverted paradigm could make some people nervous because he seems to add to the paradigm of self-consciousness something that should not be there: color, cultural specificity, racial determination, even a nationality. In principle, it is possible to have a theory of self-consciousness striving for freedom without ever having to discuss the notion of cultural or racial difference. But, Zea would respond, is it appropriate for Latin Americans to engage in the discourse of self-consciousness as if they were on the conqueror's side of history, as if the color of their skin had no historical consequences, as if colonialism had never occurred or neocolonialism were nonexistent?

Nevertheless, in interpreting Zea's philosophical perspective, we must be careful not to overlook the fact that as long as the notion of humanity on which he relies is basically a European construct, the mere addition of color or nationality as a qualifying circumstance to this "universal man" will not be sufficient to legitimate indigenous and marginalized ethnic cultures *on their own terms*. The latter can only be legitimated in terms of the paradigms of freedom and self-determination developed by European philosophy, albeit in an extended and more radically inclusive form. This means that, despite his efforts to mediate the effects of the conquest in Latin American history, the notion of reason prevailing in his work is basically a product of European culture. Still, in adapting European philosophical anthropology to Latin American conditions and needs, Zea has tried to avoid the trap of falling into a rigid dualism of good and evil with respect to culture, nationality, or race. His position moves the question of cultural diversity (albeit in a partial and restricted form) to the forefront of a Western philosophy of history. "This philosophy of ours cannot be limited to purely Latin American problems, that is, the problems of the Latin American circumstance. It must be concerned with the larger circumstance called humanity, of which we are also a part."[50]

The "For Itself" as a Culturally Rooted "For Us": Roig's Beginning Point for Philosophy

Arturo Roig, who has also contributed to a historicist perspective on Latin American cultural identity, offers another post-Hegelian approach to the study of this problem.[51] In his important work *Teoría y crítica del pensamiento latinoamericano* (1981), Roig explores the conditions marking the point of departure for a historically rooted Latin American philosophizing.[52] He notes that Hegel, who wrote about philosophy's beginning at the time of the Greeks, characterized this beginning in terms of the emergence of a self-consciousness that regarded itself as valuable and situated itself in relation to the ethos of a people. According to the paradigm we are exploring of a culturally and historically situated "for itself," Roig is saying that philosophy begins when a historically aware subject takes himself as valuable and at the same time assumes the cultural legacy of the society to which he belongs. As part of his elaboration of this model, he adds an original point about the plural nature of the cultural-philosophical subject:

> The subject that affirms itself as valuable, which according to Hegel constitutes the condition through which philosophy had its beginnings among the Greeks..., is not a singular but a plural subject, insofar as the categories of "world" and "people" properly refer to a universality that is only possible within a plurality. This is the reason why we can enunciate the anthropological a priori referred to by Hegel as a wanting ourselves as valuable [*querernos a nosotros como valiosos*] and consequently as a holding the *knowing* of ourselves as valuable [tener como valioso el *conocernos* a nosotros mismos] even when it may be this or that particular man who puts into play this point of departure.[53]

Roig transforms the notion of the subject (either in its singular form, "I," or in its abstract form, "Spirit") to a "We" [*nosotros*], a plural, culturally rooted subject whose reflexive form as a "for itself" would therefore be a "for us." The formula of self-consciousness giving itself value vis-à-vis another self-consciousness is transformed and adapted to that of a plural subject united by a cultural legacy with respect to which it places itself in the position of a "for us," or appropriating subject. Unlike Zea, Roig does not exploit the juxtaposition of the European/North American versus the Latin American consciousness. The appropriation and reappropriation of culture of which Roig speaks takes place wholly within a Latin American context. Thus his approach to the history of ideas in Latin America is more moderate in scope than Zea's. Nevertheless, there is a noticeable strength in Roig's perspective due to its methodological precision and self-contained form.

For Roig, the beginning of philosophy in Latin America, as in Greece, occurs when the philosophizing subject acquires a consciousness "for itself/for us." In Latin America, this involves turning away from a consciousness "for another," which represents the state of servitude or colonization. The Latin American subject, argues Roig, is not unique in being born into a reality he did not create. This is always the case with anyone born into a culture. One is born into what Roig calls a cultural "legacy" (*legado*), which in turn one can transform through critical thinking and creative action.[54] It would be useless, for example, to denounce the Spanish language in a gesture of rejection of the language of the colonizer. This is now our language and we must use it as an instrument of our aspiration for freedom and social change. The figure of Caliban in Shakespeare's play *The Tempest* is used as a symbol by Roig and other Latin American authors.[55] Reversing José Enrique Rodó's turn-of-the-century characterization of Latin America as existing under the sign of Ariel, the idealistic winged spirit of Shakespeare's play, Roig and others take the side of the defiant Caliban. Caliban attracts these thinkers because he has carried out an "axiological transformation" (*transmutación axiológica*).[56] In so many words, he has told his master Prospero (who symbolizes the colonizer in this set of metaphors): you have taught me your language, and now I use it to curse you. The consciousness of liberation represented by the plural cultural subject and its corresponding "for us" at the reflexive level has been described by Horacio Cerutti as a "philosophy of the Calibans."[57] Or, in Roig's words: "A new man has emerged who...does not renounce the imposed 'legacy,' in this case language and the instruments of work. But he gives them a new value, his own intrinsic value, creating a 'language for cursing' which assumes [*supone*] a spontaneous type of decodification of the discourse of oppression."[58] It is not so much a rejection of the legacy as a rethinking of it in critical terms from the standpoint of those who had been told originally that they were not capable of thinking. In Roig's account there is both an element of the Hegelian *Aufhebung* of history—whose analogue is Zea's idea of the assumptive project—and an extension of the discourse of denunciation found in the writings of Nietzsche, Marx, and Freud.[59] One could even say that Roig's "for us" is engaged in a project of the sort Nietzsche called a "transvaluation of all values" if it were not for the fact that Nietzsche's political views were strongly antidemocratic, while Roig is interested in denouncing the values of a colonialist legacy.

The paradigm of the "for itself/for us" employed by Roig and Zea is applicable to situations and actions whose original context is not Hegelian. For example, the "for us" paradigm can elucidate

Marti's concept of *nuestra América* (our America) used to designate
a perspective critical of an aggressive or expansionist conception of
the mission of the United States with respect to the territories or
societies existing south of its borders. It appears that the idea of
"our America" proposed by Martí is an example of a "for us" type of
consciousness. The use of the word "our" here suggests at least two
things. First, it suggests that in addition to "our" America there is
"their" America, someone else's America, a party that may wish to
ignore the boundaries between its America and "ours." Second, it
suggests that there are at least two interpretations of the meaning
of Latin America—"ours" and "theirs." In this second, more subtle
sense, the mere fact that a person in Latin America gives an interpretation of his or her culture does not mean that the interpretation fits into the concept of "our America." "Our America" therefore
refers to the idea of a "Latin America for us" stemming from the
perspective of an already self-conscious interpreter. "Our America"
involves a normative judgment as to whose America we are talking
about—is it America for the advocates of imperialism or America
for those who want to be free from imperialism?

It could therefore be argued that the birth of the "for us" type
of consciousness depends, to some extent, on a separation of the
individual from his or her immediate environment. It involves a
recognition of alienation in one's relationship to one's environment—the "for us" being a counterpart to the alienation, a turn in
consciousness that negates the very values that negate *our* value.
The separation of the conscious subject from his or her immediate
environment through a critical turn in consciousness constitutes a
double negation through which the original alienation may be
superseded. This type of interpretation can be used to theorize
about liberation movements throughout the world, even if the persons involved in these movements may not conceive of themselves
as negating a negation. They may conceive of themselves as negating a lack of freedom or a situation of oppression. In such cases
they may regard their action, for example, as fulfilling a need, filling an emptiness, or redressing a grievance, rather than as their
assuming a position of consciousness "for itself" in relation to an
inert or alien environment. It would seem then that the range of
explanation offered by Hegel's dialectical view of consciousness is
vast since it can incorporate other explanations into a more general and, at the same time, easily concretizable perspective. The
range of explanation of Zea's "assumptive project" is equally vast.
This explains its power to take under its wings so many other

interpretations of history—that of the colonizers, of the emancipa-
tors, of the conservatives, and of the civilizers.

Both Zea and Roig have been influenced strongly by Hegel in
their views of self-consciousness and the dialectic between conqueror and conquered, colonizer and colonized. In spite of the fact
that they both side with the colonized, a subject that, as portrayed
in their work, emerges from a situation of bondage through a turn
in self-consciousness, the reasons they offer for favoring the emergence of the colonized from their bondage are basically derived
from nondualistic and democratic paradigms of freedom and self-
worth. It is important to note this since other versions of liberation
theories—some to be considered particularly in chapter 6—will
side with the oppressed for quite different reasons.

Rational Activity Itself as the Paradigm of Liberation: Miró Quesada's View

Zea's main objective in elaborating a philosophy of Latin
American history is the achievement of a united attitude on behalf
of the defense and development of a Latin American cultural legacy and of the region's political projects for liberty and equality,
not the securing of agreement about a post-Hegelian view of the
universe. A case in point is his collaboration over the years with
the Peruvian philosopher Francisco Miró Quesada, who is quick to
reject a Hegelian approach to the philosophy of culture. In his
essay "Ciencia y Técnica: Ideas o Mitoides," Miró Quesada notes:[60]

> It seems to us that to compare culture with an organism in
> which all the parts exert functions related to the whole and to
> every other part is a prejudice derived from Hegelian philoso-
> phy and from certain theses of Spengler. In each culture, in
> addition to there being a general style, categories, forces,
> structures, and functions that are closely interrelated, there
> are unforeseen manifestations that do not harmonize strictly
> with the rest. According to the information at our disposal,
> this aspect [of culture] has not been studied sufficiently,
> although it is fundamental for understanding the evolution
> and true sense of cultures.[61]

Miró Quesada explores, in general terms, the effect of science and
technology on the evolution of Latin American and Third World cultures. He discusses the role played by technology in the region's

dependence on foreign powers. This is an interesting issue because science and technology are important aspects of modern culture and much sought-after instruments for development, as seen by those living in developing countries. Yet with respect to the issue of cultural identity the question arises: Is the technology imported from abroad value-neutral? Is its incorporation into the economic and cultural life of the developing country laden with values tilting the developing culture in the direction of the developed? It would be difficult to deny that the latter is the case. Technology is indeed value-laden. Its introduction into a new environment may easily create an attraction toward or dependence on additional aspects and characteristics of the technology-producing culture. Does this mean that Latin Americans ought to resist the advance of science and technology, as radical critics like Ivan Illich suggest?[62] Miró Quesada wishes to avoid such a conclusion. At the same time he remains alert to the fact that technology is a conveyor of values that can penetrate a culture from outside and change it drastically.

Miró argues that, in the last analysis, one should distinguish between importing a foreign country's technology and importing that country's culture. The distinction follows logically from his point that a culture is not an organism, the parts and whole of which are inescapably interrelated. It also follows rather closely the spirit of another of his assumptions, namely, that there are unpredictable factors in cultural evolution not subject to prediction by totalizing laws. Still, he considers (if only in order to refute them) a number of objections raised regarding technology's ties with dominant cultures and the latter's capacity to penetrate into developing cultures through technology's apparently value-neutral influence.

Critics have argued that when technology is imported, regardless of where it is imported from, a relation of dependence follows for the importing country. For example, together with the technology one also has to bring the foreign experts who know how to use it. Moreover, the country begins to accumulate debts, and, if it wishes to obtain better terms from its creditors, it has to learn to play by the latter's rules. This can lead to the increased influence and/or manipulation of the internal affairs of developing countries by powerful interests situated in developed countries. Miró takes these arguments to be outdated as far as the situation of Latin American countries is concerned. He does not state, however, why such arguments would fail to carry much weight. Perhaps the unstated premise is that as real as the dependence of developing countries on developed countries may be due to the importing of technology, it is reasonable to think that their dependence would be far greater if no technology whatsoever were brought in. The main issue therefore cannot be whether technology is imported or not, but on what terms, for whose benefit, and under whose control. Miró Quesada does not make any mention of such equity-oriented conditions, but his general emphasis on the rational use of resources leads one to think that he would have no quarrel with them.

The thrust of Miró's analysis revolves around an assessment of the *image* of technology that is most prevalent in the developing country, in other words, the nature of people's beliefs and attitudes regarding science and technology. Is there a scientific attitude toward technology in the developing country, or, as Miró warns, is technology the object of a more primitive type of "mythlike belief" (*mitoide*)? The term *mitoide*, roughly translated as "mythlike belief," is used by Miró to convey the uncritical trust people place on science and technology. It would appear that technology and science have become nonthreatening means for the transmission of values from one culture to another because their efficacy has become a "myth" or more properly a pervasive (and therefore "mythlike") belief of our era. Miró Quesada finds such *mitoides* much more threatening to the vitality of Latin American culture than the importation of technology, which has been the object of so much criticism.

> In our modern world, for the first time in history, myths [mythlike beliefs] are formed under the assumption that they are truly universal, accepted and lived by all peoples of the earth. And the content of such myths—[in this case] science and technology—is precisely what...has the greatest power of penetration. Thus the cultural penetration that comes to us from Europe and the United States does not have to conquer any resistance.... [O]nce accepted as cultural formations and the force of its "absolute" value generalized, everything else follows on its own. For two reasons: because the speed of diffusion of the first contents accepted by the culture...under attack is dizzying, given the existence of the above-mentioned mythlike beliefs; and because science and technology are not two accessory (*accesorias*) and peripheral formations of Western culture. They are essential to it.[63]

The principal problem, then, is whether the power of science and technology to "infiltrate" the receptor culture is due to their mythlike quality, in which case one ought to warn against it. If, however, the function they serve is one derived from the exercise of reason itself, that is, from the need to confront and solve problems of a concrete or abstract nature, then the position of science and technology is quite favorable. Their role would be one of combating ignorance and authoritarian beliefs typical of the hierarchical, pyramidal structures of societies kept "together" by myth. "One thing is science and technology lived as myths and, another, science and technology as products of reason."[64] Cultural liberation would therefore be served if one could liberate science and technology, as products of reason, from all association with mythlike belief.

Miró Quesada therefore accepts the need for technology, though he advocates a vigilant, rational control over its potentially destabilizing character. Technology must be subject to reason, he argues, since originally it is reason's offspring. The battle is not between native cultural autonomy and foreign technologies, but between reason and unreason, between rational and not so rational approaches to technology. The proper use of reason as a source of combating human ignorance and error becomes the ultimate avenue of liberation. "In its deepest sense, the struggle against myth has been understood as a struggle for human liberation. It has been said that at the bottom of all dominion of a collective character, one can always find a myth."[65]

Does this mean that the greatest problem of liberation theory is not to focus on issues of cultural conflict or oppressor/oppressed dualities, but rather to create a social order based on the rule of reason? Miró asks Latin Americans to switch their attention from revolution to rationality, for thinking, he argues, is the most revolutionary of activities: "If one forgets that thinking,...even at the most abstract levels, is the most revolutionary and essential human expression, one forgets what reason is.... We believe that the tragedy of the modern world is that it has created the ideal of the rational life but it has not learned how to live it in a [fully] conscious and universal manner."[66] In modern culture, he claims, what characterizes the "ideal of a rational life" is science and technology. To reject this is to prevent the possibility of a creative life for Latin Americans. "We are convinced that the way of reason is the only way out. We think that the transformation of science and technology into mythlike beliefs is due to the fact that a certain type of modern man, the creator of a rationalist model of society, has not known how to realize this model appropriately."[67]

It might be objected that Miró Quesada's view of reasoning itself as liberation is much too vague to be included within the perspective of Latin American liberation theories. Not only is this paradigm too vague but its content appears to be too bland. Such views about reason are often the product of the established classes, who do not perceive their standpoint to be specific to the interests of a particular class. It can be said, however, in Miró Quesada's defense that in view of the violence suffered by people whose socioeconomic situation is characterized by poverty, injustice, and repression, these are, indeed, his views on liberation. It is not as though he has no perspective on liberation and merely says, "Let us be reasonable." Reason must be used in the service of liberating social transformations. But the struggle to achieve the latter cannot take place without reason, or outside of reason and the criteria for rational deliberation. In his view, this is a message both oppressors and oppressed need to hear. And to a great extent, he is right. Perhaps fascism, conquest, and colonialism would never have succeeded if human beings had considered these thoughts and acted accordingly. Perhaps a message like this helps to prevent the recurrence of slavery, exploitation, violence, and the many massacres history has witnessed as far as our memory takes us.

A stronger challenge to Miró Quesada's perspective would be the argument that human beings are not as willing to take the path of reason as he imagines them to be. Or, analogously, it might be objected that in the wake of the violence suffered so far by the oppressed, the harmonious way of analyzing and solving problems proposed by Miró Quesada cannot fully address significant aspects of reality. Unless a method of analysis is tuned to the demands of the problem one is examining, even the finest method may afford only ineffective results. In Miró Quesada's favor, however, it can be said that he may have tuned his method of analysis to the demands of the time. For example, perhaps his moderate approach to liberation can counterbalance one of the main problems affecting contemporary Peruvian society, namely, that of violence. In this sense his appeal to reason and moderation has an existential and realistic base, in that his perspective is born out of a sensitivity to the human pain caused by the irrational escalation of violence.

Elsewhere Miró Quesada has stated that he wants to posit the ideal of "man without theory."[68] In other words, he has faith in human beings' rational faculties, but not necessarily in the theories of liberation resulting from the use of these faculties. The reason he gives for this perspective is that all too often man has forgotten that theories are incomplete and their explanatory capacity changes over the course of time. Theories are inflexible; the person who acts solely according to a theory becomes a prisoner of the theory as well as a potential danger to himself and others. "It is as if man were a spider and the theory were his web, but a web that continued to expand unceasingly until it had imprisoned him in its own strands and slowly, inevitably, asphyxiated him."[69] Moreover, history shows that man has committed the most outrageous crimes in the name of theory. For the sake of theory, he has killed, tortured, and destroyed many forms of life. "When man takes hold of a theory to justify his desire to make others suffer, he descends to the level of the demonic."[70] But here one should distinguish between the negative associations Miró Quesada has drawn from abusive and destructive approaches to "theory," and theoretical inquiry, insofar as the latter leads people to a better understanding of their reality. Just as Miró Quesada wants to rescue the ideal of reason from what he takes to be poor applications of it, so it is relevant to distinguish between the use of a theory to justify destruction and the use of a theory to assist those who would be discriminated against, abused, and marginalized if such a theory did not denounce their abuse or help them empower themselves against it. Liberation theories—among other theories—should not be simply discarded, as if no good could come out of them. If anything, they should be studied further, criticized thoroughly, and improved on. A theory should never be an excuse for failing to be in touch with reality, or with human pain, emotion, and desire.

The Humanity of *Mestizaje* and an Open-Ended Dialectics

Throughout the discussion in this chapter I have examined Leopoldo Zea's unifying conception of the philosophy of history in Latin America, based on the reevaluation of the notion of *mestizaje* and his proposal of an egalitarian position for Latin America vis-à-vis Europe and the United States. Within this broad perspective, Roig's approach to philosophy looks inward to the history of ideas in Latin America and the axiological reversal needed to establish a point of departure for Latin American thought, while Miró Quesada's looks outward to the rest of the Western legacy and modern culture in an effort to build bridges of reason between Latin America and the advanced developed world. The post-Hegelian view of consciousness considered by Zea and Roig contains a very broad principle of self-consciousness as a "for itself" that, when applied to the concrete historical situation of Latin America, is transformed into a "for us." This transformation of consciousness is mediated, in Zea's case, by the positive, transvalued idea of *mestizaje* and, in the case of Roig, by the analogous movement of a historical and cultural plural subject emerging from colonialism and needing to give itself value. In the case of Miró Quesada we see a different (nondialectical) understanding of the relation between the universal and the particular. The universality of reason transcends the specificity of the Latin American situation. Human beings recognize each other by virtue of being reasonable. The standard of rational deliberation, not that of cross-cultural recognition, is ultimately what binds together human beings from different cultures.

Criticisms of Miró Quesada based on the notion that his ideal of rational deliberation as liberation is too general to address the specificity of the Latin American situation have already been mentioned. Still, in this respect what appears as a criticism to some is considered a strength by others who prefer a more general or universal approach to the analysis of philosophical problems, including the problem of cultural identity. Criticisms of Zea's view are perhaps not so obvious. Despite the fact that Zea's position is capable of incorporating many different elements under its synthesizing power, the lacunae in his perspective should not be neglected. The strength of Zea's position is the broad, comprehensive view it takes of self-consciousness; its limitation, not surprisingly, is due to the same factors. For example, in the civil wars that have plagued Latin American history there have been *mestizos* against *mestizos*, two antagonistic "for itselves," both self-consciously Latin American, both fighting to the death for the triumph of their particular conception of cultural identity. The conflict between the Sandinistas and the Contras (christened "freedom fighters" by their supporters) in Nicaragua during the 1980s exemplifies this problem. Can the theory of the "for itself," together with the concrete addition of the specific quality of a historically rooted *mestizaje*, generate any decisive theoretical criterion to distinguish in this case who is the authentic *mestizo* who is *really* fighting for freedom? Both sides say they fight for freedom, and they are both *mestizos*. Are they both right, are they both wrong, or is one right and the other wrong? We know that Zea wants to say it is those on the side of the Sandinistas' interpretation of the Nicaraguan Revolution who are on the side of freedom. But how does this opinion follow from his theoretical criteria?

The object of Zea's theory is to pursue the implications of the ideas of unity promoted by Bolívar, in addition to the idea of equality without which, he argues, the project of unity cannot be completed. Perhaps it is then possible to say, applying these principles, that if two groups of Latin Americans were to engage in combat or in political debate against one another, Zea would support the side whose program would lead more effectively to equality among the citizens and to unity among those who share libertarian, anticolonialist, anti-imperialist goals. Liberation would be determined in terms of the project toward which understanding and action are aimed, with the principal consideration given to projects of freedom and equality for all. It is important to note that Zea does not think his views—or those of others writing from a Latin Americanist perspective in philosophy—should be so particular that they cannot be embraced by all human beings, regardless of their racial or cultural situation. "Our philosophizing cannot be so special as to reach only one type of man."[71] Neither a difference in cultural background nor a difference in political ideology should be so decisive as to prevent human beings from recognizing each other in their struggle toward autonomy and freedom. How to reconcile disputing claims regarding the meaning of freedom within such an idealistic and potentially ambiguous framework is indeed a political if not a theoretical challenge to Zea's philosophy. The political challenge arises because liberals, conservatives, and others may very well wish to advance their political interests as ends in themselves, rather than as parts of the larger "assumptive project" proposed by Zea, over whose ideological and political objectives they lack direct control. Theoretically, the challenge to Zea's unifying conception of self-consciousness, freedom, and history lies in the need to specify even further than he has done the criteria for a liberating concept of the "for itself" in its condition of *mestizaje*. The impulse and unity of vision Zea has given to this goal are commendable. There remains, however, a need to focus on particular issues that, precisely because of their particularity, may escape the categories and guidelines of his broad view.

In this context it is very helpful to consider a suggestion offered by Roig with respect to how the study of Latin American thought modifies the Hegelian conception of dialectics. Roig suggests that more emphasis ought to be placed on the key role of particularity in the dialectical process:

> A different [*distinto*] understanding of dialectics emerges...,
> deriving from the place where the accent falls. The moment of
> totalization...is not underscored, but rather the prior moment

of particularity from where it [totality] is achieved. Its legitimacy derives from the capacity for deconstruction and reconstruction of the successive totalizations. Such would be the dialectic to which [Francisco] Bilbao and [José] Martí point, examples of a *faciendum* through whose moments…it is possible to reconstruct a history of Latin American thought. The truth is not found primarily in the totality, but in determinate forms of particularity with power to create and re-create totalities from a place outside the latter, as alterity.[72]

The "for us" disengages itself from adhering to the values of an alienating totality and becomes a creator of values that affirm the possibility of a new type of human being, nourished by different social relations:

The function of such knowing is not to justify what has happened, but to contribute to the making and slow formation of man. For the same reason it is open to "what is and will be" and not to "what has been and is eternally." This consciousness of alterity assures the deprofessionalization of philosophy and reveals to us, not precisely the role of the exceptional latecomer into which the philosopher must fit, but his place *on the side of* [emphasis added] that man who, because of his state of oppression, constitutes the very voice of alterity. In his inauthentic existence is found the root of all authenticity.[73]

Dialectics thus understood shifts to a deconstruction of totalities to make room for the creation of new structures previously unthought. Philosophy ceases to remain securely fastened to its professional distance from social transformation. Most importantly, a different paradigm of liberation reveals itself in the above observations: one in which the accent falls not so much on consciousness "for itself" as on consciousness "on the side of" the marginalized, the exploited, the oppressed. Let us now turn to an examination of some aspects of this paradigm.

CONSCIOUSNESS ON THE SIDE OF THE OPPRESSED: THE THEOLOGY OF LIBERATION AND CHRISTIAN-MARXIST DIALOGUE

In the late 1960s a movement that changed prior understandings of the relationship between faith and politics gained impetus in Latin America. While this phenomenon is sufficiently important to warrant extensive study in its own right, there are interdisciplinary aspects of it that have a special bearing on philosophical theories of cultural identity and liberation. In this chapter some of these points of overlapping interest will be explored. In particular, two influential works of the Christian "Left" will be considered: *Pedagogy of the Oppressed* (1968), by Paulo Freire, a Brazilian educator, and *A Theology of Liberation* (1971), by Gustavo Gutiérrez, a Peruvian priest and initiator of the theology of liberation movement. Despite the interrelated nature of the themes approached by these thinkers, the analyses of their work will be kept as separate as possible. Such an approach is indispensable if one wishes to understand the conceptual distinctions operating in the discourse of liberation, even among thinkers whose general perspective on liberation appears to be part of the same religious or political movement.

Freire's Dialogical Method of Teaching and Grass-roots Organizing

Paulo Freire is a precursor to the theology of liberation and an important educational theoretician. His best-known work, *Pedagogy of the Oppressed*, contains principles of liberation still valid today. His theory contains both strengths and limitations deserving of critical analysis and reflection. "I consider the fundamental theme of our epoch to be that of *domination*," he states, "which implies its opposite, the theme of *liberation*, as the objective to be achieved."[1] His conception of liberation is founded on a Christian humanism. It is centered on fighting ignorance and social oppression, including all the systematic social and psychological structures in and through which human beings are reduced to things.

Freire considers the struggle against ignorance and social oppression to be a unified, two-dimensional activity. This is why his "pedagogy of the oppressed" contains four symmetrical categories with two dialectical dyads: students/teacher, people/revolutionary leader. Within these dyads, established power is on the side of the teacher and the leader, while the students and the people are on the side of powerlessness. Through a process of "becoming conscious," or conscientization (*conscientização*), Freire hopes the dynamics of oppression inherent in these types of relationships will shift to a dynamics of liberation. He believes this shift in power relations can be achieved through a changed politics of communication. From being confined to silence or to the role of passive recipients of information, students and "the people" (*el pueblo*, a term referring to the popular sectors of society) will become "co-intentional" speakers with teachers and leaders.[2] This model of dialogue is based on an absolute respect for the subjectivity of each person. The Christian overtones in Freire's message are apparent: "Human existence cannot be silent, nor can it be nourished by false words, but only by true words, with which men transform the world. To exist, humanly, is to *name* the world, to change it."[3] He uses the term "dialogue" in a specialized sense to refer to a paradigm for nonoppressive forms of human communication:

> Dialogue is the encounter between men, mediated by the world, in order to name the world. Hence, dialogue cannot occur between...those who deny other men the right to speak their word and those whose right to speak has been denied them....
>
> ...this dialogue cannot be reduced to the act of one person's "depositing" ideas in another, nor can it become a simple exchange of ideas to be "consumed" by the discussants.[4]

In these remarks Freire offers a compact summary of critiques aimed at capitalist consumerism and political dogmatism. He does not criticize by name dogmatic methods of religious instruction, although such criticism is implied by his argument. His specific concern is the welfare of illiterate and oppressed people in developing countries. His work is directed to those who take an interest in

the liberation of the oppressed, either as teachers or political orga-
nizers. One should not aspire to such leadership, argues Freire,
unless one undergoes a conversion from what he calls the "banking"
method of education to his proposed "dialogical" method. This
involves a change of consciousness—away from an elitist, authoritative control of "truth" and space—to a grass-roots-oriented
method of generating answers and insights to common, persistent
problems.

The process of conscientization is tied to the development of
critical thinking. "Arguments based on 'authority' are no longer
valid; in order to function, authority must be *on the side of* freedom, not *against* it."[5] Notice here the paradigm of a consciousness
positioned "on the side of" freedom for the oppressed. The emphasis is Freire's. The critical thinker does not view himself in terms
of some abstract standard of reasoning, but as positioned on a certain *side*. Part of the critical effort, if not the whole of it, is to distinguish between one side and another. Such a distinction is
important because critical thinking for freedom spills over into
praxis or action aimed at transforming the world. "Education as
the practice of freedom—as opposed to education as the practice of
domination—denies that man is abstract, isolated, independent,
and unattached to the world; it also denies that the world exists as
a reality apart from men."[6] According to this formulation, neither
materialism nor idealism is primary. "Consciousness and world
are simultaneous."[7] Still, Freire is an idealist. He claims that both
human beings and history, insofar as they exist in time, are
"unfinished." He insists that, although critical thinking begins
with an awareness of "man's historicity," human fulfillment does
not end there; human beings transcend history, while history is
always subject to future transformations.[8] It is important to note
that in spite of his advocating an open-ended future for man and
world, Freire does not hold a future-oriented view of history as
such. His perspective is explicitly utopian in character. In another
work, *Acción cultural para la libertad,* he states: "What distinguishes above all cultural action for freedom from cultural action
for domination is the utopic nature of the former."[9] Thus, critical
thinking is not understood by Freire only in the sense of the
human capacity to reflect critically on one's social reality or past
experience. Critical thinking is a consequence of believing in some
value or values that are not (yet) of this world. Such values can
only claim a utopian existence. In other words, they belong to an
ideal world.

Freire's vagueness with respect to the utopian quality guiding liberatory practice presents some problems in the interpretation of his pedagogical theory. In particular, it has the effect of creating a placeholder in the chain of signifiers that will serve to defer conflict over political differences among activists interested in radical social change. Christians, for example, may take "utopia" to stand for a reference to divine justice, paradise, or "the kingdom of God," while Marxists could interpret the notion as referring to a revolutionary justice to be brought about by political and/or insurrectionary action. Where the theology of liberation would later draw important distinctions between these two planes of consideration, Freire allows for the blending of the two in a manner that defers an examination of their differences. One result of the deferral is the creation of a transitory "space" wherein the belief systems of some Christians and Marxists are able to find some common ground as each group envisions the coming-into-being of a "new man" in a "new world." This sense of sharing some common interests has proved invigorating to many Marxists and Christians in the Latin American region, but the failure to distinguish between these two projects of radical change has also led to new sources of misunderstanding, confusion, and anger. One of Freire's strategies in *Pedagogy* for influencing young leftist activists is to describe Marxist leaders in terms of such widely accepted Christian virtues as love, faith, and devotion to the needy.[10] In this sense he breaks new ground in understanding the possibility of establishing some positive form of relationship between some aspects of Marxism and Christianity. Nevertheless, insofar as he does not attempt to distinguish properly between them, he blurs their boundaries at a time when greater clarity and precision would have been a vital service to those engaged in political practice.

Advantages and Disadvantages of Freire's Method

In order to consider some of the advantages and disadvantages of Freire's pedagogical approach to liberation theory, it is useful to distinguish between the two dyads—students/teacher and people/political leader—whose meaning is often merged in his exposition. The distinction suggests that while some parallels exist between teaching and political action, it is best not to confuse the two spheres of activity. Such a confusion could lead to thinking of education exclusively in political terms and of politics in educational terms. In particular, it would be useful to refrain from viewing society as one giant school, with the revolutionary leader positioned as teacher and the people (or constituents from the popular sectors) positioned as those in need of instruction by the leadership. Such a model is paternalistic. Despite Freire's insistence that he opposes paternalism as well as a "salvific" or messianic role for the political leaders, it remains to be shown how he can be truly coherent on this point.[11] In fact, nothing is added, while much is subtracted from a theory of liberation if we are persuaded to think of the relationship between a people and their political leaders in terms analogous to those of a student/teacher relationship.

Freire denounces social oppression and authoritarian education in an effort precisely to move out of paternalistic models of social control. His revolutionary theory of education (unlike his pedagogical approach to politics) is largely successful in attaining this goal. In his critique of teacher/student roles, he points to the process of subordination occurring in the classroom when knowledge is dispensed through the repetition of information, the passive compliance with an expert's authority, and so on. Freire's critique awakens his readers to the stereotypical relations that over a period of time can stifle the personal and intellectual growth of teachers and students in the educational process. His theory also contains some limitations. There is the question as to whether some areas of learning are better served than others by Freire's "problem-solving" approach to learning. For example, the project of teaching illiterate peasants how to read may benefit strongly from the use of this method, as might philosophy courses dealing with basic questions of human existence. Some science courses and other courses requiring, at least in part, efficient memorization of data, however, cannot dispense with experts' advice or with the memorizing of relevant information. This suggests that expertise is not an evil as such, but a positive good, when its knowledge and skills are shared with those in need of them.

Freire invites the teacher's expertise and authority to be placed in a broader perspective, within a larger view that takes into account some important needs of students. Among the latter are the capacity to challenge authority, the capacity to use creativity in the service of learning, the capacity, as he says, to "name" the world they see from their particular standpoint. Indeed, Freire's approach to pedagogy, with its program of critical thinking, problematization of subject matter, and dialogical pattern of interaction between teachers and students, is a healthy alternative to tediously dogmatic methods as well as boringly technical uses of education. It is not difficult to agree that the latter cover only the bureaucratic aspects of teaching while leaving the spirit of teaching and learning out of the classroom. Freire is right to call the latter approach "necrophilic" in its most extreme cases.[12] And he is wise when he warns: "Any situation in which some men prevent others from engaging in the process of inquiry is one of violence."[13]

The special case to which Freire applied his pedagogy—teaching illiterate adults to read and write—is also both significant and commendable. Here it is clear how Freire's "pedagogy of the oppressed" is designed to empower students by exposing them to a teacher who does not disseminate the ideology of domination confining them to marginality and oppression. For example, he confronts the ideology of fatalism and the belief that if one is oppressed, it must be because it is the will of God.[14] Not only does Freire's "dialogical" teacher refrain from disseminating and enforcing such views, but his or her role is to help the oppressed unmask the disabling effects of "a world of deceit designed to increase [the people's]...alienation and passivity."[15] Among these disabling ideas are those proclaiming that the society in which the oppressed live respects their freedom or that "all men are free to work where they wish," the belief that "rebellion is a sin against God," and so on.[16] Freire proves that when the teaching of illiterate adults to read and write is subordinated to a disabling ideology, it cannot be considered a responsible type of teaching. Yet, by the very same logic he uses to argue that the ideas of some human beings should not be imposed on others, he needs to be more careful in his characterization of what constitutes "correct" versus "incorrect" (true/false) beliefs, lest he himself become dogmatic about his own conception of what constitutes education for freedom. As long as his method is devoted to critical thinking and a transformative praxis based on critical thinking, it is an excellent contribution to liberation theory. But as soon as certain forms of leadership are endorsed without a critical examination of their actual or potential political consequences, the approach runs the risk of becoming too didactic, and its transformative elements are foreclosed.

Freire's application of the dialogical method of teaching and learning to broad cases of human interaction has some positive as well as negative characteristics. On the positive side, there is an important ethical principle at stake in dialogical interaction. This consists of an imperative to treat the other person as one who deserves to be heard regarding the expression of her or his own needs, desires, and ideas. The extension of this principle to all forms of interaction among persons is of the utmost significance. As

Freire suggests, dialogue rather than manipulation should not only be the ideal but the practice when it comes to interaction among human beings. But is the political sector the type of public space in which such dialogue will flourish? Does the political organizer who adopts the Christian virtues of love, faith, and humility—as Freire admonishes—become, by virtue of this alone, an authentic political leader? The situation appears to be much more complex. In direct contrast to Freire, I think it is not the function of political leaders, including leaders whose subjective state of mind may be one of comradeship with the people, to consider their relationship as fitting a pedagogical model. Such a model presupposes that the education of citizens is the proper function of political leaders, whereas, with some allowances for understandable exceptions, it is reasonable to argue that education is, more properly, the function of schools and a wide range of cultural associations.[17] To encourage the type of dialogical thinking advocated by Freire, independent, original thinking needs to be rewarded and popular culture needs to receive due recognition from academic institutions. But this is different in kind from expecting political leaders to assume a pedagogical role. Freire's theory is significantly weakened by the failure to stress the importance and value of independent thinking for a dynamic community. Instead, as we shall see, he stresses the absence of independence and the value of collectivity and "communion."

Given the utopian, overidealistic nature of Freire's analysis, it is important to stress that his proposal for establishing conditions of dialogue between the revolutionary leaders and the people is not a guarantee of or substitute for political freedom. Faith in the people and personal humility, the principal virtues he advocates for the leadership, likewise are not sufficient to guarantee the basic conditions for dialogue.[18] Dialogue requires a basic respect for difference, diversity, and otherness, that is, a basic concern for the relative autonomy of individuals and groups within a political community. A political leader—whether revolutionary, liberal, or conservative—who assumes a paternalistic relationship with members of the popular sectors does them much more harm than good insofar as he expresses a desire to maintain them in a state of dependency or tutelage. The leader, on the contrary, must help to create grass-roots democratic political structures that reinforce the people's capacity to determine their own best interests, act on their own behalf, and govern themselves accordingly. Perhaps such goals are not far from Freire's ideals for a popular democracy. But his work could suggest the notion that the people and their leader should be wedded to each other until death insofar as they are meant to exist in "communion" with each other. If read this way, this part of Freire's message would represent a disservice to liberation theory in the political sector. Such ideas reinforce a dependent role on the part of the people. They are therefore the opposite of a model aimed at promoting a dynamic, liberating praxis. Freire does not draw these debilitating inferences from his theory because, as will be shown, he stresses the spiritual aspects of the notion of communion. Yet there are important sociopolitical aspects of the communion model that he does not address. For example: How does a leader make decisions in a state of communion with the people? How does he limit his power so that they can be free? How does one determine the proper length for a political term of office? What procedures are to be used to elect a leader? And most importantly, why is the term "the people" (*el pueblo*) used in this type of discourse to refer to a relatively homogeneous block of social agents, thus ignoring both the heterogeneous composition as well as the diversity of interests of this group?

The principle of a necessary "communion" between leaders and people is pervasive in Freire's thought. While he often gives credit for the practical application of this idea to the Argentine revolutionary Ernesto "Che" Guevara, the symbol of communion can hardly be dissociated from its place in the Christian faith.[19] Communion, in this tradition, is the ultimate expression of love, faith, and self-sacrifice. Its significance goes back to the Last Supper and to the death of Christ on the cross. But in *Acción cultural para la libertad*, as in *Pedagogy*, Freire highlights the attainment of a sense of communion with the people as the mark of distinction of revolutionaries.[20] He refers again to Che Guevara as a model for this idea: "The more we study his work, the more we perceive his conviction that the true revolutionary must be 'in communion' with the people."[21] By this, Freire probably means that political activists and those members of a community in whose service they are engaged should be of one spirit in all their cares and needs. Whereas for Freire the communion model appears to denote the notion of leaders who are of one mind and heart with the people, in Marxist theory the accent on unity tends to be on the oneness between revolutionary consciousness and popular will. While, admittedly, a variety of opinions will be found among reasonable persons regarding the preferred type of relation that ought to hold between an individual and a community or group, it seems to me that the model of communion developed by Freire is not an appealing criterion from which to judge the interaction of people engaged in political activity. If an idealistic approach to political interaction is desired, it seems more reasonable to support a model of mutual understanding, where each person is enriched by appreciating the differences between self and others, than to uphold a model of relating to others in which individuality must take on a subordinate position to the spirit of the whole group.

The idea that communion represents the culmination of dialogue cannot be taken as self-evident. If he had argued that teachers and students must live in a state of communion with each other, Freire's reasoning could be considered strange or absurd. Why should this principle then appear as a sine qua non of the moral legitimacy of political leaders? If the aim is to propose a model of interaction between leaders and people that resists manipulation of the latter by the former, can it be said, objectively, that the "communion" model itself is not manipulative? Or, if the aim is to replace a communist ideology with a Christian belief in communion, why isn't this made explicit so that the merit of this proposal can be examined rigorously on its own terms? One suspects that the reluctance to face such problems directly has led to ambiguities that in the end have weakened liberation theory and practice. In order to keep the spirit of Freire's pedagogy of liberation alive, we must be able to carry the practice of critical thinking beyond what he argued, to a responsible questioning of the various models he offers of revolutionary authority. The philosophical reception of Freire's theory of liberation therefore strongly depends on analyzing some of the unexamined premises found in his thinking, while retaining his valuable insights on the need for dialogue and respect for persons, especially in contexts where one side enjoys an unjustified excess of power over the other.

The Birth of Liberation Theology

The critical spirit of Freire's pedagogical method influenced new directions in Christian social practice and created new challenges for theological reflection on the commitments of Christians to progressive social change. In 1968 the movement known as a theology of liberation was launched as a result of the work of the Peruvian priest Gustavo Gutiérrez and other like-minded collaborators. The first major impact of the group was felt at that year's meeting of the Latin American Episcopal Conference (CELAM), held in the city of Medellín, Colombia. At this meeting the Latin

American bishops addressed significant social and political issues of the region. Special attention was given to the problems of the poor. "The Lord's distinct commandment to 'evangelize the poor' ought to bring us to a distribution of resources and apostolic personnel that effectively gives preference to the poorest and most needy sectors."[22] According to the Brazilian theologian Leonardo Boff, the term "liberation," which was used at the conference, was understood in the sense of "integral liberation":

> Predominant was the perspective of integral liberation, which included political liberation, but the accent fell on liberation from sin and the consequences of sin: "the liberation of the entire human being and of all human beings." What was new in the Medellín perspective was subsumed in a perspective that was, in itself, traditional.... Medellín had the merit of consecrating, on the official church level, the discourse on liberation, and of thus lending the support of its authority to the liberating practices already undertaken by Christians who were socially involved.[23]

The decade following the conference at Medellín saw a proliferation of the theme of liberation in Latin American theology and pastoral practice. In 1979 CELAM met again, this time in Puebla, Mexico. The Puebla conference reaffirmed the liberation thematic. Leonardo Boff describes the results as follows:

> Puebla endorsed liberation theology and aroused an even deeper interest in it.... Liberation theology enters into the basic focus of evangelization in the present and future of Latin America: the creation of communion and participation of human beings among themselves and with God. Meanwhile, because communion and participation are not given, but have to be built, the process of liberation comes into the picture. The human being must be delivered *from* the impediments to communion and participation and *for* the concrete experience of communion and participation. "Our churches have something original and important to offer to all: their sense of salvation and liberation" (Puebla 368).[24]

The theme of communion, which I commented on in Freire's work, is a major focus of the discourse of liberation. The following passage is typical of those cited by Boff from the Puebla Final Document:

In a word, our people yearn for a full and integral liberation, one not confined to the realm of temporal existence. It extends beyond that to full communion with God and with one's brothers and sisters in eternity. And that communion is already beginning to be realized, however imperfectly, in history (Puebla 141).[25]

This statement also suggests that the bishops wanted to exert some influence on the direction of the historical movements of liberation that were developing in the Latin American continent.

In liberation theology, a new approach is sought to the announcement or preaching of the Christian message of salvation. The relationship between liberation, understood in a psychological and sociopolitical sense, and salvation, understood in terms of redemption from sin, opens a wide area of theory and practice centering on the balance between the religious beliefs and political involvement of Christians. At the theoretical level, a great deal of effort is spent trying to determine what boundaries and/or priorities exist between faith and politics as well as a number of other theological issues ranging from hermeneutics to pastoral work. Some of the major thinkers linked with this movement are Gustavo Gutiérrez, Juan Luis Segundo, Hugo Assmann, Jon Sobrino, and the brothers Leonardo and Clodovis Boff. Gutiérrez's work, *A Theology of Liberation* (1971), is one of the most radical as well as brilliant expositions of this intellectual movement, in addition to being the first major book to be published on the subject.[26] Of special philosophical interest in Gutiérrez's approach to liberation theology is his treatment of such topics as the meaning of liberation, the critique of development economics, the question of poverty, the ideals of the new society and the new human being, and the relation between faith and politics. Though controversial, his work has contributed significantly to a multidisciplinary understanding of Latin American social and political problems.[27]

Liberation from Capitalism

An outstanding quality of Gutiérrez's writing is its theoretical character, demonstrating his ability to investigate and reflect on issues about which he is deeply committed without losing the theoretical focus of the discussion. In the introduction to his work he states:

Our purpose is not to elaborate an ideology to justify pos-
tures already taken, nor to undertake a feverish search for
security in the face of the radical challenges which confront
the faith, nor to fashion a theology from which political action
is "deduced." It is rather to let ourselves be judged by the
Word of the Lord, to think through our faith, to strengthen
our love, and to give reason for our hope from within a commitment which seeks to become more radical, total, and efficacious. It is to reconsider the great themes of the Christian
life within this radically changed perspective and with regard
to the new questions posed by this commitment. This is the
goal of the so-called *theology of liberation.*[28]

The theology of liberation, notes Gutiérrez, does not offer so much
a new theme for reflection as "a *new way* to do theology"; theology
so understood is a "critical reflection on historical praxis."[29] "Critical reflection...always plays the inverse role of an ideology, which
rationalizes and justifies a given social and ecclesial order."[30] The
goal of the theology of liberation is not to replace "the other functions of theology" but to emphasize certain parameters dealing
with liberation in a historical context.[31] Gutiérrez indicates that
this does not mean doing theology from an armchair but "sinking
roots where the pulse of history is beating."[32] He situates the perspective taken by the theology of liberation as self-consciously
Latin American and radically tied to a human base. The Latin
American emphasis relates the theology of liberation to the much
broader movement, particularly in the social sciences, which seeks
to stress the values proper to a region in terms of its historical
legacy and cultural identity. The theology of liberation is therefore
situated within the problematic of liberation and cultural identity
I have been pursuing in this study beginning with the discussion
of Mariátegui. It is not a coincidence that Gutiérrez, like Mariátegui, is Peruvian and, like the early Marxist leader, agrees that
Marxism and religion need not be contradictory, as so many others
have thought. He accepts the relevance of Marxism in a restricted
sense, as a method for analyzing Latin American social reality.

Gutiérrez is clear that by choosing a Latin American focus he
does not wish to foresake the importance of universality. In this
respect his position resembles that of Leopoldo Zea. He tries to
seek a balance between the specificity of the Latin American position (understood historically) and the quest for universal values:

This Latin American focus would not be due to a frivolous desire for originality, but rather to a fundamental sense of historical efficacy and also—why hide it?—to the desire to contribute to the life and reflection of the universal Christian community. But, in order to make our contribution, this desire for universality...must be present from the beginning. To concretize this desire would be to overcome particularistic tendencies—provincial and chauvinistic—and produce something *unique*, both particular and universal, and therefore fruitful.[33]

Another concrete point of departure for critical reflection is the human factor, regarding which Gutiérrez makes the following comment:

What Antonio Gramsci said of philosophy is also true of theology: "It is necessary to destroy the widely held prejudice that philosophy is something extremely difficult because it is the intellectual activity proper to a certain category of scientific specialists or professional and systematic philosophers. It is necessary, therefore, to demonstrate first, that all men are 'philosophers,' establishing the parameters and characteristics of this 'spontaneous philosophy' proper to 'everyman.'"[34]

It should be clear by now that we are dealing with a revolutionary conception of theology, whose point of departure is going to be the human, historical base from which faith springs. This theology is on the side of people who are trying to transform their historical situation in order to create a more just society. It is a reflection precisely on their action, giving meaning to it—as philosophy would from a secular standpoint—in the light of the Christian faith.

What is it about the Latin American situation that makes a perspective founded on it so critical? Poverty and lack of development are taking an enormous toll on the people. An extreme situation of "poverty, alienation, and exploitation" requires an urgent demand for change.[35] Gutiérrez focuses on the socioeconomic, historical, and religious dimensions of liberation, all of which he takes to be interrelated. The economic aspect requires an analysis and critique of the policies of economic development carried out since the 1950s, which have placed the region in a situation of growing poverty and external debt. The historical aspect is concerned with realizing the political ideals of the Western humanist tradition, aimed at bringing about a just and free society where exploitation will cease to exist. The religious aspect is the Christian vision believers link to these ideals, which places an accent on the religious meaning given to these economic and social programs. Gutiérrez makes clear that he speaks of liberation in three distinct senses.

> In the first place, liberation expresses the aspirations of oppressed peoples and social classes, emphasizing the conflictual aspect of the economic, social, and political process which puts them at odds with wealthy nations and oppressive classes....

> At a deeper level, *liberation* can be applied to an understanding of all history. Man is seen as assuming conscious responsibility for his own destiny....

> Finally,...the word *liberation* [in contrast to *development*] allows for another approach leading to the Biblical sources which inspire the presence and action of man in history. In the Bible, Christ is presented as the one who brings us liberation.[36]

Gutiérrez regards the third approach as the deepest and the one that unifies the other two. In this nontheological discussion, however, I will focus primarily on the first two aspects.

Gutiérrez notes that one may think of development purely in terms of economic growth or as a more integral social process.[37] In keeping with his Christian view of the universe, he rejects the first understanding as too narrow. From the second standpoint, the relation between economics and other factors (social, political, cultural) receives a great deal of attention. But so do other aspects of development, such as the relation between external and internal elements affecting the ways in which wealth is generated in a particular country. Recent studies by Latin American social scientists and economists have concluded that "the dynamics of world economics leads simultaneously to the creation of greater wealth for the few and greater poverty for the many."[38] Gutiérrez devotes a chapter of his work to this issue, which is of primary importance for developing countries.

Following the conjectures of economic studies by Fernando Cardoso, Enzo Faletto, Theotonio Dos Santos, André Gunder Frank, and other strong critics of capitalist development theory, Gutiérrez accepts the thesis that underdevelopment occurs as the end result of development.[39] For example, Dos Santos argues that historical time is not unilinear. Societies evolve together in interrelationship with one another. Focusing on structural economic relations between the metropolises and the colonies or between central and peripheral capital, critics of capitalist development theory argue that capitalist development and Third World underdevelopment go hand in hand. They claim that Western capitalism has succeeded so far in large part because it has managed to extract value from peripheral areas such as Latin America in order to enrich the economic centers of the metropolises. Reformist measures within this model of development will not work because the problem is structural: underdevelopment in the periphery is the other side of development in the center. For any area that is being targeted as the center of development, there will be correlational areas where the obverse economic results will be manifested, that is, where poverty and exploitation will proliferate. The only way to remove these structural problems of development economics, argues Gutiérrez, is to move toward a more human, socialist economy in which the gap between the rich and the poor ceases to exist.[40] Yet, even as he recommends this radical move to a different economic structure, Gutiérrez is cautious about a few theoretical problems.

While it is important to consider the situation of Latin American countries in terms of dependence, Gutiérrez warns that more scientific study is needed in order not to fall into "new equivocations" and "new reifications."[41] One approach to be avoided is that of blaming some nations for the oppression of others. "To take into account only the confrontation between nations misrepresents and in the last analysis waters down the real situation."[42] The theory of dependence will lead to deception unless its explanations are offered "within the framework of the worldwide class struggle."[43] This position addresses a conceptual limitation on the part of the center/periphery paradigm insofar as the paradigm relies on a geopolitical as opposed to a class model of domination and exploitation. Gutiérrez accepts a Marxist class analysis of exploitation, which he considers useful as a method illuminating certain facts pertaining to a historical analysis. This does not mean he subscribes to a theory of philosophical materialism. In this respect he agrees with Mariátegui's conception of Marxism. "For Mariátegui as for many today in Latin America, historical materialism is above all 'a method for the historical interpretation of society'" not to be confused with philosophical materialism.[44] As noted in chapter 2, Mariátegui envisioned a type of Marxism that would find nourishment in the latest developments in philosophy, the sciences, the arts, and even religion, not all of which would have to subscribe to a materialist metaphysics. From a Marxist standpoint, Mariátegui paved the way for future movements such as the theology of liberation, which would draw on a Marxist analysis of exploitation and alienation but would supplement it with independently held ethical and metaphysical principles. In this case, a materialist approach to historical development is supplemented with a Christian belief in redemption.

Another point worth clarifying at length, though Gutiérrez does not take up the subject until the last chapter of his book, is precisely what meaning ought to be given to "poverty." One hears repeatedly that the theology of liberation expresses the church's "option for the poor." What exactly does this mean, or what can it mean for those committed to a theology of liberation? It certainly does not mean that the church is promoting poverty or a sentimental attitude toward the poor. Gutiérrez distinguishes between material and spiritual meanings of "poverty," arguing that Christianity opposes material poverty in the sense of deprivation. It favors a spiritual type of poverty, where poverty refers to the attitude of emptying oneself (from selfishness) so that one can more properly receive the Word of God. Spiritual poverty is an attitude of "opening up to God," of being at God's disposal.[45] In the theology of liberation, the primary emphasis is on "witnessing" poverty, that is, on acting to help eradicate material poverty while preserving a spiritual attitude of "childhood" before God. This view affirms that life is meant to be lived fully in the spirit of giving and justice inherited from the Christian faith. It is precisely because life is meant to be lived fully by every human being that the poverty and exploitation of the majority of men and women in Latin America and other developing regions by a worldwide economic system that favors the interests of wealthy minorities is such a scandal to those who believe in the Christian message of brotherhood, or human solidarity. "Witnessing poverty" therefore takes on the meaning of fighting to eradicate poverty and exploitation.

Gutiérrez mentions a third sense of "poverty" understood as a commitment of "solidarity *with* the poor and...a protest *against* poverty."[46] He interprets the Christian spirit of poverty in a most radical sense—not as the assumption of voluntary poverty but as a "break with one's social class."[47]

In today's world the solidarity and protest of which we are speaking have an evident and inevitable "political" character

insofar as they imply liberation. To be with the oppressed is
to be against the oppressor. In our times and on our continent
to be in solidarity with the "poor," understood in this way,
means to run personal risks—even to put one's life in danger.
Many Christians—and non-Christians—who are committed
to the Latin American revolutionary process are running
these risks. And so there are emerging new ways of living
poverty which are different from the classic "renunciation of
the goods of this world."[48]

Gutiérrez wants to stay away from a sentimental use of the term
"poor." He offers a class analysis of poverty:

We must pay special attention to the words we use. The
term *poor* might seem not only vague and churchy, but also
somewhat sentimental and aseptic. The "poor" person today
is the oppressed one, the one marginated from society, the
member of the proletariat struggling for his most basic
rights;...the exploited and plundered social class, the country
struggling for its liberation.[49]

In this way, the Christian who takes up the option for the poor is
simultaneously taking up the struggle for political liberation, understood from a class perspective. And, similarly, those non-Christians
who join the political struggle for liberation on behalf of the exploited
classes are living up to the Christian ideals of sisterhood and brotherhood as they acquire a new historical meaning for individuals in
societies that have become impoverished by economic and political
systems favoring the wealthy.[50] As many more Christians make personal decisions leading them to witness poverty in the sense understood by Gutiérrez, the result will be to place the church within the
revolutionary process of social transformation. How will the church
move, however, from its feudal and bourgeois mansions to its new
revolutionary camp? Can one even imagine the transition?

Placing the Church within the Revolution:
Dimensions of Witnessing Poverty

According to the analysis pursued by Gutiérrez, the situation
of poverty in the sense of severe material deprivation clashes with
both a humanistic conception of human beings as the creators of
their historical destiny and a religious conception of human beings

united under the Fatherhood of God. Gutiérrez reasons that the status quo, even if committed to reformist measures, will merely prolong the present condition of misery for large majorities of people. As a result, he argues that it is not possible to continue supporting the political and economic status quo in Latin America. As with any radical argument, Gutiérrez doesn't just denounce domination; he goes further to name the agent of domination. One therefore needs to speak of the domination *of* the oppressed *by* the oppressor. Since the primary source of misery we are talking about is that of poverty, then the primary issue to confront is the domination of the poor by the rich.

The paradigm of the domination of the poor by the rich (and the system from which the latter profit most, capitalism) is expanded to cover the relation of the Latin American continent to the more industrialized nations of the world. Latin America, notes Gutiérrez, is a poor *continent*, and it is poor in relation to the richest nations of the world. The Latin American church ought to take on the identity of its people and continent, thus witnessing to it.

> The Latin American Christian community lives on a poor continent, but the image it projects is not, as a whole, that of a *poor Church*.... The majority of the Church has covertly or openly been an accomplice of the external and internal dependency of our peoples. It has sided with the dominant groups, and in the name of "efficiency" has dedicated its best efforts to them. It has identified with these sectors and adopted their style of life. We often confuse the possession of basic necessities with a comfortable position in the world, freedom to preach the Gospel with protection by powerful groups, instruments of service with the means of power. It is nevertheless important to clarify what the witness of poverty involves.[51]

The church must place itself on the side of the people, in order to exist as *their* church. If the people are poor, the church must acknowledge their poverty as its own. The church must learn to speak *from* the position of the poor to denounce poverty and the structures that maintain it in power. It is not enough to denounce it from the side of the rich or from some third position that avoids taking sides with one or the other. Here we are at the heart of Gutiérrez's notion of liberation. Consciousness must be on the side of the oppressed and speak from that position for the general goal of liberation.

Let us follow this reasoning further. If consciousness is to position itself on the side of the oppressed, this must mean it is not yet on that side, at least explicitly and unambiguously. Among other things, this refers to a situation in which educated people—theologians, priests, laity—who have had the benefit of what culture has to offer, who are well fed and clothed, and so on, are faced with a decision to reject their middle-class status and their secure position in society in order to side with the oppressed—to think, act, and live like them. This is not exactly a case of "conversion" from one outlook to another. It is a case of repositioning oneself, one's sympathies, one's hopes. It is a case of what the Cuban poet José Martí referred to when he wrote that he wanted to share his fate with those who were poor ("los pobres de la tierra").[52] Or, it is a "realignment," to expand on a metaphor used by the Colombian priest Camilo Torres.[53] The process of "witnessing" to which Gutiérrez refers may be broken down into three moments. First, someone witnesses someone else's oppression: for example, I witness, I proclaim the oppression of others, their poverty. Second, as I witness it, I listen to what they have to say about it, how they experience it, how they would like things to change. Third, I could organize or join a group that sides with the oppressed in their struggle for freedom (here understood as liberation). The process of "witnessing" involves a form of self-decentering as one points to the oppression of another person or a group.

Two options present themselves here. First and most important is the participatory model of grass-roots organizing (supported by Gutiérrez), in which people carry out their own projects for social liberation, enjoying the power of decision making over their goals. This is a model of grass-roots democratic participation aimed at changing society from the bottom to the top. Its proliferation in Latin America is found in the *comunidades de base,* or Christian base communities, which consist of groups of believers, usually organized along neighborhood lines, who combine critical reflection on the Scriptures with organized political action on social issues directly affecting the well-being of their communities. Issues concerning public welfare, housing conditions and standards, material assistance for the needy, child care, and human rights are some of the most important.

There is also what I would call the "fusion" model of siding with the oppressed. According to this model of liberation, the priority is not given to changing society from the bottom to the top of the political spectrum by means of a united, democratic, grass-roots action. Supporters of the fusion model more commonly develop the strategy of taking over certain territories or spaces, declaring them free from injustice and appealing to those outside these territories to "fuse" with them in a struggle to destroy the perceived external menace. In the fusion model of solidarity with the oppressed, a person's consciousness will become "fused" with what she or he takes to be the voice of those in need of liberation. The model suffers from confusion regarding the distinction between ideal voices and real, empirical situations. This model is antidemocratic insofar as it does not trust individuals—not even those who are oppressed—to speak on their own behalf. Authenticity is based on self-erasure and submission to the authority of the oppressed other. Not only philosophers (because it is one of philosophy's tasks to clarify ambiguities in reasoning) but individuals (because it serves their most fundamental welfare) must learn to distinguish well between the paradigms of consciousness on the side of the oppressed and consciousness in fusion with (the alleged voice of) the oppressed. The former preserves the value of individual judgment, which can be placed alongside those in need, whereas the latter may undermine the proper functioning of this type of judgment. Under the fusion paradigm, the individual committed to liberation perceives himself or herself as acting in the name of those oppressed, as speaking with their voices, and so on. Such a model can be politically and psychologically dangerous in the sense that the self may become absorbed by the power of an idea that, in some respects, presents itself before it in the form of a compelling urgency to which one simply cannot say "No." For this reason, it is important for liberation theology to distinguish more clearly between these two models of repositioning consciousness on the side of the oppressed—the participatory model and the fusion model.

Freire, as we have seen, endorses grass-roots participation *within* the model of communion. This model operates on the basis of a "dialogical" relationship between leaders and members of a political group, according to which acts of love and faith interlock their respective consciousnesses. For example, in the model of liberation developed by Freire, the moral legitimacy of leadership rests on the leader's expression of *belief* in the people and in the sense of *communion* between the people and their leaders. But if a perfect blend between these dyadic voices were to be achieved, even momentarily, the fusion model would begin operating. The paradigm of fusion, however, is especially ill-advised as an ideal for positioning oneself on the side of liberation. To fuse with another subject, no matter how worthy the other, is an act of self-destruction with respect to one's self—a rupture with one's personal potential as a thinking, acting, perceiving, and caring being. No person, however, can be said to be empty of value. Only an extraordinary amount of perceived guilt or pain, ennobled by feelings of duty or love, would lead one to want to be totally free of oneself in such a way as to give up one's life for the sake of what one takes to be a more deserving other. This is the process of witnessing turned into martyrdom (or possibly self-destruction). Such may have been the case of Camilo Torres, a respected Colombian sociologist and priest who came to believe he had an unconditional duty to help bring about a new society under socialism. Torres first engaged in political activism, trying to convince his fellow Christians to adopt a socialist platform peacefully. When a quick, peaceful transition to socialism failed, he believed his only choice left was to join the guerrilla movement. This decision led to his death shortly thereafter. Torres's attitude and reasoning will be examined in an effort to understand the type of "hold" a fusion model of liberation can exert over some individuals.

In his "Message to Christians," dated 26 August 1965, Camilo Torres asserted: "I believe that I have offered my self to the revolution for the love of neighbor."[54] While he still sought a peaceful transition to socialism, he reasoned as follows:

> It is...necessary [in order to enact with efficacy the maxim of love of neighbor] to take away the power of the privileged minorities in order to give it to the poor majorities. If this is done quickly, this is what is essential in a revolution. The revolution can be peaceful if the minorities do not resist violently. The revolution, therefore, is the manner of attaining a government that gives food to the hungry, dress to the naked one; it teaches the one who has no knowledge; it fulfills, with works of charity, the love of neighbor—not only in an occasional and transitory manner, not only for a few, but for the majority of our neighbors.[55]

Torres concluded that it was obligatory for Christians to support a revolutionary political agenda. There is no mention of violence, only of love of neighbor.

Within a few months, disappointed with the results of the electoral process, his outlook changed. "Now the people will never believe again [in peaceful change]," he wrote. "The people know

that the legal means have been exhausted. The people know that
the only means left is the armed struggle. The people are in despair
and resolved to risk their lives so that the next generation of
Colombians will not be slaves."[56] The issues mentioned by Torres as
demanding immediate attention were education, clothing, housing,
"dignity," and a future for Colombian children free of "North American dominion." These are peace-oriented issues, and to many it
would seem contradictory to opt for a civil war in order to attain
them. But such has been the reluctance of the ruling sectors of
many Latin American countries to institute widespread policies for
social change on behalf of the nonprivileged that Torres's feelings
about the urgency of helping those in need are understandable,
even if the means he sought to correct the problems may be subject
to some important criticism.

In particular, the issue of who is to speak for those individuals or groups in need of liberation is a major point of debate in liberation theory. Torres uses the Spanish expression *el pueblo* as a
singular collective subject—"el pueblo no cree," "el pueblo sabe,"
and so on. This term refers to a collective entity or subject who is
of one mind and will. Although used repeatedly in public rhetoric
and political discourse, the term can be misleading in that it fails
to denote the diversity and/or conflicting interests of those who
make up "the people." As with other singular collective nouns,
such as *la mujer* ("woman"), often used to refer to "women," the
meaning of *el pueblo* can easily slip from the context of an empirical reference to that of a normatively constructed ideal. In the latter case, it is possible to lose sight of the sense of a people as a set
of differentially situated political actors in a given society, for
whom the terms "liberation" and "oppression" will not have a uni-
form meaning.

From this broader perspective it can be seen that the people
about whom Camilo Torres spoke, in their concrete, particular
existence, did not exactly fit into the specific vision Torres had of
them. This does not mean that the objectives he supported (at
least in their peaceful version) might never be realized, only that
his discourse was more reflective of his own sentiments than of the
state of affairs allowing for radical change in society. He attributed
to "the people" his own most passionate thoughts and sentiments.
It can be argued, though, that to be efficacious in the practice of
the love of neighbor, as he intended, one needs to be in better
touch with "reality" in the sense of being able to reach a more balanced judgment regarding the actual conditions available for social

change at a given place and time. A liberation movement—regardless of whether the focus of liberation is gender, race, class, and so on—needs to begin in the here and now. It needs to work with individuals' sense of awareness based on who and what they are today, as well as with an awareness of the major obstacles preventing individuals' desires from coming into being. The fusion model of liberation guiding Camilo Torres's decision in his last days skips over reality, especially empirical reality, in the name of a singular, idealized collective subject, "the people." The individual who takes on this collective identity may fail to understand the interests of other members of society who do not conform, or do not wish to conform, to such an identity. Moreover, failure to pay sufficient attention to social and historical conditions can severely limit the efficacy of a liberation movement. The power held by the status quo over individuals is often underestimated. Learning to respond effectively and appropriately to conditions of oppression is not a type of goal that can be accomplished instantly or by force; on the contrary, much critical reasoning and persistent reflection on experience are needed.

In contrast to Torres's approach to the problems of poverty and dependence, Gutiérrez's *A Theology of Liberation* depicts the need for Christians to choose a historical path to liberation, but it does not promote the "fusion" model of consciousness on the side of the oppressed. Gutiérrez focuses on the reality facing the church and Christians in Latin America and the enormous complexity of the situation in which they live. One of the issues faced is what the church's option can be today, realistically speaking. How can it take sides with the oppressed when the church itself is split politically, with some of its members engaged in liberation movements and others going so far as to persecute and kill them? Gutiérrez addresses the problem of the Christian conscience, inquiring whether the church is going to stand on the side of the oppressors and their system or on the side of the oppressed, with their hope for a new society? This is a serious problem for the church, because it finds itself divided.

The Latin American reality, *the historical moment* which Latin America is experiencing, is *deeply conflictual....*

The Latin American Church is sharply *divided* with regard to the process of liberation. Living in a capitalist society in which one class confronts another, the Church, in the measure that its presence increases, cannot escape—nor try to ignore any longer—the profound division among its members.... [A]mong Latin American Christians there are not only different political options within a framework of free interplay of ideas; the polarization of these options and the extreme seriousness of the situation have even placed some Christians among the oppressed and persecuted and others among the oppressors and persecutors, some among the tortured and others among the torturers or those who condone torture. This gives rise to a serious and radical confrontation between Christians who suffer from injustice and exploitation and those who benefit from the established order.... Participation in the Eucharist, for example, as it is celebrated today,[57] appears to many to be an action which, for want of an authentic Christian community, becomes an exercise in make-believe.[58]

This situation of conflict can be explained as one generated by an opposition of interests or by a failure in consciousness. Gutiérrez's point, however, is that given the weight of the Catholic church's influence in Latin America, if it were to place its solid moral and public support behind the oppressed, this in itself would generate a significant change within the (currently oppressive) system. "It is evident that only a break with the unjust order and a frank commitment to a new society can make the message of love which the Christian community bears credible to Latin Americans. These demands should lead the Church to a profound revision of the manner of preaching the Word and of living and celebrating its faith."[59]

Toward a New Society and a New Human Being

The theology of liberation takes very seriously the belief in a new society and a new human being. This desire for change stems from people's need to live in a world that is more joyful or just than the one they have known so far. A kind of utopian belief drives the Christian revolutionaries forward. They want to contribute to the creation of a society in which selfishness will have as little part as possible, while love, solidarity, brotherhood, and sisterhood will play the larger part. These Christians believe that capitalism makes the advent of such a society difficult, if not impossible, to realize. Therefore, they look to some form of socialism as the better way to achieve such a society and, hence, to bring the world closer to a Christian ideal of love.[60] How is socialism understood from such a standpoint? How does this socialism differ (as one assumes it must, due to the Christian emphasis) from the predominantly non-Christian socialisms we have known so far? Not only the political transformation of Christianity, but that of socialist ideologies, is at stake.

Gutiérrez does not stress the differences between Christians and Marxists, but focuses rather on the characteristics of the theology he is articulating. His first remarks about socialism show the pairing of the concepts of "socialist" and "new" society. "Only a radical break from the status quo, that is, a profound transformation of the private property system, access to power of the exploited class, and a social revolution that would break this dependence [the dependence of some countries on others] would allow for the change to a new society, a socialist society—or at least allow that such a society might be possible."[61] With the change from a capitalistic to a socialistic mode of production, says Gutiérrez, human beings will have "controlled nature, created the conditions for a socialized production of wealth, done away with acquisition of excessive wealth, and established socialism."[62] He acknowledges that the term "socialism" means different things to different people. In a brief section of his study, where he attempts to clarify what the Latin American socialism advocated by those who share his views might mean, Gutiérrez refers extensively to many documents published by clergy in different contexts, in an effort to offer provisional suggestions about the characteristics marking a specifically Latin American socialism.[63] This implies that, for Gutiérrez, the nature of the specificity of a Latin American socialism—or a plurality of Latin American socialisms—is still a topic of current discussion. The theoretical lines regarding the specific nature of a Latin American socialism, responsive to the economic, social, political, and cultural characteristics of the continent, have not been defined yet.

A major aspect of the transition to the new society would be related to "the progressive radicalization of the debate concerning private property."[64] While in some portions of A Theology of Liberation Gutiérrez suggests the need to narrow the excessive gap between the rich and the poor—a position that does not necessarily refer to the abolition of the private ownership of the means of production—the latter idea is important to Gutiérrez's vision of the new society and the new human being. The transformation of the status quo "ought to be directed toward a radical change in the foundation of society, that is, the private ownership of the means of production," he states.[65] The ultimate justification he gives for this belief rests on the interpretation given to the Christian mandate of love and human solidarity in today's world. "It is...necessary to avoid the pitfalls of an individualistic charity.... Indeed, to offer food or drink in our day is a political action; it means the transformation of a society structured to benefit a few who appropriate to themselves the value of the work of others."[66]

Just as the Christian radicals view the abolition of private ownership of the means of production from the standpoint of ideals mandated by love of neighbor, so they argue that as these measures are taken, the new society will give birth to a new person who is the possessor of many ideal Christian virtues. The transformation of human beings must be pursued with an enthusiasm equal to that directed toward the transformation of the economic structures. "We do not believe man will automatically become less selfish," states a document cited by Gutiérrez, "but we do maintain that where a socio-economic foundation for equality has been established, it is more possible to work realistically toward human solidarity than it is in a society torn asunder by inequity."[67] (The revised edition of *A Theology of Liberation* [1988], adopting gender-inclusive language, uses "persons" instead of "man" in the just-quoted sentence.) At the time of the democratic victory of the socialist leader Salvador Allende in Chile, many statements of support for socialism were elicited from Chilean Christians. The Catholic Workers Action Movement stated: "This fact embodies a great hope and a great responsibility for *all* workers and their organizations: active and watchful collaboration to bring about a more just society which will permit the integral liberation of those oppressed by an inhuman and anti-Christian system such as capitalism."[68]

The logic of the coupling of socialism with the advent of the "new human being" becomes clearer. If capitalism in its competitive and exploitative aspects is typified by inhumanity, then socialism, its economic antagonist and/or alternative, will supplement this deficiency by reversing the inhuman aspects of the capitalist system. A new economy, argues a group of Chilean priests in 1971, "should also generate new values which make possible the emergence of a society of greater solidarity and brotherhood in which the worker assumes with dignity the role which is his."[69] The focus on community and giving provided by these Chilean Christians contrasts sharply with the dominant image of Christianity thriving in capitalist societies. Under capitalism, economics is restricted to profit making, while compassion and humanist sentiments are kept in separate compartments, such as community service or charity. The "integral liberation" of which these Christians speak overcomes this split in the consciousness of capitalist Christianity. The new human being of which they speak does not have to enter a system of exploitation in the material aspects of her existence in order to be delivered from it by participating in separate spiritual exercises. The material and spiritual dimensions of a person's life would be better integrated, as would the social benefits enjoyed by each individual in relation to those of all others in the community. In other words, Christianity would cease to justify the division between the rich and the poor as an inevitable matter.

Democratic participation in the process of constructing the new society is essential in Gutiérrez's view.

> Finally, the process of liberation requires the *active participation of the oppressed*; this certainly is one of the most important themes running through the writings of the Latin American Church. Based on the evidence of the usually frustrated aspirations of the popular classes to participate in decisions which affect all of society, the realization emerges that it is the poor who must be the protagonists of their own liberation....
>
> ...At Medellín, a pastoral approach was approved which encourages and favors "the efforts of the people to create and develop their own grass-roots organizations for the redress and consolidation of their rights and the search for true justice."[70]

Popular participation, of course, is assumed to follow in conjunction with a process of conscientization that will enable the people actively to analyze and confront their situation with a degree of critical consciousness.[71] In these respects, the positive aspects of the consciousness-raising methods developed by Freire would therefore prove to be most helpful in guiding people through the initial stages of conscientization.

This brings to a close this examination of Gutiérrez's contribution to liberation theory, including some of its most debatable features. My discussion sheds light on his initial definition of the term "liberation" according to three distinct senses: economic-social-political, historic, and religious. Subsequent developments of liberation theology and the experience of the Nicaraguan revolution, which took most of these precepts of the theology of liberation to heart, have produced specific results. In particular, a form of socialism committed to democratic popular participation was developed by the Sandinista liberation movement (and later political party) in Nicaragua, where the effects of liberation theology were felt strongly during the 1980s.[72] In Cuba, religious practice has become more acceptable since the mid-1980s. On a more individual level, some persons have paid an extraordinary price for their commitment to liberation theology, as was the case of the Jesuits murdered in El Salvador in 1989, along with two women in their household. Ignacio Ellacuría, a leading scholar in the theology of liberation, was one of those killed. In Peru, however, an internal war conducted by an extremist rural guerrilla movement has caused enormous damage to the civilian population. Under such conditions, advocates of the theology of liberation need to be especially cautious that their message is not misunderstood.

The consequences of this theory have also had important repercussions in the United States, for example, in the development of the Sanctuary movement, wherein Christians have provided refuge to Central Americans seeking asylum in this country. The Sanctuary movement, too, has taken the option for the poor of which liberation theology speaks. In this case, it has addressed the combined plight of poor and displaced persons. This movement reveals a positioning of consciousness "on the side of the oppressed" of the type explored in this chapter. It shows that it is possible for supportive groups in North America to care decisively for Latin America's casualties of economic/political oppression, even if they have to dissent from the present government's views.

On the other side of the spectrum, however, conservatives have strengthened their hold on the Latin American church in a way that restrains the expansion of liberation theology. In addition, conservative fundamentalist groups, often based in the United States, are proliferating in many parts of the continent and gaining membership from among the poor and the economically disadvantaged. There continues to be a divided opinion among Latin Americans about how best to solve the huge problems of poverty and economic deterioration felt in many parts of the region. There has also been a tendency in the late 1980s to place the larger part of the blame for each country's economic difficulties on those responsible for the management of resources within each Latin American country (rather than on the unequal and exploitative structure between central and peripheral capital). The pendulum of economic culpability swings toward the least advantaged as conservative ideology gains power both in the United States and abroad. The ethical aspect of the problem of the oppressive conditions of poverty found in dependent capitalist economies, however, remains intact. The moral question of siding with social changes that will help the vast marginalized sectors of society pull themselves up from their subordinate social roles, therefore, continues to be at the center of any radical theory of liberation claiming to be rooted in specifically Latin American sociocultural conditions. If liberation theology is, as it claims to be, a genuine perspective born out of important social conditions in Latin America, its message will no doubt continue to be relevant for some time to come.

In any case, the number of Christian base communities formed in some Latin American countries like Brazil and Nicaragua has been impressive. The theology of liberation has been able to articulate certain needs and beliefs of the Christian community and, more importantly, its leading exponents have been able to stay in touch with these community groups so that their theoretical work is closely connected with social practice. There is no analogous situation in philosophy for this unusual connection between a group of committed theologians and the popular sectors of the community. Liberation theology therefore provides a unique paradigm for grass-roots-based theorizing for which, at present, there is no counterpart in philosophy.

A Brief Assessment of Issues Highlighted by Liberation Theology

An interesting methodological feature of liberation theology is its reliance on the social sciences for an analysis of social problems, their root causes, and some potential ways of improving the quality of life of the people. While there has been a strong interest in thinkers like Marx and Gramsci, however, relatively little has been done to relate the specific problems addressed by a Latin American philosophy of history or culture to the "option for the poor" that, arguably, is rooted in the sociohistorical conditions marking the countries of the region. Yet, philosophers, too, have had long-standing concerns for examining the topic of social liberation in a Latin American context. It is appropriate to offer some suggestions that may help to clarify some of the commonalities and differences between philosophy and theology in this respect and to situate some of the arguments given by Gutiérrez in particular or by liberation theologians in general in a critical philosophical perspective.

One might ask, specifically, what kind of long-term effects may be expected from the contribution of liberation theology? Among its foreseeable effects, should the accent fall on the changes this movement will bring to an understanding of theology or on those it will bring to an understanding of the meaning of liberation?

To clarify the terms of these questions, a distinction should be drawn between two types of effects following from the engagement of Christians in the theology of liberation movement. One has to do with the impact of the theology of liberation on the structure of the Catholic church itself (or on other churches, as the case may be). This means one would have to study and analyze the effects that the "option for the poor" would have within institutions where other options for commitment are also available. Gutiérrez's notion that the theology of liberation is not a different theology but a new approach to theology would be relevant to this concern. For example, one advantage of a theology of liberation—and the religious, moral, or social practices connected to it—is that it could enrich the plurality of options within the church with respect to the representation of different approaches to social problems and the renovation of church structures and policies. Responding to questions of material need and other grass-roots concerns of the more marginalized members of society would be part of the accent brought into the life of the mainstream church via the work of liberation theology.

In this context, liberation theology would act as an internal lobby within the church, putting pressure on church authorities to respond to matters considered of top priority by the liberationists. As one competing interest among others within the church, however, liberation theology would be subject to attack by other interests, particularly conservative interests, which view it as a threat to their power over matters of policy or doctrine. Indeed, there has been an active campaign by conservative elements within the church to dismantle or at least restrain as much as possible the influence of liberation theology within the institution itself.[73] Given the hierarchical power structure of the Catholic church, it is unlikely that liberation theology will be able to grow fast enough to become a majority influence within the institution. Still, the institution may provide spaces where liberation theology is able to function in a relatively self-determined manner as long as it does not deviate significantly from previously established ecclesiastical policies. In other words, liberation theology can open up new spaces for creative reflection and action within an institution like the Catholic church, but it will also be limited in its full possibilities for development as long as the structure of power in the church remains authority-oriented, strongly hierarchical, and institutionally conservative. Gutiérrez recognizes this dilemma when he refers to the conflictive nature of church membership. Whether liberation theology can develop fruitfully side by side with church dogma and authoritative ecclesiastical structures is a question theologians and Christians involved in these popular movements will need to face. The concerns of a philosophical reading of liberation theology are different, however. They fall primarily within a second set of considerations, namely, how this approach to theology affects an understanding of the relationship between ethics and social change in contemporary Latin America.

A different set of implications, therefore, may be derived from liberation theology if, rather than being considered from the standpoint of an intra-institutional option for the poor, it is viewed as an ethical perspective aimed at the renewal of the whole society by means of a practice aimed at radical social change. Here the accent falls on the relationship between ethics and social change, a question of broad interest to individuals regardless of their religious affiliation. One important characteristic of Gutiérrez's analysis of liberation is that it brings to the forefront the importance of an ethical perspective on social problems.

In Gutiérrez's analysis, ethics supersedes economics, politics, and the study of history (even though the latter are used widely to enhance his arguments) as a ground from which to draw a solution to the region's condition of poverty. This is so insofar as he claims that the specific conditions of economic and social injustice in Latin America demand an existentially rooted ethical response from the Latin American church and the region's Christians. This implies that it is no longer sufficient to be a Christian (understood in a universalistic, cosmopolitan sense). One must relate the expression of one's faith to the special problems affecting one's society. The argument behind this approach is that a new ethical "world" with new responsibilities and duties becomes apparent to the individual who reflects deeply about the nature and causes of poverty in the region. But, if Gutiérrez is right, the option for the poor, which involves the recognition of the difficult economic and social conditions in Latin America, could not be confined to Christians living in the region. The meaning of Christian ethics would have to change all around the world and not only in a specific geographical area. Contemporary economic (capitalist) relations interlock poor and wealthy nations together into a single system, so that whoever reaps the largest benefits from the system becomes responsible for the witnessing of poverty of those who are less fortunate. Moreover, the meaning of an ethical state of mind such as solidarity with the oppressed cannot be so easily accommodated to a location inside a nation or even a culture's "borders." An ethical concern of this type cannot be the special prerogative of Latin Americans alone. A philosophical assessment of the option for the poor, then, would upgrade it from a regional to a worldwide concern. But it would also question—more than theology has already done—the use of "poverty" as a single issue and/or theoretical category in this worldwide ethics of social justice. Although Gutiérrez has widened the meaning of poverty well beyond its most literal meaning, addressing conflicts of class, nationality, and ethnicity in his analysis, continued broadening of the type of groups or social agents whose needs call for radical social transformation seems to be warranted. Giving such social agents specific names other than "the poor" (or as Freire did, "the people," or "the oppressed") is essential if their concerns are going to receive the attention required for widespread social transformations.

Indeed, many other problems besides poverty would need to be brought to the forefront by this radical Christian perspective. The list is not new, but it is important to be reminded of some of its principal components: issues of discrimination against many groups, including women, ethnic and racial minorities, refugees and migrants, the handicapped, the young, the aged, and those of gay or lesbian sexual orientation; issues of human rights, including rights to education and health care; issues regarding the treatment of animals, the protection of the environment, and so on. Whereas, on the whole, there is support for many of these issues within liberation theology, within the church there are some doctrinal constraints on how far these topics can be developed. Continued emphasis on this expanded list of social priorities, nevertheless, is necessary, since the type of ethical awareness that is demanded for responding to the needs of the poor in the manner expected by liberation theology cannot be satisfied with a single-issue approach to social justice.

Ultimately, this also means that various concepts and paradigms of "socialism"—or the "socialisms" mentioned by Gutiérrez—would have to be examined critically in terms of whether any or all of them would be likely to generate new kinds of oppression or to reinforce certain kinds of oppression already existing under capitalist conditions. It cannot be taken for granted, as some conceptions of a socialist utopia would have us believe, that a change from capitalism to socialism is equivalent to the difference between selfishness and unselfishness. Moreover, the existence or nonexistence of private ownership of the means of production cannot be taken as an objective indicator of the degree of selfishness or unselfishness found in a given society. Many ethical problems demand solutions in capitalism, but the same can be said about socialism. It cannot be argued that socialism is a more ethical system unless one first describes what kind of socialism is meant by the term, since, as Gutiérrez observes, there are many forms of socialism. But obviously there are some strong affinities between a Christian ethics of care and a generous socialist vision of social justice, insofar as both stand in sharp contrast to the type of ruthlessness often associated with the profit motive.

From the above it is arguable, then, that while the relation between ethics and social change may be considered central to a perspective of solidarity with the oppressed, it does not follow from this that poverty will be the single issue to be considered or that the political and economic mediations for bringing about a more just society are easy to decide on. For many, poverty may be the single most important issue of human marginalization and exploitation; for others, however, it may be gender, ethnic or racial discrimination, freedom for political prisoners, assistance to refugees and migrants, and so on. While these problems certainly fall within the scope of the object of study and action by a theology of liberation, an ethical philosophical perspective would be freer in its capacity to address them, insofar as it would not have to confine itself to boundaries established by a certain dogma or faith. This point is especially important with respect to the struggle for women's rights, and, in particular, their reproductive rights, given that male-dominated religious institutions have little incentive to examine this problem objectively.

Liberation Theology and Its Relationship to Philosophy

The theology of liberation, in the form pursued by Gustavo Gutiérrez, Hugo Assmann, Leonardo Boff, and others, is an exciting theoretical contribution to an analysis of Latin American social problems. Theology and philosophy can work together in many instances to provide methods of critical analysis and models for practical action whose goals are to defend the cultural, political, and economic integrity of the people of the region. One important difference between the two disciplines is the religious orientation of theology. Philosophy, in contrast, has no equivalent place for the role faith plays in theology, unless it be its own faith in the critical exercise of reason. Similar issues, however, may be pursued by both disciplines, for example: the theme of deliverance from the system of exploitation of human being by human being, the affirmation of an enlightened, humanistic struggle for freedom in history, the importance of critical thinking in the evaluation of social structures and actions taken to transform them, the extension of rights to the poor and marginal sectors of society, to women, and so on. In the field of philosophy and the history of ideas, Leopoldo Zea comes to mind as someone whose work has addressed many of these issues, though not all of them. Other issues such as the philosophical study of popular culture and the relation between ethics and social change require further investigation.

One intellectual movement that attempted to fill some of these gaps was the self-denominated "philosophy of liberation" movement that arose in Argentina in the early 1970s. In contrast to Zea's approach to liberation, which takes a historically based notion of self-determination as constitutive of the idea of freedom, the Peronist-influenced Argentine group worked with symbolic constructs of ideas such as "the people," "the Other," "the poor." Through a hermeneutical unravelling of this symbolism, they brought to bear on the discipline of philosophy some politically charged thoughts about the meaning of liberation. This type of approach (as practiced in South America) has tended to be politically conservative and traditionalist in character, even when it calls itself a "philosophy of liberation." A contradiction is noticeable between its self-image as a progressive or even revolutionary theory and the actual conservative or even reactionary ideological function its discourse can play in social analysis. In the next chapter a critical examination of this interesting and controversial intellectual and political phenomenon will be offered.

THE PHILOSOPHY OF LIBERATION
IN CRITICAL PERSPECTIVE

In the 1970s, shortly after the theology of liberation began gaining ground in Latin America, a movement known as the philosophy of liberation was launched in Argentina. In a recent study, Hugo Biagini notes that if the banner of liberation was first raised from a theological standpoint in countries like Peru and Brazil, it was in Argentina that the question of liberation first acquired a "nucleus" of philosophical meaning. "At the beginning of the 1970s," he recounts, "a group of young thinkers came together and worked together until the differences among them became acute."[1] As Biagini describes it, the intellectual movement, induced by the "heterogeneous" political forces of Peronism, actually began to gain ground just after the death of Perón in 1974. Yet, also at that time, there was an intensification of the power of the political Right that put liberation thinking in jeopardy. The Right targeted the government and the universities as objects of its control.[2] A study of the Argentine political scene explains that under pressure from advisors, the late president's widow Isabel Perón "exacerbated the [political] situation by moving further to the right rather than seeking some compromise with the left. Intolerance of opposition led to the establishment of paramilitary groups for its suppression, most notably the Argentine Anti-Communist Alliance (AAA)."[3] A right-wing military coup followed in 1976. The coup led to very serious divisions among philosophers. Some proponents of liberation sided with groups supporting the coup, while others were ostracized or persecuted by the forces of repression. The former "went so far as to favor the dismissal of their colleagues and former associates" from university positions; they also collaborated with the military in various ways.[4] At this time many faculty members lost their jobs, and large numbers of students were expelled from the universities.[5] Arturo Andrés Roig, Horacio Cerutti Guldberg, and Enrique Dussel were among the philosophers forced to leave the country. State terrorism ruled Argentina from 1976 until 1983, when military rule ended and there was a return to democracy.

Understanding the philosophy of liberation involves being aware of the repression scattering the intellectual forces that came together to examine the relationship between philosophy and liberation in the early 1970s. These groups were part of a social movement of renovation taking place within some sectors of Argentine society. Part of their agenda included comprehensive grass-roots-oriented proposals for university reform.[6] Perhaps due to the persecution and repression suffered by professors and students and the exigencies of relocation and exile faced by the more progressive members of the group in the years that followed, a fundamental task of the young philosophical movement remained unfulfilled: namely, that of analyzing with critical rigor the theoretical coherence of the intellectual movement they had initiated in the midst of changing political and social conditions. Cerutti's *Filosofía de la liberación latinoamericana* (1983) is the only major contribution made so far on behalf of this critical task.[7] Yet if one looks at the original articles and pronouncements on liberation, it is clear that, from the very beginning, the phrase "philosophy of liberation" covers positions that are theoretically incompatible with one another. It is true that, broadly speaking, all thinkers shared a concern for the problem of liberation. Nevertheless, a careful reading would show that Roig's and Cerutti's positions were markedly different from those of Ardiles and Dussel, for example. Perhaps if censorship and persecution had not thwarted the development of this intellectual movement, the internal oppositions and differences among the philosophers would have yielded more positive results. Perhaps such differences would have enriched and strengthened liberation thinking in Argentina. As it happened, however, the impossibility of an internal critique forced those with more critical, independent positions out of the "philosophy of liberation" movement, a situation that persists until the present time. Thus we see two liberation thinkers such as Cerutti and Dussel part ways—the first insisting on maintaining a critical perspective on liberation, the latter following an absolutist path.

Elsewhere I have offered, from a polemical standpoint, a rather detailed analysis and critique of Dussel's ethical theory and an overview of Cerutti's critical perspective.[8] Some elements from my earlier critique will be used in the present discussion, but in the present analysis I shall not focus primarily on Dussel's theory.

Instead I will address wider issues in the philosophy of liberation that will help to place the work of individual contributions to the movement in a historical and theoretical perspective.

After a brief overview of information relevant to the historical origins of the movement, two principal problems will be addressed: the question of Latin American identity and its effect on the philosopher's view of liberation, and the implications of "not being European" in Argentine liberation thought. In the course of the discussion several related topics will be touched on, among them, the role played by some liberationists' critique of modernity and modern rationality, the issue of the rupture with "totality," and some questions about the political implications of Dussel's thought. The primary focus will be on a collection of articles published in 1975 in Argentina by the *Revista de filosofía latinoamericana*. The *Revista* was a philosophical offspring of the journal *Nuevo mundo*, which had published the first collection of writings on the philosophy of liberation in 1973. At the time of its appearance, the editorial council of the *Revista* was composed of five active contributors to liberation thought: Osvaldo Ardiles, Mario Casalla, Enrique Dussel, Aníbal Fornari, and Juan Scannone, S.J. The first issue, from which some themes will be selected for discussion, featured articles by Osvaldo Ardiles, Mario Casalla, Horacio Cerutti Guldberg, Enrique Dussel, Daniel Enrique Guillot, Rodolfo Kusch, and Arturo Roig.

Early Precedents

Prior to 1975, much work had already been done in the philosophy of liberation. According to Cerutti, it was the journal *Stromata*, published by Jesuits, where, beginning in 1970, the first articles appeared on the question, "What is Latin American?"[9] This problematic, as we shall see, both preceded and incorporated itself into that of the philosophy of liberation, insofar as the latter wanted to serve as a paradigm for Latin American philosophy. In the first half of 1972 *Stromata* published proceedings from academic meetings on the subject of "Latin American Liberation."[10] In early 1973, the Franciscan journal *Nuevo mundo* published the first collection dedicated to the philosophy of liberation, a large part of which later appeared in an anthology, *Hacia una filosofía de la liberación latinoamericana*, by Osvaldo Ardiles and others. Several other publications quickly followed, including the first issue, in 1975, of the *Revista de filosofía latinoamericana*.

Some of the authors who contributed to the first statements of a philosophy of liberation or were instrumental in shaping its development have already been mentioned. The list should also include the names of Julio De Zan, Antonio Kinen, Alberto Parisi, and Carlos Cullen.[11] Among the theoretical influences making an impact on the philosophy of liberation were the theory of economic dependence elaborated by Latin American social scientists in the 1960s and the theology of liberation. The polemic between the Peruvian philosopher Augusto Salazar Bondy and the Mexican Leopoldo Zea regarding whether there could be an authentic Latin American philosophy within a culture of dependence seems to have been influential to some extent. Furthermore, as Cerutti notes, several international events provided a political context for the deliberations, among them, "the failure of Torres's government in Bolivia, the fall of the Chilean government of Salvador Allende, the first attempts at a nationalist politics in Peru and Panama, and the frustrated possibilities in Argentina."[12] But the most important influence was that of the internal political situation of Argentina itself. This involved, in particular, the desire on the part of many intellectuals—whose political orientation ranged from conservative to radical populist—to rethink the meaning of an Argentine national identity in relation to the idealized image they constructed of the popular sectors.[13] This "popular" influence can be found in Dussel's description of the basic theoretical and political elements of the movement when he states: "The philosophical formation of its components is predominantly Hegelian and Heideggerian…, while its concerns are raised out of the Argentine political praxis: a praxis that is popular, national, of liberation."[14] Yet, as I shall argue, Dussel's argument on behalf of national-popular liberation is a problematic one.

From the beginning, Dussel's approach to a philosophy of liberation has been marked by at least two disturbing characteristics. The first is the postulation of an absolutely untainted source for, or undisputed authority at the origin of, its claims to truth or justice. For Dussel, philosophical truth is a matter of deriving various imperatives from a set of uncontaminated first principles. This approach allows him to be critical of many things, but not of the view that an absolute criterion of truth is available to the philosopher "of liberation." Second, the ethical and political theory emerging from this approach is marked by a dualistic understanding of good and evil. Ethically, there are two principles: totality (evil) and alterity (good). The scenario of world history is background to the struggle between these two mutually exclusive forces. This is translated politically into the absolute mandate to support the struggle of national liberation movements (alterity) against imperialism (totality). Thus "alterity" ceases to refer to an otherness or a difference thought to lie "beyond absolute knowledge," as interpreted by postmodern writers.[15] It also ceases to refer to the marginalized, particular other whose ethical as well as empirical presence keeps the circle of knowledge from closing itself off from reality in the form of an absolute knowing, as understood by Roig.[16] Instead, "alterity"—as used by Dussel and several other members of the Argentine group—comes to designate the ground of a new absolute, but one constructed in the name of the poor, the exploited, and the oppressed.

One of the problems with the epistemic schema employed by Dussel is that in some respects it is similar in structure to that used by some of the most fanatical ideologies in modern history. To be sure, the theory claims to be fighting totalitarianism in the name of alterity or otherness. Yet it is not unusual for an absolutist and dogmatic cause to appeal to the highest-sounding principles in defense of its operation. It is not necessarily what an absolutist ideology says it is fighting for or defending itself against that ultimately determines the merits of its cause. When dealing with this type of ideological framework, one must question and disassemble critically the mechanism by which the world has been cut in half in the first place—with an undisputed source of truth and the good on one side and a delegitimized rationality and/or evil totality on the other. This is the unpleasant but necessary task with which one is faced when analyzing the basic tenets of the more radical—or, better yet, fundamentalist—wing of the philosophy of liberation movement.

It takes an especially critical perspective to notice the authoritarian and traditionalist nature of Dussel's reasoning, since he writes on behalf of such progressive political and intellectual movements as the theology of liberation. One must distinguish between the legitimate aspects of Dussel's collaboration with the theology of liberation, where he basically supports the notion of a Latin American church as a church of and for the poor, and his elaboration of the concept of national-popular liberation in ethics and political philosophy. The present analysis is concerned only with the latter. In *Introducción a la filosofía de la liberación*, the strategy of appealing to an absolute source of truth and dividing the world into two mutually exclusive spheres of good and evil can already be observed. For example, referring to the 1968 episcopal conference of Medellín, Dussel states: "It is God himself, the Bishops proclaim, who, in the plenitude of time, sends his son so that, made flesh, he can come to liberate all men from all forms of slavery to which they are subjected by sin, ignorance, hunger, misery, and oppression."[17] Here "God himself" is described as activating the basic principles from which the legitimacy of the national-popular political movement will be deduced. A decade later "Marx himself" would be invoked as the guide to Dussel's commentary on the *Grundrisse* in support of the same political cause. "In this work we offer a direct entry into the essential moment of [Marx's] theoretical production, for whoever wants to 'get into' Marx *himself*. And we say 'essential' in the sense that in the *Grundrisse* the reader...will be led by Marx *himself*, with his own pedagogical hand, to his central, fundamental discoveries [emphasis in the original]."[18]

The ethical complement of this epistemically uncontaminated source, whether it be God or Marx, is the privileged site of oppression, which is juxtaposed to a foreign, dominating evil. As early as 1971, a presentation delivered at the National Congress of Philosophy in Córdoba concludes on the following note: "The task that a Latin American philosophy attempting to overcome modernity and the subject must impose on itself is that of detecting all traits of this [modern] North Atlantic, dominating subject in our hidden, dependent, and oppressed Latin American being."[19] Of interest in this formulation is the view that the critique of imperialism is tied to a critique of modernity; in practice, "modernity" will often be equated with a secular approach to existence or a favorable attitude toward science. This view will result in the pursuit of a highly traditionalist conception of "Latin American being," based on such values as the procreation-oriented or "pro-life" family, the rejection of individualism, the critique of a secular-scientific education, and the repudiation of a philosophical materialism. As envisioned by Dussel, the socialist revolution resting on these traditionalist values would be a completely separate political phenomenon from "totalitarian" Marxism. It should be emphasized that Dussel was actually trying to construct a religiously grounded socialist theory that would serve as an alternative to Marxism. "Marxism is ontologically incompatible not only with the Latin American tradition but with the metaphysics of alterity," he wrote in 1974. And again: "Shall we opt for the Marxist way, where one has to kill the other as oppressor, in order for us to become the new oppressors? [Or] shall we opt for a philosophy in alterity?... This would be a totally distinct way, another program...a socialism unlike any other."[20] Dussel's most important philosophical work from this period is *Para una ética de la liberación latinoamericana*, published in 1973 in two volumes.[21] Numerous publications followed guided by a strong Heideggerian and phenomenological influence, until the mid-1980s, when he developed a considerable interest in Marx.[22]

Let us now turn to the first issue of the *Revista de filosofía latinoamericana* (1975) and consider these initial observations in a more detailed way. Appropriately, this issue of the *Revista* was concerned primarily with the problem of where and how to establish the point of departure for a Latin American philosophy of liberation.

Identity and Liberation

The "point of departure" (*punto de partida*) for a Latin American philosophy can be discussed from many different angles. They range from relatively formal discussions of the logical status of culturally specific truth-claims to more broadly defined approaches focusing on the nature of a Latin American philosophical identity.[23] Assuming that it is possible for at least some philosophical claims to have a culturally specific logical status, one may proceed to inquire, given the variety of positions found in Argentina during this period, how the differences between superficially similar perspectives are constituted. Insofar as "the philosophy of liberation" is often presented as a theoretically homogeneous movement, the critical issue is to identify and distinguish from one another the various philosophical/ideological perspectives and tendencies within it. This can only be done by paying close attention to their differences. Just as an outsider to feminism or Marxism may believe all positions are alike within such theoretical movements—when in fact we know that there are different kinds of feminisms and Marxisms—so there are different philosophies of/for liberation, or rather, different philosophical positions on liberation. Within the so-called philosophy of liberation, the differences are seldom discussed. This discussion, however, is necessary, not only for the sake of clarity, but in order to reach an adequate understanding of the conflicts that generated the various positions.

Broadly speaking, in the philosophy of liberation developing in Argentina there are two principal approaches to the "starting point" of a Latin American philosophy. The first is historicist or post-Hegelian; the second, metaphysical or "ontologicist," a recognizable product of Heideggerian thought. The historicist perspective is more accepting of past cultural traditions, especially those of the modern period, as well as more progressive with respect to present-day social change. The post-Heideggerian position, in contrast, places itself at a radical distance from modern values at the same time that it tends toward political conservatism. Both approaches have in common a rejection of the universalist thesis that truth-claims are independent of time, place, history, culture, economics, and so on. Both are largely concerned with what it means to do philosophy "from" (*desde*) a Latin American standpoint. Moving well beyond the historicist position of Leopoldo Zea, which conceives the Latin American perspective as mediated by the progressive actualization of the ideas of freedom and equality in Latin American history, the outlook of the ontological-foundationalist sector of the philosophy of liberation stresses the need for challenging Western reason from the standpoint of the oppressed or popular sectors of the society. Zea had examined Western reason's failure to deliver to Latin American and Third World people the same liberties granted to the dominant sectors of industrial societies. The ontologicist wing of the philosophy of liberation questions Western reason in principle, a move that finds some important theoretical precedents in Heidegger.

Both the post-Hegelian and the Heideggerian approaches contest the universality of philosophical discourse. The first appeals to the notion of a concrete or historically situated, in contrast to an abstract, universality; the second attempts to situate itself in a different order of being than that represented by a universal reason. From this last point, the Heideggerian wing of the Argentine philosophers extrapolated the view that if Europe and European philosophy stood for "universal" reason, Latin America and its philosophy would be the site of a new revelation of truth or being. In short, while, for some, Latin American philosophy represents or ought to represent a development of Western culture (taking into account the need for a transformation of this culture in view of various requirements for social liberation found in Latin American societies), for others, Latin American philosophy ought to represent a radical otherness to Western culture. Such an otherness, it is claimed, can still be found in the region's indigenous heritage, ancient myths, popular culture, religious beliefs, and national-popular political movements. The ontological-foundationalist sector believes itself to be the direct interlocutor of the people and their beliefs; this sector also tends to believe that an authentic Latin American culture is homogeneous rather than heterogeneous in character.

Some positions come closer than others in approximating this general sketch, which one should not expect to find instantiated in a pure form. Still, the sketch serves to place various positions within a certain continuum in the history of ideas. The specific view of liberation emerging from a philosopher's writing may then be traced to the notion of a philosophical identity found therein. In practice, the starting point is not Hegel, Marx, or Heidegger, but the place or position wherein a given philosopher situates himself in his discursive narrative. At least four different positions can be identified in the first issue of the *Revista*: (1) situating one's philosophical discourse in the context of the history of ideas and institutions (Roig, and, to some extent, Cerutti); (2) situating one's discourse within the politics of a popularly based "national project" (Ardiles); (3) situating one's discourse in politics and justifying the latter with a combination of ethical and metaphysical principles (Dussel); and (4) situating one's discourse in a cultural-ontological "place" called "the American," or *lo americano*, and privileging this site as a starting point for philosophy (Kusch).[24] For some, a historical identity prevails. For others, a political, culturalist, or national identity prevails. Each position will then maneuver the notion of liberation differently. Each has its own style of delivery and works from a different (though at times interrelated) set of postulates.

Arturo Roig, whose essay on university reform does not discuss the topic of a philosophy of liberation as such, offers a clearly defined historicist perspective.[25] His discourse is unambiguously situated in the history of ideas and institutions. Roig follows a critical position in which the notion of effecting a change of values within the culture and its institutions is paramount. With a standpoint firmly rooted in Argentine history, he avoids the guilt-ridden discourse characteristic of those who desire to possess the elusive "being" of "being Argentine." Although he finds some appeal in the notion of utopia as a ground for the critical discourse of philosophy, he bases the possibilities for social change on current historical circumstances. Humanistic proposals for the transformation of the university are offered in view of the service they might provide for students. The emphasis is strictly on social liberation, in this case, liberation from authoritarian or exclusivist traditions in higher education. The provision of wider educational access to students, the expansion of interdisciplinary studies, and the development of work-related programs are some of the notions discussed. This article carries such a distant tone from that found in contributions by Dussel, Ardiles, Casalla, and Kusch, that, without saying so, it puts in question Roig's relationship to the "philosophy of liberation" group. Some years later he would summarize his differences with this intellectual movement, rejecting any further association with it: "Those of us who have been fighting...[on the side of the history of ideas] ended up looking suspiciously, if not at the problematic of liberation, most assuredly at the 'philosophy of liberation,' from which, at a given time, we felt the decisive need to be liberated."[26]

Much more representative of the movement is the position of Osvaldo Ardiles in his article "Basic Lines for a Project of Latin American Philosophizing."[27] Ardiles offers an almost quintessential statement of the basic orientation behind the 1970s movement when he argues that a Latin American philosophy must face a radical choice between dependence and liberation. He argues that the present "subject" of philosophizing—for example, the individual philosopher employed at a university—is part of the system of oppression and dependence in which the country is situated. Thus the philosophy of liberation rejects this subject and searches for a new one, which it finds in the notion of "people-nation" (*pueblo-nación*). The philosopher of liberation is envisioned as someone who must speak exclusively for this subject, which is generally conceived as lying outside himself. A new "horizon of understanding" is postulated for philosophy, namely, that of a national project "conducted by the popular masses as the meaning of Being and the way of action."[28] The goal of the project, he adds, is to break with dependence, defeat imperialism, and place the nation's cultural, political, economic, and social power under the control of the popular sectors.[29] Ardiles's position appears to imply that the philosophers of liberation and other intellectuals siding with the same cause would be the only legitimate interlocutors for the "national project" in the universities. The image of liberation philosophy that is promoted is therefore exclusivist rather than inclusivist in character.

The category "people," like that of "national project," appears to be set up so as to include only those individuals and groups whose interests can be linked to the support of certain designated political struggles. Ardiles states: "By People we understand the *ensemble [conjunto] of exploited social sectors in struggle against Imperialism as well as internal and external dependence* [emphasis in the original]."[30] This means that a person's political affiliation and activity would determine whether or not he or she is considered a member of "the people." Among the political causes that have served to give meaning to the term "people" in Argentine history, Ardiles names the indigenous rebellions, the struggle for independence from Spain in the nineteenth century, the early twentieth-century social movements, and more recent popular movements, including Peronism. He therefore places emancipatory and populist movements in the same category, describing them as "organic expressions" of various distinct sectors of the popular base of the nation.[31]

In a similar vein, it is argued that there has not yet existed an "organic" philosophy in Latin America, namely one that serves as the direct expression of the cultural values of the popular sectors, or *pueblo*. Neocolonialism has created a culture of dependence in which philosophy is entrapped. Within this culture of dependence, philosophy "has acted as an alienated and alienating consciousness."[32] It has been a concealing logos in the interests of domination. Against this dominating logos the new horizon of understanding "is established beginning with the popular praxis [a partir de la praxis popular]"; the revolutionary theory that will guide it will be "pre-ideological" and "prescientific."[33] The new theory does not come from the philosophers themselves. "It is the social group that produces a determinate representation of the world. The task of intellectuals is to express it coherently and vigorously on the conceptual or imaginative levels."[34] All this must also be done "according to the light of the superior rationality of the National Project."[35] If philosophy begins with the "liberating praxis of this new historical subject—the popular masses—the dichotomies of modernity... [subject/object, theory/praxis, and individual/society]" will be overcome.[36]

Ardiles's approach—nationalistic, populistic, "prescientific"— is typical of the "radical" wing of the liberationist philosophers. This wing is radical in its stand against imperialism but conservative in its stand against modernity, whose progressive stance it rejects as *totalizadora* (a term best translated as "producer of totalities," in contrast to *totalizante*, or "totalizing," used favorably by Ardiles to depict the major syntheses of which the philosophy of liberation is capable). In other words, on one side there is a correlation between the "liberating praxis" of the people and the "totalizing synthesis" of the philosophy of liberation,[37] just as on the other there is a correlation between the dominating order of modernity and the discredited culture of dependence currently guiding the practice of philosophy. One will notice here a powerful, schematic dualism between good and evil. Modernity and dependence demarcate a totality of evil, which one can exit only by joining the national project of the people against imperialism (in this particular case, Peronism, but any other political movement with a national-popular base and with an "anti-imperialist" self-image will fit in its place).

The "totalizing synthesis" proposed by Ardiles is probably the least critical theoretical feature of his perspective on liberation. Prone to reductionism and oversimplification, this engulfing logic is incapable of distinguishing well between particular aspects and general characteristics of various problems under discussion. Whole epochs of history and entire civilizations are looked on with disdain, and past Argentine philosophy is scorned. Yet there is little justification for such sweeping conclusions, especially in view of the fact that throughout its history Argentina has produced many outstanding thinkers, who, even if highly influenced by European thought, have left their mark on the development of philosophy in Latin America.[38] As Ardiles sees it, however, only what is judged to promote the cause of national-popular political movements is considered worthwhile. From this standpoint, it is only a small step to Dussel's position, which will place this political dualism under the gaze of an absolutist ethical and cosmological optic.

Dussel takes the logic of Ardiles's political discourse one step further by *justifying* the national-popular project with a metaphysical and ethical arsenal of symbolic constructs. The name given to the principle justifying this standpoint is that of alterity. In religion, this refers to God as the absolute Other, from which all moral commands emanate. In philosophy, it is the Other as oppressed, who nevertheless is the earthly revelation of the absolute Other.[39] From this standpoint, the earthly Other's demands signify the absolute Other's commands. The supreme law of Dussel's ethical system is "service to the Other," a maxim that may include the duty to lay down one's life for the Other. But "the Other" is only a metaphysical term which, like its ethical counterpart "alterity," serves as a placeholder for a vast number of metonymic replacements. So "the Other," depending on the context, will be substituted for "the people," "the poor," "the hungry one," "the child," "the oppressed," "the periphery," "Latin America," "the Third World," and so on. Through the strategic placement and development of the formula "the Other demands justice," it is possible to move from a religious context to a political, social, economic, or metaphysical context without engaging in a detailed elaboration of arguments in support of particular claims. At the end of this process of conceptual replacements—from "Other" to "poor" to "Latin American," and so on—one comes back to the original equivalence between liberation and a national-popular political project. There is, fundamentally, a double reflection from the political to the religious and then back to the political. But little is gained theoretically in the movement insofar as we remain caught within the same circle of definitions from which all else follows.

"Latin America is 'the Other,' the *poor*," writes Dussel in the first issue of the *Revista de filosofía latinoamericana*.[40] He argues that the region's political situation is such that it faces only two options: "The dilemma then must be defined as follows: national popular liberation or regression to dependence. There is no other possibility!"[41] To act against the interest of the Other (in this case, Latin America, the poor) is evil. Using a text from the nineteenth-century utopian socialist and Christian thinker Aloisius Hubert, Dussel notes that "individual private property is the exclusive cause of division, hatred, and struggle" and that "it is the only source of all evils and tyrannies."[42] Moreover, in Hubert's statement "Doing evil is acting against the interest of the Other," Dussel sees a precedent for his own ethics of alterity.[43] Incidentally, Hubert does not capitalize "other" (*d'autrui*), whereas Dussel's rephrasing of Hubert's statement does. "To say 'yes-to-the-Other,' to the political Other," Dussel concludes, "is the *absolute criterion* of a political ethic [*eticidad política*]."[44] Combining these elements into an ethical imperative, he interprets Christian thought as carrying an absolute mandate on behalf of the cause of national-popular liberation. In his concluding paragraph, he states that "Latin American liberation is impossible [*sic*] if it fails to be a national liberation, and every national liberation is [only] definitively such if it is a popular liberation, that is to say, [a liberation] of the workers, peasants, and marginal [sectors].... Only the poor, the Other, the people have sufficient *reality, exteriority and life* to accomplish the construction of a new order."[45]

One will notice three levels of absolutism in the discourse employed by Dussel. The first is political, and it is based on an "absolute criterion," which, as stated, guides the political ethics of liberation. The second level of absolutism is a religious one. It is based on the absolute rejection of evil and the correlative wholehearted embracing of the good (interpreted here as a profound divestment of self and possessions in an act of service to the

Other). The third level unites the religious and the political in an absolute ethics of service to the Other, which is translated into the political goal of serving the people and their national-popular revolution. The political and religious levels move in strict parallelism to each other, reflecting the same ideas back and forth, so it is difficult to say which of the two has priority. Since the narrative is filled with political references and abstains from a proper theological analysis of the problems, it would not be unreasonable to deduce that both religion and philosophy are used here primarily as intruments in support of the political cause of national-popular liberation, bearing in mind that both "national" and "popular" are understood in predetermined ways.

If the political aim of Dussel's use of the "Other" is to promote the cause of religious, national-popular liberation movements, the rational tool used in support of this aim is the so-called analectical logic of "exteriority." In *Philosophy of Liberation*, Dussel distinguishes between "dialectics" and "analectics" (otherwise referred to as "anadialectics") as methods of philosophical inquiry. "Dialectics," whose metaphysical counterpart is the category of totality, is associated roughly with the most prominent methods of philosophical investigation from Aristotle to Marx. In contrast, "analectics" is posited as the method that would allow us to theorize about the exteriority or alterity that lies beyond totality.[46] The categories of exteriority, totality, and alterity used by Dussel are borrowed directly from the work of the French philosopher Emmanuel Levinas, but these categories are then applied to a different and, indeed, contradictory end, insofar as they are subordinated to a political platform of national-popular liberation.[47] The result is that Dussel employs the term "analectical" both to refer to the unpredictable and differential quality of that which lies outside dialectical totalities (e.g., the poor person in relation to the system of wealth) and to dictate the terms under which alternatives to present economic, social, and political systems must be considered if such alternatives are to qualify as emancipatory. I would argue that in the second function of the term "analectical," a new foundationalism is operating. This new foundationalism encloses us within an intricate array of newly given totalities to which we must conform if we are to be "liberated": for example, "the new home," constituted by the obligatorily procreative couple, becomes paradigmatic for liberation.[48] An essentialist and highly normative discourse of liberation, through the mediation of analectic logic, comes to replace the so-called metaphysics of totality. In this way the notion of alterity loses its critical quality, becoming part of a dogmatic and moralizing discourse.

It may be argued that the category of "exteriority," when used in conjunction with analectical logic, carries little philosophical weight. The argument that exteriority is always logically privileged rests on an artificial premise, namely, the ability to set up a certain logical space (the position of the Other), which by definition is external to a given "totality," or system of domination. Thus, according to analectical logic, the oppressed must always speak "from the exteriority of the established system."[49] To do so, they must be represented as morally privileged prior to entering into "the system." According to this formula—to use an example from Dussel's 1970s pedagogical ethics—the preschool child (designated in the text as masculine, *el niño*) is said to be external to the domination he will encounter when entering the school system. Yet, if we follow this example, it is not difficult to see that, while there might be some important structural as well as empirical elements of domination in a given school system, it is too farfetched to suggest both that the child's mind is uncontaminated before he steps into the school and that the school is so perverse that everything taught therein is part of a culture of oppression.[50] In the same vein I would argue that the standpoint of a pure, uncontaminated "exteriority" does not exist and that a much more empirically informed and critical use of the concept is needed before it can serve as a tool of analysis for a theory of liberation.

The process of appealing to the logic of exteriority can easily constitute an evasion when it comes to analyzing the actual social relations of domination and the corresponding struggles for freedom found in human existence. For example, in Dussel's sexual and pedagogical ethics, the child is always situated in a privileged space: "What is certain is that the son-child-student is never an equal or someone different.... The child is *distinct* from [the very moment of] his origin, someone new, a messianic and eschatological history."[51] At times he speaks as if, somehow, a child could exist prior to conception. Contraception is viewed as morally offensive, and abortion is regarded as cold-blooded murder. "The son is there. He might not have been there, because he was unwanted, because he was always prevented [from coming into being], or because he was assassinated through abortion."[52] This type of reasoning, in which the category of exteriority is superimposed on a number of complex problems so as to yield a simple solution, is not unusual as an applied instance of analectics.

The application of the logic of exteriority to moral reasoning has not been exempt from the use of some puzzling forms of argumentation. For example, the idea of doing what is *right* has not been distinguished properly from that of being in a certain *place* or that of holding a certain *position*. The fact that something is described as being outside of something else, however, does not make the former a privileged moral subject. Nor does being in a particular place condemn one to a special fate or predisposition. Through this careless form of reasoning, place and position are overdetermined with ethical and political value. In *Philosophy of Liberation* it is said that a person born in New York City is likely to become "a hunter of men," while an African person will be a hunter of animals. "The world...gives a privileged place to the past as the 'place' where 'I' was born. The 'where-I-was-born' is the pre-determination of all other determinations.... The one born among the pygmies will strive to become a great hunter of animals; the one born in New York will strive to become a great entrepreneur (a hunter of persons)."[53] This type of reasoning does violence to our most basic expectations regarding a philosophy of liberation. Philosophies of liberation are meant to *prevent* people from being discriminated against on account of race, national origin, or place of residence, rather than reify the basis for such prejudice. There is much confusion in Dussel's thinking between the part and the whole, between a designated space and those who occupy it. The prolific use of "metonymic reasoning" is most disturbing insofar as whatever is associated with "totality" becomes a candidate for destruction, while anything associated with "alterity" is thought to carry an absolute mandate for justice on its behalf. When used in conjunction with certain intransigent political positions—how else would an absolutist ethics function in society?—the practical results of "the philosophy of liberation" as elaborated by Dussel and other exponents of this type of analectical reasoning appear truly frightening.

Ontological America

Another defense of a national, popular perspective was offered by the philosopher Rodolfo Kusch, who, strictly speaking, was not a member of the philosophy of liberation group, but nevertheless exercised a great deal of influence on it.[54] Kusch's discourse is situated in the problematic of what it means to "be American," with a strong accent on "being." His reflections on the point of departure for a Latin American philosophy are rather provocative. He claims that the problem of philosophy in the region is that one still does not know who the subject of philosophizing is. Kusch argues that in Latin America there is a gap between the thinking subject and the subject of culture. He also thinks there is only one cultural subject, even though empirically there are many thinking subjects, or individuals.[55] The reason the gap exists between philosophy and culture is that intellectuals are alienated from popular beliefs described by Kusch as "American."

In Latin America we [philosophers] are not the subject of culture, only thinking subjects. We feel the cultural subject is another, and this other puts pressure on us.... Peronism arises as a pressure of the Latin American cultural subject on us, the thinking subjects.

And in philosophy the situation is the following: despite our being the thinking subjects, the pressure of the other makes us unable to assume the cultural subject, and, as a result, we don't get to do philosophy. Since philosophy is the cultural discourse that finds its subject, even though we are thinking subjects we cannot do philosophy, because the subject is the other, the one who is putting pressure on us, who in sum is the true cultural subject of Latin America.[56]

When an Argentine philosopher tries to do philosophy, Kusch goes on to explain, he feels not only the pressure of what is "popular," but also his "interior unpopularity."[57] With this pressure that the other—who is now called "people"—places on the philosopher, the philosopher discovers he is not a cultural subject. Furthermore, if an Argentine philosopher feels he is a cultural subject, he is only such because he assumes "a culture that is not ours, a culture for which we have opted, believing in its universality."[58] In other words, there is a displacement, Kusch argues, between the philosophical subject and the cultural subject—the philosophical subject taking on a European cultural identity and the "true" cultural subject, the non-European "American," simply being there, not yet attaining the status of a thinking subject. If this is the problem, the solution offered by Kusch is simply for the philosopher to find the true cultural subject—not the people in a political sense but the "other" in a cultural sense. "The pressure of the popular is the pressure of the American."[59] This cultural other privileged by

Kusch as the true Argentine cultural subject is someone from the popular sectors, someone whose culture differs from Western European culture and its reified view of the world.

As a case in point, Kusch offers the example of a seventy-year-old Bolivian man from the popular sectors named Felipe Cota. He proceeds to reconstruct this man's cultural universe, which is largely dependent on mythlike beliefs. Cota's very conservative beliefs are thought by Kusch to be quintessentially Latin American. What does the authentic subject of Latin American culture believe, in contrast to the fake European-identified thinking subject?

> The principal characteristic of such a mythical consciousness is that it integrates the totality of the cosmos with weights of signification [*cargas significativas*]. The latter are not static but dynamic. The themes of the Lord and the Virgin polarize the dynamic of the whole, to such an extent that everything situated in the mythical field is able to become dynamic according to certain themes such as the seedtime, the fiestas, etc.

> There can also be established certain semantic channels by which signification is distributed. These derive from an existential level inhabited by Cota. This is the level of situated being [*estar*], taking this as his everyday life and habitat. From here two planes are embraced: one comes from heaven and the other from below. The theme of the Lord...spreads toward heaven. At the level of situated being, or daily existence, the theme of the Virgin unfolds, and from below there operate the dark forces, translated into fear and punishment.[60]

Interestingly, Kusch integrates the mythical beliefs of someone like Felipe Cota into an essay on the topic of the point of departure for contemporary Latin American philosophy. The thesis proposed by him is that, even if one has to begin again "from zero," philosophy in Latin America should rethink its beginning and stake out its roots in the cultural universe of a peasant like Cota. Appropriating a Heideggerian perspective, Kusch links this point of departure to a "pre-ontic" level of awareness.[61] He argues that such a pre-ontic level should be included in Latin American philosophical investigations "as a chapter forgotten by Western thought."[62] Behind the façade of things, he says, is "where we discover what is essential in myth, the difference that constitutes it (which is always unforeseeable), that which is unsaid, that which science cannot determine."[63]

This pre-ontic level, according to Kusch, is reachable not by a reason (or type of rationality) through which what is ontic is understood (*razón de ser*) but by a *razón de estar* (a reason of situated being). He speaks about "a sense of finding ourselves captives of a new vision that passes behind the objectual façade imposed by the West."[64] Ironically, his description of "authentic culture," that is, non-European culture, is largely dependent on Heidegger. He himself speaks of this sense of being held captive as an *Ereignis,* or appropriating event (as articulated by Heidegger).[65] Through this *Ereignis* in which the culturally differentiated other gives himself to us and constitutes us as ourselves, "and only in this way," claims Kusch, shall Latin American philosophers find the path to liberation.[66] He believes this new appropriation will result in the destruction of the concept "people," which was of colonial European origin, and its replacement by the "other," who in turn constitutes the authentic "us." In this sense he differs from Dussel, who uses the category "other" in just the contrary way: to reinforce the notion of "people" in the national-popular political sense of the term rather than to strengthen a culturalist sense of the term "us."

Before moving on to Horacio Cerutti Guldberg's contribution to this collection of articles, I should mention another criticism arising from the positions taken by Ardiles, Dussel, and Kusch with respect to the relationship of philosophy to the popular sectors or to popular culture. Apart from the blind spot involved in failing to recognize the value of cultural contributions not strictly identifiable with the popular Other, there is a politically questionable side to the issue of privileging that discourse that is labeled "popular" as the exclusive source of meaning for philosophy. A type of paternalism emerges when philosophers or other intellectuals decide they will be the official cultural interpreters of the people's beliefs. Regardless of good intentions, this attitude can easily degenerate into the practice of "keeping the people in their place." By defining and interpreting "the" meaning of the popular for "the people" and by discrediting other kinds of knowledge as antipopular—particularly modern European thought, "bourgeois" thinking, or scientific knowledge—this approach confines the horizon of legitimate popular knowledge to those belief systems that are compatible with the philosophical orientations of the liberationist philosophers. Or, to put it another way, it is one thing to pay attention to popular thinking, including various kinds of mythlike beliefs, within a pluralistic horizon admitting of a diverse range of beliefs and values, and another to say there is only "one" cultural subject in Latin America and that *his* beliefs (for this subject is generally depicted as masculine) must be evoked as ontologically or politically privileged if Latin American philosophy is to be authentic. Again, there is a confusion between the part and the whole, between unity and plurality, between the present and the past. The silencing of many voices, particularly women's voices and voices of dissent, is a necessary part of this process of privileging the "one" subject, whether this be a cultural, popular subject, a philosophical subject, or a combination of both.

Popular Wisdom or Ideology of the Popular?

Apropos of the lack of a self-critical perspective, characteristic of positions where the "turn" to the popular is perceived as a kind of epiphany or road to salvation and never questioned rigorously as an ideological construct, we now look at the contribution by Horacio Cerutti Guldberg, which is unique among this group in raising the issue of ideology.[67] Cerutti addresses the problem of liberation from the standpoint of a political philosophy, specifically one situated in a Latin American history of ideas. The problem of ideology is situated in the context of the prior analysis of related issues by Latin American philosophers such as Arturo Roig and the Uruguayan Carlos Vaz Ferreira. There is no departing from zero here or from a purist position of "exteriority." One will recognize at once a philosophical discourse rooted in the texts and ideas of Latin American philosophers such as Roig and Vaz Ferreira as well as the critical perspectives of Marx, Nietzsche, and Freud. The concept, argues Cerutti, is never pure or neutral. It does not have an abstract origin; it is grounded in life. This grounding positions conceptual thinking at the same time that it attaches to it a concealing—ideological—element. As Nietzsche, Marx, and Freud have shown, "conscious 'life' in its expression hides a 'will to power,' 'an economic structure,' 'an unconscious.'"[68] Philosophy, therefore, is always ideological, because conceptual thinking fulfills simultaneously both an unveiling and a concealing function.

The ideological content of philosophy must be exposed in order to arrive at a proper understanding of reality. "A clear view of reality is acquired only by conceptual means, but, at the same time, there is in the process of conceptualizing an approach that hides aspects of the same reality."[69] All conceptual thinking is positional; philosophy is both political and ideological in nature. Though limited in this sense, philosophy can still be instrumental in analyzing reality and contributing to social transformations in a Marxian sense.[70] If it learns to sharpen its self-critical capacity and thereby avoid the self-assuring role of negative ideology, it can contribute all the better to advancing human knowledge and social change.

Cerutti situates the philosophy of liberation in the tradition of a Latin American political philosophy. He raises the question of the relationship between a political philosophy and a political praxis. In this regard, he advocates the development of a "political philosophy [intended] for Latin American liberation."[71] While Cerutti agrees with Ardiles in thinking that there are basically two options—either supporting the status quo or working toward a transformation of the current political structures—his understanding of the Latin American tradition and the nature of political praxis contains two significant theoretical differences. In the first place, Cerutti understands "praxis" in the context of a historical/anthropological process rather than as directed specifically toward a national-popular political movement. "The political philosopher should break with the closure of being in the very praxis where its meaning is acquired, and he ought to let his engaged voice be heard in the *actual historical process*. He should think the very process of collapse, openness, and closure of dialectical totalities in the light of a *new anthropological stage* [emphasis added]."[72] These statements show the influence of Roig, who, as may be recalled, argued for a reading of Hegel from the standpoint of an "anthropological a priori" that would override the absolutist orientation of the dialectic.[73]

Second, Cerutti opposes the paradigm that advocates a sharp rupture with modernity, the European philosophical tradition, and the rich tradition of Latin American thought. He argues, on the contrary, that doing Latin American political philosophy is a way to be united with this tradition, particularly that of the nineteenth and twentieth centuries. Citing a passage from Frantz Fanon's conclusion to *Black Skins, White Masks*—"I am a man, the whole past of the world belongs to me"—Cerutti emphasizes that one cannot construct a Latin American political philosophy based on a select ontology or a strictly ethnic view of history. "Applying by analogy what Fanon has said to a Latin American situation, we find it unworkable from a historical standpoint for a liberating process to pretend to bring back...a pre-Columbian cultural past that is no longer...recoverable."[74] The Latin American philosopher needs to be able to recover "the whole human past."[75] Thus, there is a place for pre-Columbian thought, but also for colonial thought "and the whole of our intellectual past" insofar as it forms part of the development of a Latin American history of ideas. The issue therefore is not whether philosophy should begin with "the American" or "the popular" instead of the European or national-bourgeois, but whether a political philosophy for liberation should have a firm grasp of the ideological, historical, and anthropological forces constituting its vision of the world, in contrast to exhibiting an uncritical ideological and/or ahistorical focus.[76]

The Weight of Not Being European and Its Political Implications

Just as the Mexican philosophers had struggled with the problem of their relation to Europe earlier in the century, so many Argentines were eventually forced to face the same question. But Argentina and Mexico are two different countries, with different political and intellectual histories. The Mexican approach to resolving the problem of cultural identity was less traumatic than the Argentine because Mexican philosophers never felt fully identified with Europe. Argentina, on the contrary, had often been viewed as the most "European" of Latin American republics. The question of "not being European" came to be perceived by Argentine intellectuals as a profound cultural crisis. This crisis was already evident during the post-Peronist period of 1955–58.[77] But insofar as this situation affected philosophers, and the development of Argentine philosophy in particular, a rather interesting factor is observable in the differences between the Mexican and Argentine approaches to cultural identity. In the case of Mexico, the figure of Leopoldo Zea stands out as the most important contributor to this inquiry. It will be recalled that Zea studied under José Gaos, one of a distinguished group of Spanish intellectuals given refuge in Mexico at the close of the Spanish Civil War. Zea's relationship with European philosophy was therefore mediated by an antifascist, progressive view of history. He saw that it was in the interest of Latin Americans both to insist on the critique of Eurocentrism and to absorb as much of the European political heritage of equality and freedom as would be conducive to solving important problems affecting Latin American societies. In Argentina, as in Mexico, the question of identity has been approached from many different standpoints since the nineteenth century.[78] But since the 1930s, there has been a powerful conservative nationalist presence in Argentine philosophy. This has compounded the problem of interpreting the work of someone like the German philosopher Martin Heidegger, whose ideas were influential in some of the formulations of liberation philosophy.[79] As will be shown, some of the theories emerging from a post-Heideggerian perspective in Argentina have been marked by a questionable mixture of ontology and politics.

Among the ontologically oriented thinkers, a philosophical position was developed that advocated a total rupture with modernity. In a stance highly reminiscent of Heidegger's "Letter on Humanism" (1947), there came to be a very strong rejection of modern values and the modern understanding of subjectivity. This position appealed to both conservative and radical sectors of the philosophy of liberation. These philosophers claimed that modernity was an expression of the European will to power (also referred to as the North Atlantic ontology of domination). Rather than seek out the causes of domination and exploitation in empirically verifiable conditions affecting the relations between individuals, classes, and peoples, they argued that the culprit for the existence of "domination" in America—as manifested in the conquest, colonialism, and neocolonialism—was nothing less than modernity. With religion, myth, the popular sectors—and, for the right wing, the military—to the rescue, perhaps a new order could be imposed that would allow Argentine society to get in touch with its "authentic" past and thereby emancipate itself from a decadent foreign culture.

From a radically oriented standpoint, Ardiles, for example, argues on behalf of the thesis that imperialism is the outcome of modernity, as if a category such as "modernity" could be held accountable for the development of a particular economic or political system.[80] In order to overcome the state of dependence affecting Latin American societies, a complete rupture with all the "inherited [theoretical] currents" found in academic philosophy is proposed.[81] Ardiles specifically rejects the study of a Latin American philosophy in the sense of an analysis of the history of philosophical ideas in Latin America. "When we speak about 'Latin American philosophy'…it is not a matter of studying [Latin American] authors or investigating Latin American currents [of thought]," he claims; what is at stake is only the construction of an "organic synthesis" for the liberation of the masses.[82] Despite his rejection of all European "isms" and schools of thought, Ardiles states that Latin American liberation philosophy might use a number of acceptable methodologies ranging "from hermeneutics and analectics to dialectics and the philosophy of praxis."[83] Ironically, the claim to be speaking for the true interests of Latin America can only be made by rejecting the fragile yet nevertheless important tradition of Latin American philosophy developed up to that time, replacing it with an uncritical and highly politicized application of (European) post-Hegelian and phenomenological thought.

Another important European tradition that is redefined and given a populist Latin Americanist image by some of the liberation philosophers is that of Christianity. Though associated historically with the conquest, Christianity can be exonerated from its partial complicity with an order of domination since it can be argued that modernity alienated it from itself. Here the radicals have something in common with the conservative philosopher Mario Casalla, who writes in the same volume that one of the essential aspects of modernity is "the rupture of the Western European project of existence."[84] By this he means the separation of reason from faith. It is revealing that while Descartes and Nietzsche are favorite targets of criticism for this group of philosophers, no attempt is made to analyze their views in relation to the repressive power of the Inquisition (contemporary with Descartes) or the critique of slave morality in Western culture (expounded by Nietzsche).

In response to the objection that modernity divorces reason from faith (conservative version) or alienates intellectuals from an organic relationship with the people (radical version, often interchangeable with the former), it can be pointed out that the dichotomy between reason and faith attributed to modern thought is a false one. Where one may find a dichotomy is between a critical, progressively oriented rationality and an authoritarian, traditionalist faith. A dogmatic rationality and an authoritarian faith do not come in conflict with each other; neither do a critical rationality and a reformist faith. By a reformist faith I do not mean Protestantism as opposed to Catholicism; there are reformers and traditionalists within both belief systems. It is more a matter of how one goes about believing something. A similar situation occurs in the Left, where one can also find political reformers and traditionalists. By a reformer at the level of faith I mean someone who questions authoritarian interpretations of belief systems. In religion, for example, authoritarian belief systems are those laying particular emphasis on obedience to established authority, predestination, punishment, and guilt. Thus the belief system of the peasant Felipe Cota used by Kusch to illustrate what he took to be paradigmatic of an authentic Latin American culture has a strongly traditionalist orientation. This can be seen in the importance given to fear and punishment. Within this belief system individuals feel that their lives are guided by forces beyond their control. The theology of liberation, in contrast, is reformist-oriented in the sense that it empowers the poor to come to a critical awareness of their social exploitation and to take action to remedy it.

Unlike the traditionalist, the advocate of reform has a democratic orientation and does not seek to impose her or his own personal beliefs on the totality of members of a community or a nation. This is precisely the perspective missing from the ontological-foundationalist wing of liberation philosophy, with its division of reality into totalized totality and analectical alterity. A crucial political issue behind the "radical" critique of "modern North Atlantic thinking" offered by Ardiles and Dussel is whether the (leftist) political process in Latin America will be traditionalist in its response to authority or critical of new absolutes. The basic choice for liberation theory is whether, in its claim to defend freedom and social justice, it will position itself on the side of absolutism or on that of critique. In this context, a position arguing for national-popular liberation may well prove itself, through its absolutist ideology, to stand in opposition to the goals of a social liberation movement. Let us take this interpretation one step further and see where Dussel's philosophy of national-popular liberation has stood on some issues related to social change.

Is Coercive Service to Otherness the Answer?

It should be clear by now that the belief that there is such a thing as a North Atlantic *ontology of domination*, which must be rejected on behalf of a Third World ontology of liberation, is far from credible. Political problems of domination and struggles for liberation surely exist, but it is not helpful to depict them in such loaded terms. To understand such a statement, one must rephrase it in ways that make sense with respect to empirical claims and particular details. When this is done, the much-discussed "totalized totality" falls apart. What remains is a will to believe in a totalized totality, and ultimately the best that can be said about such a will is that it is engaged in a search for meaning to the point of absurdity. This reveals a crisis in cultural identity of extraordinary proportions. Our task as philosophers, however, is not to be consumed by this type of crisis but to find a basis for cultural identity that is in tune with reality, even while keeping in mind that Latin American societies, in their social reality, need to undergo major changes.

Empirical reasoning can point to the damage that can result from the social and political implications of a philosophical position such as Dussel's, where a revolutionary leftist perspective and an absolutist moral code are mixed together with little or no awareness of what the combination may bring. It is a serious matter of principle to argue against imperialism, which in the context of a Latin American political scenario refers to a policy or practice of systematic intrusion on the part of the United States government on the right of self-determination of the people of the region. The conditions leading to the phenomenon known as imperialism have to do with very specific issues regarding the political, economic, and military use (and abuse) of power. When a theory begins to confuse the greater part of North American and European culture with imperialism, or the position of individuals living in these societies with an imperialistic ideology, or the whole of modern rationality with an ideology of conquest, such a misunderstanding causes concern. The explanation given for the sources or causes of injustice is closely tied to racial or cultural ascriptions, and this in turn reminds us of a phenomenon such as fascism.

Of course, Dussel's intention is not to promote fascism; on the contrary, he is arguing for liberation from totalities, including totalized thinking and fascist ideologies. But his argument is seriously flawed, regardless of the intention. The flaw has to do with the manner of perceiving relations between parts and wholes, or between an ethical position and a physical, or spatial, location. In a way this confusion is the other side of the "fusion" ideal in which intellectuals, the people, and their leader(s) supposedly become merged within an invulnerable "organic" whole. Both the fusion model and the method of representing differences as manifestations of the totalized "other" are evasive, uncritical ways of conceiving highly complex individual, social, and political relations. The question needs to shift to what a political platform for liberation ought to accomplish in terms of specific issues and empirical goals. The specific objectives of working for a nonracist, nonsexist, nonexploitative society should take precedence over metaphysical ideologizing and political oversimplifications.

A number of social issues require philosophical attention in Latin America, among them questions regarding democracy, racial and sexual equality, child care, elimination of poverty, access to and funding for education, provision of health care and benefits, peace, protection of natural resources, care of wildlife and the environment, safety from nuclear and toxic hazards, protection of basic freedom of expression for individuals and groups, workers' rights, basic security and services for senior citizens, and so on. In regard to all of these issues a liberating political process would encourage the greatest possible use of decision-making power by individuals and relevant groups. Decisions should be understood as contributing to the life of the society rather than to the demands of an externally situated Other. Dussel's use of the principle of alterity works against the concept of a democratic national unity and also against a policy of centralizing the social interests and benefits named above into a unified political platform. In Dussel's *Philosophy of Liberation*, there is also an excessive emphasis on the conflictive relations between central and peripheral power. The center is defined as a dominating force, while the periphery is depicted as morally worthy. Through this paradigm of liberation, the fragmentation of the Left remains assured. This is so because the "periphery" is given a bad conscience if its demands are presented as "central" to a society's political future. To be in the center, let us recall, is to be an exploiter; thus one must remain on the periphery if one is to receive the moral blessings associated with alterity. The migration of ideas from periphery to center and from center to periphery, which is one of the signs of a healthy culture, remains impeded by this excessively positional view of right and wrong.

What this creates, in effect, is a national political impasse in which little or nothing can be done to promote social measures against oppression until a peripheral group that claims it will liberate the nation from *all* injustice first takes power over the whole, establishing the longed-for organic community. This model can be used by anyone from the extreme Right to the militant Left. The model as such is no guarantee that either national or social liberation would follow from its application. On the face of it, it seems to work against majority rule. This is all the more reason why, in order to understand how this type of theory would affect the quality of life in a society, it is essential to inquire about how the principle of alterity is to be applied to specific issues. What does it mean to talk about an organic community or women's liberation, for example, from the standpoint of Dussel's ethics?

Feminist Concerns and Liberating Social Change

How Dussel would translate his vision of national-popular liberation into a program of social reforms that would benefit the popular sectors and society as a whole is not clear. He has been an opponent of state power as well as a strong critic of capitalism. One wonders how social reforms would be brought about in the organic community envisaged. For example, how would education and health care be distributed as equally as possible to all citizens if, as it is argued, centralization is wrong and equality inadmissible?[85] The pedagogical section of Dussel's ethics dismisses the value of a secular, state-sponsored education, and the section on "erotics" has been used to condemn contraception and abortion, as well as any sexual practice not conducive to procreation (homosexuality is singled out as the most important example).[86] Sometimes these points are missed because they are inserted as parenthetical remarks in the midst of an extended discussion on behalf of the notion of alterity. He stresses that modernity and the Cartesian "I think" bring about a totality in which alterity is denied by sexual or educational practices. Yet I think it is important for liberation theory to be explicit about where it stands on specific social issues. This is not only a necessary exercise when it comes to understanding the actual contents of a particular theory; in many cases it is necessary to examine the differences between what one would like to believe a theory of liberation is saying and what it actually says. Moreover, without an understanding of what a theory advocates with respect to specific issues, it is impossible to contribute to its improvement through criticism or logical analysis. In this context, it is appropriate to note some of the ways in which the principle of alterity is applied to specific social and moral questions in Dussel's writings on sexual ethics from the 1970s and 1980s.

In his ethical works from this period, a time when important struggles against right-wing political regimes in the region were taking place, Dussel held the view that abortion is murder, that contraception is a denial of Otherness, and that homosexuality is a perversion. In response to criticism received primarily from North American students, radical philosophers, and feminists, he has stated his intention to write a "new erotics" in which his position will be modified to some extent.[87] While acknowledging his intention to rethink these points, it is, however, important to look at the logic of the positions defended in the past, since they are typical of what the philosophy of liberation has been articulating for close to two decades with respect to sexual morality. Dussel's early position reflects the conservative views still held by large numbers of Hispanics (including high-ranking members of the clergy) who have not had a serious opportunity to consider alternative conceptions of sexual and reproductive ethics. Dussel's early teachings on sexual morality support a concept of sexual normativity that is shared by the political agendas of the Far Right. The Other has not been represented in this theory as the woman who needs an abortion or the socially excluded individual of a gay or lesbian sexual orientation. No considered notion of alterity functions in such an ethics of liberation, only an appeal to alterity as a rigid formula that in fact erases the very concept of otherness as difference.

In response to the possible objection—held by some who have intransigent views on these subjects—that the questions of abortion and homosexuality are not Latin American issues but reflect primarily North American concerns for social liberation, it should be noted that neither problem can be so easily confined to a geographical location. As Oscar Terán notes, since the 1950s the Argentine political Right as well as the sexually conservative Left have voiced objections to homosexuality, and this outlook has been prevalent within the military.[88] With respect to abortion, it is well known (but difficult to document) that countless Latin American women die each year as a result of clandestine abortions. Yet, appealing largely to people's religious sentiments, political opponents of abortion have carried out an extensive campaign against legalizing abortion. It would be ahistorical as well as empirically incorrect to claim that issues such as homosexuality and abortion are relevant only in North America. Any ethical theory with a realistic, practical orientation has to deal with these issues in Latin America; it is therefore all the more important that a so-called ethics of liberation deal with them without prejudice.

A woman's right to make decisions over her own body, especially as this applies to sexual and reproductive issues, can be denied or obstructed in different ways and through the use of a variety of "justifications." In his sexual ethics, Dussel applies the macrostructural distinction between "totality" and "alterity" to two types of sexual behavior, defined as "impulses": a "totalized" sexual impulse (sexual activity engaged in with no intention of having children) and an "alterative" impulse (sex open to procreation).[89] Not surprisingly, the former is condemned as perverse, and the latter is considered the only morally worthy way to relate to the erotic Other. From these premises it is deduced, among other things, that "feminist homosexuality concludes by summing up all perversions."[90] In addition, any sexual activity engaged in for nonreproductive purposes is labeled "homosexualizing" (*homosexualizante*).[91] This means that, in this alleged philosophy of erotic liberation, even a married couple practicing responsible sex with the use of contraceptives can become the target of homophobic allegations. While Dussel's work is not without a critique of machismo, the critique is feeble. It confines this attitude to European males, especially those influenced by Cartesian rationalism. The account ends with the words of a gaucho who laments his woman leaving him, perhaps for a wealthier man.[92] Despite his claim to be offering a theory of women's liberation far superior to feminism, Dussel fails to address the fundamental problem to be considered by such a theory: the need to reverse the effects of the sexist-laden content of popular and mainstream culture and to guarantee prompt and efficacious legislative measures on behalf of women's rights.

The Rejection of "Difference"

One of the most important conceptual flaws in the framework of alterity as used by Dussel is the refusal to accept the legitimacy of the concept of difference. In place of the category of that which is different (*diferente*), he substitutes the category of "what is distinct" (*lo distinto*). Difference, it is said, negates the possibility of recognizing true distinction, since any (one) difference may be conceived as interchangeable with any other. The move to the category of distinctness, however, only exacerbates this problem. Under this category, everything called "distinct" operates in a monolithic fashion without the possibility of internal diversity, conflict, and so on. Ethical duties and roles are stratified and placed in elaborate hierarchies that control even the most intimate aspects of a person's life. According to this model, ethical relationships are not conceived in terms of a person's decision to undertake certain responsibilities in the context of various specific circumstances, but only as responses (of service) to the analectically determined needs of an alteratively positioned Other.

The use of analectics as a radical-separatist, absolutist logic yields an understanding of alterity or otherness based on traditionalist beliefs since it refuses to concede that the category of "difference" is relevant to an ethics of social justice.[93] By definition, in Dussel's view, differences can only exist within totalitarian systems, which are the logical extension of "totalities"—or so it is argued. To break out of the closed belief-system advocated by Dussel, the first step is to acknowledge the moral and political legitimacy of perspectival differences. Then it is easy to see that various categories such as "child," "people," "woman," "other," and so on will hide a vast multiplicity of differences and that not only is it a distortion of empirical circumstances to forget these differences but, worse yet, there is a heavy price to be paid politically for such a distortion.

Today the process of liberating human beings from various forms of oppression needs to be considered from a more realistic standpoint. It needs to be stated that a people, as a political body, is constituted empirically in and through the differences of all its members. There need to be social provisions in a society for the legitimate expression of such differences. When conflicts arise between individuals, groups, classes, and various other sectors of a society, appropriate mechanisms should be in place for their resolution. Informal mechanisms, the courts of law, and various forms of arbitration should be as open-minded and fair as possible so as to accommodate the different needs of the members of the society, with an eye to the common good. The dream of establishing an organic community in which individuals' interests harmonize according to some ethical notion of the good is very unrealistic. The more aggressive goal of attempting to destroy the totality of evil so one can establish the true social good is not only unrealistic but violently disruptive. Where there is life there are differences and potential conflict. To have total control over what happens within a certain social space is a sign that one is living out of touch with reality and life.

A philosophy of liberation, if it is going to respond to the types of concerns named above, needs to begin with an acceptance of life rather than with the rejection of undesirable "totalities." The acceptance of life is not to be interpreted as a mandate to bring every conceivable child into existence but as an acceptance of difference. This brings up the issue of one very important cultural difference—the sexual or gender difference—and the role gender can play in nonsexist liberation and cultural identity theories. In order to understand gender properly it is necessary to maintain a critical distance with respect to the position of normative sexuality elaborated in theories such as we have been examining. Accordingly, in the next chapter I consider women's participation in Latin American social movements, based on the assumption that women are free human beings whose bodies and minds belong solely to themselves and over which they have the full right of expression and choice in accordance with a carefully reasoned standard of conduct.

CULTURAL IDENTITY, LIBERATION, AND FEMINIST THEORY

Economic dependence, political subordination, and cultural marginality—issues of central importance for Latin American theories of cultural identity and liberation—also play a central role in the lives of women, with a significant difference. Women will often experience their negative position not only with respect to a foreign culture or an exploiting class but within their own culture and class. A woman's economic, social, and political status—if oppressive—is complicated by the factor of gender. Thus we come to a crucial point in the consideration of Latin American theories of cultural identity and liberation, namely, the issue of conceptualizing the problem of gender oppression, and the possibilities for rectifying this problem within the context of a Latin American culture and its traditional concepts of freedom. This is the task pertaining to feminist theory, whose role in a theory of liberation will now be examined.

Latin American feminisms have their roots in the analysis of gender issues and the struggles for women's social and political equality that have taken place in the continent since the early part of the twentieth century. The suffragist movement united the various feminisms that constituted the women's movement in the early decades of the century. A period of relative quiet followed after the vote was won. In the 1960s radical movements around the world, including the political waves created by the Cuban Revolution of 1959, spurred more decisive action on behalf of women's rights. Subsequently, the Decade on Women (1975–85), sponsored by the United Nations, had a significant impact on the region. Today, while the role of women in society is in the process of change, the paradigms used to measure and assess these changes may themselves be in a process of fluid transition. Nevertheless, it is possible to identify certain feminist theoretical achievements—

particularly from the last two decades—as well as some of the research strategies responsible for them.

In this chapter an analysis of issues of special relevance to recent feminist theory in Latin America will be offered in four parts: (1) philosophy and feminism: historical and contemporary precedents; (2) research strategies in feminism; (3) the question of specifying the situation of women in Latin America; and (4) the search for conceptual models that deal appropriately with Latin American women's specific situation of oppression. This discussion gathers together some of the theoretical conclusions I have reached in the process of trying to understand a variety of problems faced by Latin American women and some of the strategies used to solve them. Keeping in mind the diversity of women's experiences and backgrounds, I attempt, nevertheless, to provide a framework for discussion whose principal purpose is to show some of the major sociocultural conditions affecting the quality of women's lives. For this reason I make special use of various practical issues and theoretical perspectives arising out of Latin American discussions of feminism, particularly in the social sciences. While some of the authors cited are social scientists who have made important contributions to their respective fields, it is not my goal to pursue or document material pertaining to the social sciences as such. The intent is to highlight selected approaches to gender identity that may prove to be of significant philosophical interest.

Philosophy and Feminism: Historical and Contemporary Precedents

In Latin America, feminist theory has not advanced as rapidly in philosophy as it has in the social sciences, an area where important topics such as women in society, women in culture, and women in development have been investigated at length from informed gender-conscious perspectives. Prior to the 1980s, when feminist ideas began to gain some ground in philosophy, only one well-known twentieth-century Latin American philosopher had published a book on feminism. This was the Uruguayan Carlos Vaz Ferreira (1872–1958), whose treatise *Sobre feminismo* first appeared in 1933. The book is a compilation of a series of lectures given by Vaz Ferreira in 1918. In this work Vaz Ferreira adopted a position that he called "feminism of compensation," or compensatory feminism, which he distinguished from "feminism of equality" (egalitarian feminism), or feminism as commonly understood. He

outlined three distinct positions: antifeminism, the view that men
are superior to women biologically, together with the view that the
same difference should be maintained in the social order; egalitarian feminism, the view that biological differences between women
and men are insignificant, and that the social sphere should reflect
conditions of equality; and compensatory feminism, the view that
women are biologically disadvantaged in relation to men, but that
society through its laws and institutional structures should compensate for this disadvantage.[1] Among women's biological disadvantages Vaz Ferreira noted such factors as relatively less physical strength and having to bear the greater part of the biological
burden of reproduction (pregnancy). In intellectual matters, he
observed that although women had not reached the category that
the cultural tradition assigns to geniuses, this limitation was irrelevant. In terms of being able to accomplish all important social
tasks, women have proven themselves just as capable as men.

Vaz Ferreira supported women's suffrage, education at all
levels for women of all social and economic classes, and women's
unconditional right to divorce. He argued on behalf of marital
fidelity and held that marriage should be entered into freely by
both partners. He also argued that women should receive a good
education and be prepared for a life of economic self-sufficiency.
He was concerned about the fact that many women were forced to
enter unhappy marriages because marriage was their only socially
accepted economic option. Vaz Ferreira's work is conservative by
current standards, but some of his positions were liberal for his
time. So far, his work has had little impact on contemporary discussions, although the distinction he drew between a feminism "of
equality" and a feminism "of compensation" continues to be theoretically relevant.

Vaz Ferreira's discussion of feminism can also be read in the
light of a variety of feminist social mobilizations that took place in
Uruguay in the 1910s. Starting in the 1900s, there had been a visible feminist movement among socialists as well as a position sympathetic to feminism among the supporters of "Batllismo" (named
after José Batlle y Ordóñez, Uruguayan political leader and president, 1903–7 and 1911–15).[2] Several feminist organizations were
founded in the 1910s. In 1911 the Uruguayan branch of the Federación Femenina Panamericana was founded with the objective of
fighting for women's civil and political rights. Several years later,
in 1916, the larger and more politically effective Consejo Nacional
de Mujeres del Uruguay was founded by Paulina Luisi, a member

of the Uruguayan Socialist party. An offshoot of this organization, the Alianza Uruguaya por el Sufragio Femenino, was established in 1919. Still, given the conservative opposition prevalent in other political sectors of society, Uruguayan women did not obtain the vote until 1932. The dates of Vaz Ferreira's lectures (1918) and publication of *Sobre feminismo* (1933) are therefore indicative of the political situation prevailing in Uruguay with respect to women's rights in the early part of the century.

Today as in the past, feminist philosophy develops in response to major political and social issues and movements. Liberalism, Marxism, and the women's movement (both national and international) have been the principal influences on feminist theory, with some new interest now developing in postmodern theory. Feminism began to make its presence felt in philosophical circles through the work of women who organized conferences, special panels, and seminars around gender-related issues. For example, in 1979 over twenty women participated in a roundtable discussion on femininity organized as part of the annual meetings of the Mexican Philosophical Association. The proceedings have been published in *La naturaleza feminina*.[3] In this work, the problem of whether there is such a thing as a "feminine human nature" is discussed from a variety of historical, sociological, and critical perspectives.

A field closely tied to the development of feminist theory in the continent is the field of women's social history. A major source of feminist philosophizing stems from a consideration of not only present but past practices of women's resistance to patriarchal domination and oppression. By "patriarchal" domination, or "patriarchal" relations of power, I mean that type of domination resulting from masculinist-authoritarian sociopolitical, ideological, or conceptual structures and value systems that have prevailed in Latin American history. Alternatives to or criticisms of this system of values and social relations offered by the women's movement and early "feminist" figures in the cultural history of Latin America provide contemporary feminists with contextual sources.

The best-known historical figure who serves as a precedent for feminist thought today is the Mexican Sor Juana Inés de la Cruz (1651–95). Sor Juana was a brilliant nun who suffered severe discrimination during colonial times in Mexico due to her passion for science and learning.[4] (Her life is the subject of a recent powerful film, *Yo, la peor de todas*, directed by the Argentine filmmaker María Luisa Bemberg.) In her occasional poems, Juana denounces the double standard of value used by (sexist) men to control the lives of women. For example, in one of her best-known poems, informally known as "Hombres necios," she writes that foolish men accuse women of wrongdoing without reason, not seeing they are the cause of the same things they condemn.[5] In the preface to a contemporary edition of Sor Juana's partly autobiographical narrative, *Respuesta a sor Filotea de la Cruz*, the editors state: "If by feminist we mean a woman who has become conscious of her oppression as a woman and who tries to exert her influence in some way so as to transform this reality, we can say that Juana is a feminist to the extent that a woman, alone, could be a feminist in the second half of the seventeenth century."[6] Other studies have begun to document the involvement of women from ethnic minorities and economically disadvantaged groups in various political struggles for self-determination, for example, women's participation in South American indigenous rebellions in the eighteenth century.[7]

More recently, the women's movement in its local, regional, and international expressions has served as an important source for feminist theory and reflection. Feminism acquired a significant boost in Latin America as a result of the impact of the United Nations Decade on Women, which redefined the situation of women in non-Western and Latin American societies in terms of the global themes of "Equality, Development, and Peace." From this standpoint, feminist consciousness-raising begins with the denunciation of violence against women in developing countries and with the social impact of the women's struggle for the attainment of basic economic, social, and political rights. Gender consciousness is born from women's experience of discrimination and oppression. But in this case its point of departure is not so much an abstract humanist ethics as a social perspective gained from studying the specific limitations characterizing the position of women in the less-developed nations and regions of the world. At the grass-roots level, one important continental event that has taken place since 1981 is the Encuentro Feminista Latinoamericano y del Caribe.[8] Numerous other meetings are taking place among women writers, artists, and intellectuals, demonstrating an increasing awareness of feminist positions and issues. Journals and other feminist publications such as *fem* and *Debate feminista* (Mexico), *Feminaria* and *Hiparquia* (Argentina), and *Mujer/fempress* (Chile), contribute to an expanding role for feminist awareness in the region.

The cultural significance of the growing visibility of women in social movements has had a noticeable impact on academic studies. The question therefore is not whether or not there will be feminist studies but what form these will take and at what pace they will grow in relation to other methodologies and disciplines. It should be noted that at the same time that there is a growing interest in women's studies and in feminism in Latin America, there are important obstacles to the development and institutionalization of feminist philosophy in Latin American universities. In view of the economic difficulties affecting most Latin American countries today, resources are limited for any professional work in philosophy, including the development of such a new field as philosophical feminism. A related problem in Latin American philosophy is the lack of a theoretical tradition dealing with such issues as women's rights. Some of these limitations can be remedied. New courses on gender-related issues are gradually being introduced into the curriculum. Women philosophers are beginning to form regional and national associations focusing attention on these issues. National associations of women in philosophy are currently organized in Mexico (Asociación Filosófica Feminista) and Argentina (Asociación Argentina de Mujeres en Filosofía). In cooperation with the U.S. Society for Women in Philosophy, international conferences on feminism and philosophy have been held in Mexico City (1988) and Buenos Aires (1989).[9] Given the expanding interest in gender issues in Latin America and the Caribbean (as elsewhere around the world), it is logical for philosophers to intensify and expand their research on these topics.

Feminist Research Strategies

Today feminist philosophy in Latin America has many sources for the reflection on and analysis of the condition of women. A pluralist perspective focused on key issues of concern to feminists combined with respect for the diversity of women's experiences is the best comprehensive research strategy at our disposal at this time. Building on this concept, I offer some specific suggestions.

A fundamental aspect of feminist theory is developed by incorporating a feminist analysis of issues into an already established field or area in philosophy, such as ethics, philosophy of education, or sociopolitical philosophy. Graciela Hierro has developed this aspect of feminist theory in Mexico in a number of contexts. For example, in *Etica y feminismo,* based on an analysis of women's social condition and of key ethical questions in Western philosophy, she argues for an ethics of equality and an end to discrimination against women.[10]

Another point of departure for feminist theory is the international nature of the feminist movement. The influence of a wide variety of perspectives, from radical feminism to Marxism, is felt in the region. Translations of selected works by feminist authors from North America, Europe, and elsewhere are available for use by Latin American feminists. For example, the Mexican journal *fem* has published translations of articles by Marilyn Frye, Susan Griffin, and Adrienne Rich. Bibliographical sources list Spanish translations of works by Simone de Beauvoir, Alexandra Kolontay, Betty Friedan, Sheila Rowbotham, Juliet Mitchell, Elizabeth Janeway, Kate Millett, and others.[11] More recently, the academic Mexican journal *Debate feminista* has been established, with a focus on regional issues as well as trends in European cultural studies. In Argentina, the journal *Feminaria*, founded in 1988, carries an impressive variety of theoretical articles, poetry, humor, reports on national women's meetings, working bibliographies, and so on. The publication *Hiparquia* has carried selections from papers presented at international conferences on feminism and philosophy.

Feminist research is also characterized by its interdisciplinary nature. In Latin America, sociology, anthropology, psychology, and literature are some of the more prominent fields contributing to feminist theory. Philosophy can work in conjunction with these other disciplines so as to contribute to the development of women's studies programs in the region. At the present time, women's studies programs focus primarily on research in the social sciences and in literature, but some programs are beginning to incorporate philosophy as well.

One final point: feminist theory is existentially rooted in women's personal experience. This aspect of feminism is explored in fiction and poetry as well as in the genre of the testimonial narrative, which includes both fiction and nonfiction.[12] Perhaps no other genre is as capable of demonstrating concretely the feminist maxim "the personal is political." There is also a political type of existential experience that is born primarily out of women's participation in social and political movements against oppression. In the latter context, philosophy studies the relationships between feminism, democracy, and socialism. Whether there is any genuine democracy or democratic socialism without feminism is one of the issues at stake in this type of discussion.[13]

As mentioned, it is important to root a Latin American feminist theory in the specific situation of Latin American women, as
opposed to judging it by paradigms imported from other parts of
the world. I will now attempt to delineate some of the features typifying the situation of women in the region.

The Specificity of the Latin American Situation
in the Context of Gender Issues Worldwide

In Latin America, as in other parts of the world, the critique
of a patriarchal or male-oriented conception of "woman" and the
demand for the legal and social recognition of women's full rights
as persons constitute the foundations of a feminist perspective.
Latin American feminists have challenged the patriarchal conception of power that grounds the oppression of women as well as that
of other oppressed groups. Graciela Hierro notes that the patriarchal or masculinist socioeconomic order both profits from women's
subordination and keeps itself in place by educating women to
accept it willingly. Hierro notes that the norms that govern the
condition of women today are founded on biology. This morality,
she argues, "obeys masculine economic interests [that have the
preservation of the existing order at stake] while it is maintained
and reproduced through the education given to women."[14] Another
feminist philosopher, Fernanda Navarro, has pointed out that the
conception of nature operating in patriarchal ideology is a function
of the patriarchal use of power.[15] This use of power seeks to deny
women the freedom to decide matters affecting their own bodies.
Abortion is seen as an offense against nature, whereas the control
over women's lives and bodies is regarded as good and just. Feminist emancipation begins with the critique of patriarchal ideology,
she observes, because the social changes desired by women will
require an ideological change. This change in ideological perspectives will also affect the status of other groups seeking liberation.
Navarro is among those feminists who see a strong connection
between the women's struggle and that of other oppressed groups.
As part of her critique of patriarchal ideology she argues that the
struggle for the liberation of women is intimately linked to the
struggle for the liberation of human beings "from all types of
oppression, subordination, and exploitation."[16]

Because Latin American women generally suffer from more
than one type of oppression or discrimination, it is important to
understand their concrete situation and some of the specific forms

a regionally based feminism is more likely to take. The issues I will discuss now have been addressed by feminists (as I will point out). But they are also part of a broader type of "gender consciousness" that is prevalent in the region. Many women understand the importance of these issues even if they have never thought of calling themselves "feminist." These issues therefore speak to the existential situation of a large number of women. While these are not the sole issues affecting women and while some of these issues are also of concern to women in other parts of the world, nevertheless it is possible to understand the birth and formation of a Latin American "gender consciousness" from these examples. My discussion of gender consciousness focuses on three important and interrelated issues: violence against women, women and development, and women and domestic work. This discussion is followed by a brief section on the repression of feminine sexuality, which is a problem not so much unique to the region as it is a characteristic aspect of patriarchal and masculinist cultures.

Violence against Women

The most extreme form of suffering inflicted on women falls under the category of violence against women. Acts of violence directed against women provoke conscientious persons to denounce the ideology of machismo and/or authoritarianism linked to such violence. The cruelty inherent in sexual abuse, sexual coercion, and rape awakens in the human mind a repulsion against the abuse of women. This abuse is often caused by behavior or acts representing an illicit or immoral use of force. When a society and the state cooperate in legitimating such abuse against women either by failing to defend and protect women's rights or by showing leniency toward their abusers, we tend to condemn both the society that furthers this injustice and the political structure legitimating the society itself. In Latin America, political protest has been one of the options taken by women who wish to denounce violence—whether this violence has been directed against women themselves or against their children or other victims. The movement of the Madres de la Plaza de Mayo in Argentina is an eminent example of this type of social protest. In defiance of the repressive military government of the 1970s, these brave women publicly denounced the disappearance of their children and relatives in spite of government orders strictly prohibiting such demonstrations.[17]

In Latin America, violence against women means much more than rape. During parts of the 1970s and 1980s systematic violence against women was carried out by repressive governments. For example, women reportedly were tortured in Chilean prisons and elsewhere by means that defy the human imagination.[18] During the military repression in Argentina, an estimated one-third of the thirty thousand persons who "disappeared" were women.[19] Women who have spoken out in defense of human rights or have joined progressive organizations have run the risk of being kidnapped, tortured, or killed. Two examples will suffice here. One is the case of Marianella García-Villas, a Salvadoran graduate in philosophy who went on to become a lawyer. In 1978 she became the cofounder and president of her country's nongovernmental organization for human rights. Under her leadership this organization received several distinguished international awards. In 1983, while she was documenting the government's use of illegal chemical weapons in rural conflicts, Marianella García-Villas was killed by government forces.[20] Another case is that of Alaide Foppa, a Guatemalan feminist intellectual who resided in Mexico and was one of the founding editors of the journal *fem*. During a visit to her country in 1980 to see her family, she was kidnapped by the state police.[21] She was reportedly tortured and killed. Her name is among the many that fill the lists of the disappeared. Today, even in countries where democratically elected governments are in existence, those who defend human rights and other politically outspoken persons continue to be at risk from sporadic, yet no less intimidating or destructive, forms of violence.

Many women are spared direct violence against their own bodies, but fewer are spared some form of violence to their children or relatives. Such was the plight of the Madres de la Plaza de Mayo who took to the streets in Argentina in defiance of the military government. It is not possible here to comment at length on the various forms of violence suffered by Latin American women. The point is to show that there are forms of violence widespread in Latin America that transcend the cases of rape that form the paradigm example of violence against women in the United States, although Latin Americans are also victims of domestic violence and rape.[22] And there are still other kinds of violence. Some count the marginalization or outright repression experienced by many lesbian women as a kind of psychological violence.[23] To this may be added the psychological violence suffered by mothers who do not know whether their children can survive or reach adulthood in the midst of conditions of extreme poverty and/or underdevelopment.

Adult men and women, as well as children, are also the victims of random violence, including street violence, resulting from widespread poverty and unemployment. Women who are the sisters, mothers, wives, or loved ones of victimized men and children identify strongly with their suffering. This experience serves to defuse some feminist analyses of violence—in particular, those that focus directly on the suffering inflicted on women by men. More prevalent in Latin America is the view that a fundamental cause of human oppression lies in the disparity in privileges between the rich and the poor. Removing the category of domestic violence from its relative invisibility is still an on-going task. At times feminism is erroneously viewed as a luxury associated with the lives of middle-class women. Important feminist programs such as the movement to legalize abortion are sometimes regarded suspiciously as an expression of bourgeois selfishness.

But it is a mistake to identify abortion with selfishness. One must include among the victims of violence against women those who die in the process of attempting illegal abortions. It is not the case that the legalization of abortion would benefit primarily bourgeois women, since they are in a relatively better position to obtain safe abortions. The actual victims of anti-abortion laws tend to be the most economically disadvantaged women—poor women and teenage girls. In Mexico, where there is a limited abortion law, it has been estimated that abortion is one of the highest causes of female mortality.[24] In Argentina it is estimated to be the leading cause of female teenage mortality, although the clandestine nature of abortion does not allow for accurate statistics on the subject. It should be noted that the political Right, which is the strongest defender of repressive governments, also represents one of the strongest voices against legal abortion, although it should also be emphasized that opposition to legal abortion does not come from these sectors alone. A more significant objection to legal abortion comes from those who esteem women's commitment to the defense of life, a theme that has mobilized Latin American women on behalf of human rights and peace throughout the continent. It would seem that the defense of life is a principle that ought to be extended to the unborn. Yet this argument fails to take into account the illegitimate control over women's bodies, and particularly over women's reproductive powers, that has been one of the major legacies of patriarchal domination. The control over women's fertility—whether exercised in terms of obligatory pregnancy or the enforced sterilization of women—is a particularly repressive and invasive form of power.[25] If a society grants that women, because of their role as mothers, are specifically called on to defend life against systematic and senseless cases of repression and violence, then such a society must first of all grant women's right to self-defense when they themselves are the victims of such repressive practices. Feminist theory must continue to denounce the actual or potential violence against women implicit in laws and actions that deny women the right to their own physical and mental integrity. Moreover, the connection between all forms of violence against women, from the cruel and inhuman torture and violation of women in prisons to the most common cases of sexual coercion and abuse, needs to be given greater exposure.

Women and Development

One major characteristic of the situation of Latin American women is that their progress toward equality takes place in (to use the current expression) "developing societies" (sociedades en vías de desarrollo). Development-oriented studies often evaluate women's progress in terms of their participation in the economic life of their societies. This means that the index of women's success is measured by the index of their economic participation. But some critical questions are left unanswered. What kind of society is the target of the policies of development? What kind of economic participation will be made available to women? Two feminist critiques of the development-oriented model will be considered—one drawn from criticism offered in the 1970s and the other from more recent sources.

Arguing from a feminist perspective, the Mexican anthropologist Lourdes Arizpe has noted the ambiguity of the ubiquitous theme "Women and Development."[26] Arizpe points out that at a time when the concept of "development" (*desarrollo*) has met with strong criticism in the social sciences, it is emerging as a focal point in the movement supporting the economic and social advancement of women. She suggests that it is not possible to reach conclusions about the benefits women might derive from "development" as long as this term is abstract; one must question what kind of development is at work in a particular society. If development is tied to advancing capitalism, to what extent are the models proposed actually helping the disadvantaged economies of developing countries and, in particular, the situation of women?

Focusing on the impact of programs of development in rural areas of non-Western and Latin American societies, Arizpe notes that prior to the implementation of these programs women often "participate in agricultural cultivation, in wage work in the fields, in the transformation of natural products, and in the making of [utensils and] crafts."[27] But when this type of rural economy is penetrated by capitalism, many of these activities are transformed. With a slow process of industrialization, there come to be more workers than jobs. When this occurs, men are chosen as the group to work with the new technology, and women are displaced from their old economic roles in production at the same time that they are marginalized from the best of new opportunities.

Arizpe concludes that the goal of integrating women into a life of full economic participation in their societies requires a political solution and not merely an economic solution. "More serious than the actual situation of women in production is the low level of public and governmental consciousness regarding this matter. [In Mexico for example] the proof is that no policies are proposed regarding the regulation and creation of jobs for women."[28] More recent studies on the subject of women and development concentrate on documenting the impact of the new international division of labor occurring in various industrialized areas such as the U.S.-Mexican border and the free trade zones in developing countries. These areas have attracted multinational capital. A pattern has emerged wherein women are considered a new source of cheap labor. In a recent study focusing on industrial subcontracting of women's work in Mexico City, Lourdes Benería and Martha Roldán note that the "intensification of investment on a world scale that has taken place since the mid-1960s and throughout the 1970s has resulted in new processes of proletarianization of women, particularly in the industries that have relocated from high- to low-wage countries."[29]

Several questions emerge from the accelerated expansion of these recent phenomena. One is the extent to which the forces of the "free market" allowed to operate in "free trade zones" coincide or fail to coincide with the best economic interests of developing countries. Is it in a country's best interest that a sector of its labor force is controlled directly by management in the United States and tied to a temporary and rotating type of job market, where there is virtually no chance for permanence, promotion, or internal decision making? Even if some short-term benefits for the region may be generated by this type of arrangement, how does this economic practice affect an area in the long run? Is the problem of dependence alleviated, or is it complicated further? And to what extent is the exploitation of women's labor an important feature of this new international division of labor?

In Mexico, up until the 1980s, it was the policy of the *maquiladoras*—as the industrial plants in the free trade zones are called—to hire mostly single women between sixteen and twenty-six years of age. They are young and relatively inexperienced, and their wages can be kept lower than those of Mexican men. The Border Industrialization Program, which began in 1965, has undergone several stages, including a major shift in 1983 that brought with it the gradual masculinization of the work force. According to Jorge Carrillo, an expert on the free trade zones, the Mexican government changed its policy with respect to the Border Industrialization Program in August 1983. (In 1982 the country had suffered a major economic setback.) The shift in policy involved viewing the *maquiladoras* as a "stable industry." "For the first time in history," Carrillo notes, "the *maquiladora* is considered a permanent industry and the base for the development of the border zones."[30] Another shift—not specifically associated by Carrillo to the shift in policy, though significant from my perspective—occurred at the same time. This shift involved a masculinization (*varonización*) of the work force. Between 1974 and 1982, women and men constituted 87 percent and 13 percent of the work force, respectively. By 1985, there had been a reduction in the percentage of women workers (and a corresponding increase in the percentage of employed men) of eighteen and a half percentage points.[31] During this period, more women were hired when the government viewed the *maquiladoras* as a transitory source of employment, while the gradual increment of male jobs coincided with the decision to consider the *maquiladoras* the permanent base of development for the region.[32] María Patricia Fernández Kelly has noted that the great majority of managers and engineers in these factories are male, showing that "jobs in the *maquiladoras* are clearly differentiated with respect to the sex of the personnel, the ladders of supervision, and technical qualifications."[33]

Just as the majority of Mexican workers have little decision-making power over the policies by which the *maquiladoras* are run (major decisions are generally made in the United States at the corporate level), so some studies show that the young women who enter into the *maquiladora* work force have little or no decision-making power within their families, although they are the principal breadwinners in their respective homes. In fact, since they are potential breadwinners, more family control is exercised over them. "Normally, women workers hand over their weekly salary, intact, to their mother or older brother, who is responsible for managing it. The young woman does not take part in decision making regarding the family's priorities for consumption or its place of residence. The latter continues to be under the strict guidance of the father or, in the case of his absence, the oldest brother or the mother."[34] Thus, gender restrictions remain in effect for many working women even if their employment profile is changing. The young woman working at the *maquiladora* or the woman doing piecework at home is still caught in the exploitative network of the division of labor by sex. Confirming the conclusions drawn by Benería and Roldán, the Mexican economist Estela Suárez warns that "the expansion of [piece]work done in the home and of part-time work may mean a real danger [for women] and the immediate return to the more traditional forms of the division of labor within the couple; this would reinforce the traditional role of women and would constitute an important restraint on women's reinitiating full-time work outside the home."[35]

The findings of scholars who offer a critical feminist perspective on women and development appear to be taken into account by United Nations specialists who evaluate such programs. "The root of the differences in the development of women's activities," one UN study concludes, "lies, as has already been said, in the social division of labor, with its specific allocation of tasks by sex and the different value attached to such tasks."[36] The fact that there is already documented evidence available to prove this point strengthens the argument that a political solution is needed to solve the problem of women's marginalization in economic production.

Building on these sociological data and perspectives, one could characterize the existential situation of women in underdeveloped countries as one of privation. The overall economic situation of the countries is characterized by limited resources, to which other significant problems are added, including the burden carried by nations forced to import the latest technology and pay interest on foreign debt. The division of labor and the devaluation of women's work in relation to that of men place a special burden on women, but the gravity of the situation of women is less visible because of the large number of men who are also jobless and poor. The solution to these problems would require that genuine efforts be made to improve the economic situation of the popular sectors while taking additional compensatory measures to assist women in gaining access to job training and to good jobs.

Women and Domestic Work

So far I have spoken about the general condition of women in developing societies as one of relative privation. Women's lives suffer a double privation since the quality of their lives is limited both in relation to the opportunities available to men and, more broadly, in terms of the limited resources characterizing these societies as opposed to the effective wealth enjoyed by the industrialized nations of the world. By focusing on domestic work as paradigmatic of the division of labor and the correlative devaluation of women's work, some of the structures of oppression and subordination affecting women's lives can be studied more concretely.

Perhaps nowhere in either the public or the private sectors is the division of labor so evident in Latin America as in the case of domestic work. Domestic work can be paid or unpaid depending on whether someone is hired to perform jobs such as cleaning, cooking, washing, ironing, taking care of young children, and shopping for food, or whether the same work is done without pay by the women of the household. Hired domestic work is almost always performed by women. Household "servants" are often women from rural areas who have come to the cities in search of work. In countries where the indigenous population is large, many indigenous women fall into this category. In virtually all cases they are poor, unskilled women with little or no economic mobility and with few prospects for a better life.

The proportion of Latin American women employed as domestic workers is high. According to the 1980 Mexican census, 52 percent of women there worked in the service sector. Of these, 35 percent were employed in domestic work. Domestic work, in turn, is a "feminized" occupation, with women representing nearly 84 percent of all Mexican domestic workers.[37] It is not difficult to see that while domestic work "exploits" the labor of rural migrants and poor urban women, it "liberates" higher-income women by allowing them to spend more time on their own self-development and the pursuit of jobs in the public sector. In the case of domestic work in Latin America, class and ethnic oppression supersede gender oppression. Since most women who are self-consciously feminist also belong to the middle or upper classes, this means they are employers of female domestic workers, a situation that obviously leads to some contradictions. In the absence of widespread social transformations that would offer a systematic solution to this problem, however, these women generally opt for a personal solution. They continue to hire domestic workers because it frees them to pursue other tasks they consider more valuable.

The issue of the exploitation of women through domestic work does not stop here. In working-class families where both husband and wife work outside the home, there is the widespread phenomenon of the *doble jornada,* the "double shift" to which women are subjected because men do not think it is part of their responsibility to share in the housework. Marxist feminism has addressed this problem, which is widespread among workers. Building on Engels's observation that in the family the husband is the bourgeois while the wife represents the proletariat, Marxist critics point out the double exploitation of women workers—their labor is exploited at the factory by capital, while at home it is exploited by the partner or husband. Theoretical studies showing the contribution of women's domestic labor (cooking, ironing, cleaning, raising children) to the reproduction of the labor force are especially important in this regard. (More on this will be said in the next section on the search for models of interpretation.) At the practical level, feminist groups try various methods to awaken the consciousness of working-class women with respect to the way their labor is exploited at home. For example, in Colombia a women's group has published a collection of cartoon-like sketches in magazine format on the theme of the need for working women to unite and speak up against wife abuse and the sexist division of labor in the home.[38] Centers for battered women are operating to assist victims of domestic violence.

One country in the region where systematic steps have been undertaken to resolve the problem of domestic work is Cuba. The Cuban Revolution of 1959 abolished the old economic and social structures that led large numbers of women to seek employment in paid domestic work. At the same time, the Marxist government has sought to assimilate women into the mainstream labor force of the new society. Initially, women were recruited to fill gender-stereotyped jobs (such as work in the textile industry), but gradually they were encouraged to gain employment in previously male-dominated occupations. Moreover, relying largely on theories by Engels and Lenin on the oppression and emancipation of women, the mass-based Federation of Cuban Women (Federación de Mujeres Cubanas) organized the nation's women and lobbied over the years for just and equal treatment of women in Cuban society. During the Second Congress of the FMC in 1974, the organization moved toward a more feminist orientation, focused on the aim of securing women's "full equality."[39] In a period when Cuba's economy was stable, much attention was paid to avoiding sexual discrimination in the workplace and to promoting an equitable division of labor in the home.

The Cuban Marxists have worked with two strategies. One strategy has been to bring women in massive numbers into the public sector to participate in the nation's economic production and, in compensation for this, insofar as it is possible, to free them from unnecessary chores at home (for example, by providing day care centers for the children of working women). The second strategy has been to make men aware of the fact that if women are bearing the burden of production just as men do, then the men cannot take for granted that only women will perform the household chores. In 1975, on International Women's Day, Cuba's "Family Code" went into effect.[40] This law made it a central responsibility of the husband to contribute equally with his wife to household work and the care of children. But legal reforms alone cannot change individuals' behavior unless they themselves stop viewing some tasks as "women's chores." While there has been an improvement over prerevolutionary gender stereotypes, gender roles in Cuba today are influenced by sexist prejudice inherited from the past. These still have a very strong hold on gender identity. For example, many aspects of the popular culture take for granted the view of women as sex objects, and at all levels of social activity a heterosexual identity is strongly reinforced.

Despite these limitations, however, Cuban women under socialism have achieved a high level of public recognition, and they have been recipients of significant benefits from the state. These have included free education and access to specialized training, job security, paid maternity leave, free health care for themselves and their children, free legal abortion, child care for working mothers, and so on. Much attention has been given to maintaining a low infant mortality rate, and life expectancy has been high. Thus within the parameters of a socialist society, Cuban women have had access to a broad and significant spectrum of social benefits and public responsibilities. But the achievements of the 1970s and 1980s are threatened by substantial cutbacks in the 1990s as the country is affected by the combined effects of a relentless U.S. trade embargo and the collapse of the advantageous system of Soviet aid. In the event of an end to the Marxist government in Cuba, Cuban women could once again find themselves in a position comparable to that of other Latin American women. Current access to contraceptives and legal rights to abortion and to equal pay for equal work could be either eliminated or curtailed.

Returning to the issue of domestic work, we see that in other parts of the continent, where a systematic political solution to the problem of domestic work has not been attempted, the issue continues to be a major object of feminist analysis.[41] A general strategy followed by researchers has been to situate domestic work within the general problematic of the sexual division of labor. Some analysts emphasize the distinction between domestic work as socially necessary labor that must be performed by someone and the perception that domestic work is "naturally" gender-based, or "women's work." In terms of securing practical results for an equitable distribution of household chores, however, this approach is far too abstract. More concrete studies examine the gender stereotypes created by this particular form of the sexual division of labor in terms of the repercussions on children.[42] In any case, we need to begin to understand domestic work (cleaning house, shopping, rearing children) as *work*, not as a natural imperative, an idealized vocation, or an activity denoting leisure.

Sexuality

Women's equitable participation in the economy makes possible their creative development as social beings. But there is a less visible form of sexual discrimination taking place in the depths of the human psyche. It has to do with the way in which sexual desire, pleasure, and reproduction are understood. Within this sphere, a politics of self-determination needs to come into dialogue with popular notions of morality in order to liberate the latter from patriarchal conceptions. Thus, to emancipate women from oppression at the level of sexuality, there needs to be a shift of attitude with respect to traditional morality—or a readjustment within practical morality—that will take into account a woman's needs for sexual satisfaction and emotional happiness as fundamental rights of a fully autonomous person.

Whereas political and economic changes affect a woman's place in the public arena, the world a woman inhabits begins with her perception of her own body. Her body constitutes her most intimate world. It is a world that patriarchal morality has broken into parts and parceled out for the satisfaction of others (the advertising media knows how to exploit this well). Sexual liberation, in contrast, involves the recovery of the world that is one's body; it breaks sharply with the perception that a woman's body exists for the purpose of satisfying the needs of others or that her desire for pleasure, to be morally valid, must be legitimated by someone in a position of patriarchal authority or power, such as the father, husband, judge, or priest.

Cut off from the purview of the Law of the Father, desire follows a path unique to each person. By resisting situations and values that alienate her from her desires, a woman may draw important insights about the needs for sexual satisfaction, companionship, and intimacy that take priority in her life. A feminist morality accentuates the fact that the nature and object of desire will vary from person to person. For this reason, desire ought not be regulated or governed through a series of impersonal moral rules thought to apply invariably and equally to all persons of a given sex, regardless of their individual personality and needs. Feminism does not argue, as it is sometimes thought, for a world in which all women must comport themselves sexually in the same way—as if turning oneself into the copy of some previously defined model would prove to be liberating to a free person. Feminism acts to empower women to choose the meaning they want to give to their own sexuality, emphasizing that the process of recovering their "sex" from patriarchal appropriation cannot take place without a definitive break with gendered rules of behavior dictated by a masculinist culture.

Without trying to construct a universal model that must be followed to the letter by everyone in order to assure liberation, let me sketch a possible approach to the task of the recovery of a woman's body for a life of freedom. This approach follows three steps. First, there arises a perception of the alienation suffered by women in their bodies; second, a process of recovery from this alienation is attempted; and third, the process of disalienation reaches stability and fulfillment through the transition to a new sexual morality. From this new sexual morality, recommendations for various political and legal changes may follow, for example, with respect to the legalization of abortion, the availability of contraceptives, the strict enforcement of penalties for rape, and so on.

Alienation of women's bodies. The world a woman inhabits begins with her own body. This is why, from a theoretical standpoint, to speak about women's liberation is to defend the integrity of women's bodies and women's right to exert full control over their sexual lives. The control exercised over a woman's sexuality by persons other than herself, by religious teachings or by the laws of the state, is not limited to Latin American societies. What is at stake is the much more universal problem of gender domination, inherited from patriarchal cultures and preserved historically by means of various social, political, and economic arrangements that subordinate the freedoms and responsibilities of women as social beings to the needs and interests of dominant males.

The control over a woman's body is not limited to her sexuality. It extends to her appearance and mobility, and it begins early in life. For example, there are expectations about what a woman's body ought to look like—size, weight, texture of skin, color of hair, type of dress, and personal adornment, e.g., the use of jewelry or makeup. Her mobility is restricted, either directly or indirectly, by the assignment of a place of privilege in the home. Her use of speech is also traditionally limited compared to that of a man. She is taught at an early age to be more silent in public than her brothers; her tone of voice is expected to be moderate, and the volume is to be kept low. A woman who breaks these restricted patterns of behavior is often perceived as being sexually "looser" than her more composed sisters. The ultimate dichotomy resulting from the regulation of a woman's appearance is the double standard of morality that assigns some women the role of virtuous wife and mother, while others are left to the role of sex object or even prostitute. This polarization of roles restricts a woman's access to the range of possibilities and capacity for personal satisfaction found in human existence.

Recovery from alienation.   Earlier the term "privation" was used to refer to the economic situation of women in a position of dependence. Analogously, and at an emotional level, a woman in a sexually subordinate position is likely to experience her sexuality in terms of a certain feeling of incompleteness. The biologist Noemí Ehrenfeld Lenkiewicz ponders why a human female, whose capacity for orgasm is high by virtue of her biological constitution, must enter into conflict when relating her sexual identity to her maternal role.

> We could say that all of us, men and women, are immersed in a universe in which the practice of the erotic enters into opposition or generates conflict with the practice of maternity. In this sense, and obviously there are some exceptions, the image of the woman-mother is not usually the symbol of an erotic woman.

> If the construction of sexual identity comprises the harmonic interactions between what is biological (sex and reproduction), sexual roles, and what is erotic within a [certain] sexual orientation, what is the reason for the apparent need

to construct the feminine out of an option that limits this integration? How has feminine experience been transformed [from its social beginnings] until our time, so that in order to "be" it must..."lose" some of its capabilities?[43]

This lack of integration gives rise to a sense of dissatisfaction or incompleteness, which is only compensated for by the strong reinforcement a woman gets from her peers when she conforms to the traditional feminine role. The social aspects of traditional gender-based behavior—even if alienating or limiting with respect to the type of happiness they can provide—serve as a kind of security blanket to women suffering from gender alienation. But what some women perceive as a vaguely felt dissatisfaction, others sense as a violation of their inward personality. What is for some a problem of lack of opportunities for development is for others a problem of outright repression of vital needs. The more distant a woman finds herself from the gender ideals provided by the culture of which she is a part, the more she will be aware of her dissatisfaction and of the need to engage in political movements for women's rights. Also, the more patriarchally oriented or masculinist a culture is in its production and enforcement of gender roles, the more limiting the opportunities will be for the self-development of women. From the dissatisfaction felt by women in such circumstances, there emerges the question of the social construction of gender. Women begin to question the discrepancy between their personal needs for fulfillment and their socially assigned gender roles.

Replacement of normative sexuality by a code of personal integrity and happiness. Let me now give a name—"normative sexuality"—to the traditionally stratified sexual morality that splits the human personality into two well-defined and opposite genders, and proceeds to tie the role of the feminine gender to its maternal or reproductive function and to conceive of sexual relations as morally justified only in view of their procreative aim. Normative sexuality involves a basic disintegration and fragmentation of the human personality in the early years of life (little boys are taught to withhold emotion and display aggressiveness, and little girls to become domestic and obedient to their fathers), while later in life each gender is given incentives to find its completion in its now excluded opposite, through a sexual practice directed at reproducing the species. Normative sexuality is both a psychological model for regulating sexual relations and a moral doctrine aimed at securing the hegemony of its psychological model over the society at large. Personal happiness, particularly with respect to sexual matters, counts little in this kind of morality. What is attempted is that the individual conform herself to a type about whose characteristics and obligations she was never consulted.

Without discarding the social importance of morality or failing to respect a person's right to practice her own religious beliefs, it should be observed that if such beliefs create an unjust burden for half of the population—in this case women—revisions are needed to remedy this unfairness. An excess of duty with a minimum of happiness is not a balanced recipe for leading an integrated moral life. A feminist approach to morality, therefore, creates two significant changes in the inherited patriarchal model, at least insofar as the role of women in society is concerned. In the first place, there is a renewed emphasis on individuation, in the sense that women, in their gender and sexual identities, move toward the fulfillment of their personal needs as individuals and away from the previously mentioned normative type. This move toward individual fulfillment has repercussions at the social and political levels, as a parallel movement occurs away from the position of political silence or marginality and toward one of public involvement and responsibility. The dichotomy between the individuated male and the undifferentiated female breaks down. And, as a woman becomes an individual, she will experience the need to control the reproductive system that would turn her into a mere instrument of the species. A feminist morality is not necessarily individualistic, but it is proindividual, in the sense that it has a profound respect for the individual's right to choose what she will do with her own life.

The practical results derived from this type of morality are feared by some, but, in a sense, what is at stake is a more honest, less hypocritical morality. Such a feminist morality involves an effort to accept a perspective of sexual difference distributed across persons of both genders, as opposed to one of sexual sameness instantiated in every member of each gender. This is a prodemocratic and antiauthoritarian morality that complements Latin America's ideals of democratic reform. It is inconceivable that "democracy" should be limited to the notions of a free press, a free market, and a system of "free" elections, as the concept of Western democracy is currently understood and applied in the region, in conformity with a conservative U.S. model. The limited concept of democracy is noticeably incomplete because it is disconnected from the existential needs of the people for health care, education, basic economic security, and so on. Among women's security needs is that of not being faced with an unwanted pregnancy. At the same time, legal abortion continues to be unavailable with few exceptions. Its absence could be considered a crime of neglect, for women's personal need in this regard is indeed extraordinary. In a culture where men are often expected to initiate sexual relations, where little, if any, social pressure is placed on men to use contraceptives, and where divorce in many cases is either frowned on for moral reasons or unfeasible due to economic need, a large number of women who want to maintain a marriage or a heterosexual relationship are going to suffer forced and unwanted pregnancies. Why should they pay for this unfair distribution of gender roles with their lives? This personal problem reveals the political structure of an imbalance of power between the genders. The political marginality of women and the denial of their basic right to bodily integrity go hand in hand. But, on the positive side, there is room for change. Women's psychological embracing of an ethic of personal happiness and individuation is complementary to their political participation on behalf of the expansion of democratic rights in the public sphere.

Conceptual Models and Regional Needs

The solutions for women's problems need to be given within the societies in which they live. They cannot be imported from elsewhere; they are part of the social and cultural evolution of each society. Currently, there are economic, cultural, and psychological pressures leading to an expansion of women's rights in Latin American society. But the equality of rights comes slowly, and the best means to accelerate this process is political change. For this reason, feminism seeks not only the participation of women in politics at the ground level but as leaders who support the implementation of programs that will promote equality of rights and opportunities for all members of society.

I will now turn to two kinds of theoretical models that attempt to assess, from different feminist positions, some of the strategies for political change available to (or perhaps desirable for) Latin American women. Both types of analysis call for a reformulation of gender identity as well as a transformation of the division between the private and public spheres. I designate these two approaches or perspectives the *participatory* and the *evaluative* models. In general, the object of participatory models is to document various patterns of political and other socially transformative action by and for women, while that of evaluative models is to offer a conceptual analysis of gender domination or oppression. There are obvious points of intersection between the approaches, but it is of theoretical interest to note the aspects in which they differ.

By *participatory models*, therefore, I mean those that emphasize the direct and active participation of women in public projects. Their primary theoretical insistence is that at all levels of responsibility women need to be able to exercise decision-making power about matters that affect their own lives. Supporters of a participatory model worry little whether women need to achieve some kind of purity of consciousness prior to their participation in new projects and activities. They rely on the view that women will learn by doing and that a feminist gender identity will develop gradually out of experience. The Argentine sociologist Elizabeth Jelin observes:

> The broadening of spaces for women's action as well as traditionally feminine roles, both in the sexual division of labor and in the public and private spheres, takes place gradually in the daily practice of the popular sectors out of necessity, because women must attend to the exigencies of survival. This implies that such changes are not presented as demands or achievements based on a conscious awareness of a situation of subordination. Their transformative potential, however, is significant.[44]

Participatory models contain an evaluative assessment of women's oppression insofar as they hold that exclusion is a major feature of domination. This explains why this type of feminist theory pays so much attention to the actual level of women's participation in decision-making activities and to the expanding character of women's roles, rights, and responsibilities. There is no effort to reach a "correct" theory of gender identity but rather to document strategies by which women can have a more effective voice in determining policies affecting their lives. Participatory models as such tend to be more value-free than the specifically evaluative perspectives, but they tend to be combined with the latter. Among the combinations of participatory and evaluative theories most often encountered at present are liberal, Marxist, and independent feminist views of women's participation in social processes.

By *evaluative models* I refer to those whose point of departure can be traced to a desire for a certain theoretical correctness. Feminist progress is measured in terms of whether a theoretical model of women's liberation has been met in practice. Evaluative models are epistemologically perspectival, although some may not view themselves that way. They range from flexible approaches, such as those offering a critical evaluation of the roles played by gender, ethnicity, and class, to purist approaches that claim that only if a certain perspective is followed will there be a true solution for women's problems. Just as participatory models may have an evaluative component, so evaluative models may display a participatory dimension. For example, a theory holding that the division of labor by sex is the root of women's oppression may promote women's participation in activities previously reserved for men, and conversely. As in participatory theories, the expansion of women's social roles follows, but the latter's significance is both assessed and articulated differently.

To build a broad democratic movement in favor of women's rights, a participatory approach is indispensable. At present, feminism as such is a minority perspective that has not kindled the interest of the majority of Latin American women. Convincing large numbers of women that feminism speaks to their legitimate interests would therefore seem to be a fundamental practical imperative for feminist theory. Unless feminism is to remain the theoretical property of a few intellectuals, it must have practitioners in the society in order to have an impact on the social transformation needed to achieve justice for women. Moreover, for participatory theory to be specifically feminist (and not merely democratic or socialist, for example), it must have a way of balancing the goal of increased participation of women in social projects with the indispensable goal of transforming the male-dominated fabric of society. In Latin America, the link between these two components is most often mediated through a critical discussion of the relation between the private and the public spheres. As I will show briefly, feminism is said to constitute itself theoretically as the ideology of the private, in contradistinction to masculinism, which represents the ideology governing public discourse and the public sphere.

Gender Identity and Public Participation

Participatory feminist theory (or the view that patriarchal relations of power begin to be dismantled as women emerge from their "private" condition as housewives to occupy active roles in the public sphere) requires a reformulation of gender identity. Currently this refers primarily to a redefinition of women's roles as mothers and their roles within the family. This familial role is intrinsically linked to the private, or domestic, sphere. The family is an ambiguous site, insofar as it can operate either as a unit of possessiveness, property, and sexual dominance or as a set of relations fostering mutual care, intimacy, and community. When Latin American women move out from their domestic roles to the street in order to protest against oppression, they often do so as an extension of their traditionally homebound roles as mothers and family members. From this traditionally recognized "gender identity," they take to the streets to demand a good life for their children, better living conditions in their neighborhoods, the return of family members who have disappeared due to political oppression, and so on. Some researchers note that in many cases women do not try to state their demands in terms of the policies of any existing political party.[45] Their social, economic, and political demands seem to take place in a new space that has not yet been structured by the rules of the public sphere. The language in which the demands are formulated may come from the private sphere—it is the language of immediacy, not the official language in which public transactions, including bureaucratic ones, take place. Arizpe observes:

> What is important...is that if the market and the political regimes create conditions that are ever more intolerable for the private sphere (the domain of women), the latter with all due right are going to move into public places to denounce this and make demands *in the very language of the private sphere*. Why is it then that they are criticized and ridiculed when they use this domestic language? The answer is clear: the political parties and labor unions do not understand how the public and private spheres are interconnected. And if they don't begin to understand it soon, they run the risk of being left to a small corner of politics.[46]

The demands mentioned here represent a twofold challenge to patriarchal power. One is related to the content of the demands, while the other relates to the form. Some participatory feminist theoreticians, such as Arizpe and Jelin, argue that form cannot be disassociated from content, that the process itself of women's dismantling previous limitations to public access is both message and goal. The eruption of the "private" consciousness of women into the "public" world has been analyzed by Jelin within the broad categories of the impact of new ethical perspectives on social change. But from a sympathetic feminist standpoint, this phenomenon can also be interpreted as a concrete expression of the feminist maxim that "the personal is political." In this case, "the personal is political" does not mean that a personal situation is analyzed in terms of political categories developed in the male world (such as liberal, socialist, or Marxist categories) or against this world (as in radical feminism). It means rather that when the personal is brought out into the open, into the public sphere, the traditional power relations governing patriarchal society begin to break down.

If women's participation in a variety of public forums has any impact on the public sphere, in the long run a redefinition of both the private and public spheres will take place, including a redefinition of women's role as mothers, of the role of the family, and so on. Participatory approaches do not simply theorize about women's participation in the public sphere. Indeed, a basic feature of these approaches is to apply the same method to the struggles women face in their personal lives. Women are viewed as active rather than passive subjects in all spheres of life. "The counterpart of women's (economic and domestic) double shift," argues Arizpe, "is, undoubtedly, their double militancy, the political and the conjugal."[47]

A major characteristic of Latin American feminism in particular and more broadly of the women's movement in the region is the fact that a large majority of women hold on to their identity as mothers and/or family members at the same time that their assertive participation in social life is intensified. Many strive for independence and autonomy within a readapted or reconstituted notion of the family, rather than discard the notion of the family. For these women, the preservation of the integrity of the family (under redefined conditions) is an essential part of their feminist praxis. (Others, of course, choose different life-styles, especially if they have the means to do so.) The family-connected aspects of significant portions of Latin America's heterogeneous women's movement are likely to be misunderstood in the United States, just as the individualism that marks North American and Western European feminism is not readily translatable into a Latin American cultural context. There is still much that individuals living in various cultures can learn from each other without necessarily having to adopt the others' paradigms as their own. I would suggest that, in Latin America, women's linking of the demands they formulate in the public sphere to their identities as family members has represented a consciousness of community gained in the family that they find absent in the public sector and that they seek to see realized there. That many women perceive their growth as feminists as an extension of their family identities does not mean, however, that the family is the only social structure defining the lives of women. The significance of gender issues clearly transcends issues concerning the family. Research methodologies in the social sciences or humanities that limit women's identity exclusively to their role in the family hinder the advancement of feminist research.

Gender Liberation and the Abolition of Exploited Labor:
A Marxist Evaluative Model

In *Hacia una concepción científica de la emancipación de la mujer*, a work coauthored with her husband John Dumoulin, the Argentine sociologist Isabel Larguía offers an example of what I have designated an evaluative model of feminist research.[48] Larguía, who spent many years living in Cuba and whose study reflects this experience, has produced an interesting Marxist approach to the question of women's liberation in Latin America. Her standpoint is purist insofar as she claims that only this theory will explain women's oppression scientifically and thus help remove it. She has been critical of Western feminism as a middle-class social phenomenon. But she has also been critical of Marxism when Marxist methodology is not applied properly to analyze and alleviate the specific oppressions affecting the lives of working women.

Drawing largely from Engels's *The Origin of the Family, Private Property and the State*, Larguía begins her argument with the claim not that women are at the margin of production, but rather that their work within the family is part of the process of production itself.[49] She notes that the division of labor has forced women to work at the level of creating use values for the direct and private consumption of the household. The fact that women perform domestic work (without pay) frees up men's time to work as long as is needed in the factories and to return home and rest before the next work day. Larguía adopts Marx's theory of the exploitation of labor by capital through the extraction of invisible surplus labor in salaried work. She then extends the notion of "invisible" work to the work performed by women in the working-class household. The extraction of surplus labor from the worker by the capitalist could not take place, she argues, without the "invisible" domestic work performed by the worker's wife at home.[50] If this is right, then women's domestic work is not marginal to a capitalist (or any other) economy but is an integral (central) part of it. Under capitalism, women's housework is exploited just as much as the invisible work of the worker at the factory. Larguía's thesis implies that women could continue to be exploited under socialism if significant measures were not taken to relieve women of the excessive burden of domestic work. As noted, some such measures were adopted in Cuba, where Larguía resided when she developed this theory.

Larguía also offers a strong criticism of the manipulation of gender roles at the ideological level. Here again, in her view, the division of labor plays a fundamental role. Using a materialist method, she argues that the division of labor is the cause of the opposed gender typologies of masculine and feminine. "We would note that the opposing typologies we know today are not so much due to basic biological differences but to the millenary effect of the division of labor."[51] She observes that morality, the law, and culture consolidate and sharpen these dual typologies.

Larguía's analysis falls within the Marxist feminist tradition. Significant for the purposes of this study, however, is the crucial role played in her theory by the category of invisible work. This emphasis coincides with a theme found repeatedly throughout feminist writings in Latin America: the relationship between invisible work, the private sphere, and domestic work. Her approach, like that of participatory feminism, insists on making women's "invisible" contribution to social life "visible." But her analysis does not address a participatory model of action as I have defined it. Larguía's specific concern is only to produce a correct scientific theory to define the liberation of women and the causes of women's oppression. This position forces her to be critical of anyone—man or woman—who continues abiding by the old standards of the division of labor within the home. Within the parameters of a Marxist analysis, her major emphasis is on eliminating dual gender roles. Her theory, therefore, is prescriptive of social values, regardless of whether the majority of Latin Americans are ready or able to adopt the position she has outlined.

Concluding Remarks

This discussion of participatory models and of one Marxist gender-egalitarian position brings up the problem—also arising in North American feminist theory—as to whether feminism should aim primarily at equality of the sexes or at affirming gender and sexual difference. The participatory theories I have cited stress the notion of sexual and gender difference but always in the context of a feminist critique of patriarchal (or masculine-authoritarian) relations of power. On the one hand, the egalitarian model is limited insofar as it regards men (who have been taken as the standard defining what it means to be a human being) as the standard measuring what women shall be equal to. Although this provides a good rule for equality of rights in society, it also creates the concern that in order to gain equality women must somehow become "like men," a stereotype many women (including many feminists) wish to avoid. On the other hand, it can be argued with justification that emphasizing sexual difference without further considerations derived from a critique of patriarchal relations of power will only serve to invite more discrimination in the future. If this proved to be true, women could never escape the double standard ruling their lives and the double exploitation they face at the workplace and in the home.

As I have noted, many Latin American women seem to be redefining their gender identity both in the public and the private spheres without giving up their family identities. As women continue to do this, however, the very meaning of "family" will be transformed. New understandings of "family" will arise not only in terms of internal structure and form (as in the emergence of a more democratic rather than authoritarian concept of family), but in terms of content. For example, single mothers and their children, married couples without children, and, as in the past but with perhaps new variations, long-standing members of a single household will also be considered families. At any rate, the fact that large groups of women who are aware of the need for democratic social changes continue to hold on to their family identities suggests that they may want to affirm the value of community in the face of what is perceived as a distant, impersonal, and, for many, an exploitative public sector. For these Latin American women, seeking equality of rights is not disassociated from raising the quality of life of their communities. These communities are their families, their neighborhoods, their villages and sustaining environment, and their ethnic heritage. As I see it, this is the symbolic value that the "maternal" gender identity holds for them.

Today Latin American social structures are in a stage of transition due to new emphases placed on economic development as well as on social and political reform. The increased visibility given to women's issues as a result of the UN Decade on Women as well as the internal changes occurring within each country will have a demonstrable effect on new formulations of gender identity in the years ahead. Philosophy should contribute to the emancipatory project of women, who constitute approximately half of the population, by readjusting its vision of cultural identity and liberation so that the articulation of women's rights is central to its concern. The future course of Latin American nations is not simply a matter for men to decide, but a basic life project of all those who participate in and contribute to the future of their societies. Latin American philosophy, responding to this concern, needs to make space for women's ideals of justice and freedom within its formulation of the region's cultural heritage and its hopes for the years ahead.

CONCLUSION

The issues and debates highlighted in this study, which covers the period from the 1920s to the present, show that there is an established tradition in Latin American thought dealing with the questions of cultural identity and social liberation. The diverse and often highly specialized approaches taken by various schools of thought and political movements toward an analysis and resolution of these issues surpass the capacity of any one study to do them justice, especially in terms of their individual contributions to knowledge. Yet, as I remarked at the outset of this investigation, it is appropriate to bring together different perspectives on cultural identity and liberation in one single study since the ideas that connect them to one another stand the test of time and criticism. It is also important to keep an open mind about the regulative concepts used to assess the meaning of cultural identity, especially insofar as cultural identity is seen to function as a motivator or supporter of social and political change. Too strict a paradigm of cultural identity can stifle change and development in the region, while the disregard for cultural identity can lead to the erosion of historical roots and loss of inherited values. In regions of the world subject to foreign debt and economic dependence, disregard for a community's inherited values can easily conspire with the penetrating force of outside influences (the mass media, the entertainment industry, external political agendas, and so on) so as to destroy the community's heritage.

A basic human right that individuals need to protect from erosion is the right to the expression of their cultural heritage, including the new needs for creative expression that may emerge within their culture. In order to protect and assure the exercise of this right, tolerance of cultural variations should be practiced internally, within one's own group, just as the recognition of and respect for cultural diversity should be extended to other groups. Religion should promote tolerance of difference, rather than intolerance or compliance with only one "correct" view of the world. Cultural identity should not be used as a pretext to block the process of social liberation in a particular culture. For this reason, it is good to emphasize that both cultural diversity (when cultures are seen from without) and cultural integrity (when they are seen from within) are rooted in the human need to give meaning to one's existence, and that human life and its cultural expression belong together even if differences exist within and across cultures. Thus the process of women's emancipation from social oppression is a cultural expression of the love of freedom and social justice inherent in many cultures. It is misguided to think that social changes broadening the rights and liberties of members of a community are intrusions of foreign cultures on one's autochthonous culture. Ultimately, a culture should respond to the needs of individuals. Freedom of expression and the capacity to accept novelty and change are constitutive aspects of a humanist, dynamic culture.

The dreams of those who would settle for nothing less than the culture of an "organic" community (in the sense of a community where the beliefs of all its members would ultimately have to mirror one another) would seem to place those who believe in these dreams in a new dependency. The human freedom to create would be compromised by a new normativity that would interfere with the free exercise of the creative process in the name of the importance given to preserving or constructing an "organic" culture. Much more on target seems to be the perspective of José Martí, who portrays cultural inauthenticity in terms of putting on a mixed bag of clothes, none of which belongs to those who wear them. A culture needs to be a spiritual expression of the people who give it birth, but the people certainly do not have to dress according to one fixed outfit. Latin Americans need to strengthen the cultures that may be called theirs—but this does not mean that such cultures must be "organic" in order to pass the test of authenticity. It is enough, as has been pointed out, that they have left a legacy for others to consider or challenge in view of new perspectives or problems. The cultural identity of a people is the sum of their creative legacy, which, as part of a creative process, is always in a state of evolution or transformation.

Latin American cultures, in their heritage and plural contemporary expressions, cannot thrive in a future world through the strategy of assuming an essentialist or separatist character, especially since cross-cultural communication will take an even more significant role in the future than it does today. A "pull" of attraction has always existed toward Europe and more recently toward the United States, because of the many cultural affinities of the region with the former and the economic ties it has developed with the latter. The new, economically strengthened Europe of the 1990s, in the form of the European Community, will most likely increase its cultural interaction with the Latin American republics. At the same time, the geographical proximity with the United States will continue to play a role in the development of economic ties, although so far an imbalance of power between North and South has allowed U.S. investment to impose those arrangements that it finds most convenient. The very "pull" of these Northern and European forces, however, creates a consciousness of resistance among many Latin Americans committed to the preservation of their cultural heritage. This heritage is one of *mestizaje*, which refers to a combined assimilation of various cultural traditions and today includes a recognition of the special importance of the indigenous and African heritages of the peoples of the region. But it is also one of an anticolonialist *mestizaje* that is aware of the region's vulnerability to being penetrated by "imperialist" forces from abroad and therefore acts so as to establish egalitarian avenues for cultural exchange with both developed and developing countries. For this reason, North-South relations can no longer be considered a one-way relationship in which the ideas and products of the more developed countries simply find their way into passive or dependent receptors in the Caribbean and Latin American region. Cultural exchange needs to be guided by egalitarian values that promote reciprocity, lest the more powerful economic forces end up imposing their values on the less powerful.

This task cannot be accomplished by the economically disadvantaged countries alone, precisely since they find themselves in a position of need. Their negotiating power for the preservation of their cultural traditions and future potential rests primarily on the weight of social institutions and on public sentiment and opinion, and this power, which to a great extent is idealistic in nature, may be easily overridden by such material needs as the need for relief from hunger, disease, or poverty. Latin American solidarity groups functioning in the developed countries—also fueled in large part by idealistic sentiments—need to refocus their efforts on assessing the criteria used to evaluate material aid assigned directly or indirectly to Latin America. One important test of such criteria is the beneficiary's record with respect to the social liberation of the people from various kinds of oppression.

In this respect, conservative ideology—which has been occupying the center of political power in the United States especially since the 1980s—proposes that as long as a country is represented by a system of a "free press," "free elections," and a "free market," it is the worthy beneficiary of support. These values are not altogether unreasonable, particularly if "free" were to cease to carry a class connotation or a masculine accent. But as long as a wide gap in power exists between the rich and the poor, as well as between the rights enjoyed by men and those enjoyed by women, such criteria are minimalist in character and assure no real democracy or self-development at the level of the everyday life of individuals. What they assure is an appearance of democracy, a problem that, to be corrected, requires the enactment of important revisions in gender role expectations and in the distribution of wealth. The conservative concern for capitalist freedoms and male hegemony in the public and private sectors needs to be questioned in the light of the broader freedoms demanded by a social, participatory democracy.

For this reason, a theory of cultural identity advocating flexibility in the development of multicultural liaisons needs to be backed up by a strong commitment to programs ensuring social liberation. To argue, on the one hand, for an open policy of economic and cultural development in cooperation with Western capitalist powers—as conservatives and even some liberals do—without insisting on the requirements aimed at guaranteeing social liberation is, for the most part, merely to support the status quo together with its widespread structural injustices. To argue, on the other hand, for a total break with Western powers in the name of strengthening national liberation movements is to amputate part of the strength of the Latin American and Caribbean societies. The inadequacy of these two positons leads one to postulate yet another option: the development of a theory of a Latin American cultural identity that assumes a positive relationship with the whole cultural legacy of humanity, including the legacy of non-Western traditions as they apply to the region, but that also places its learning in the service of the social liberation of the people, especially minorities, women, and those in need of material assistance. This theoretical position is progressive with respect to social and political change, at the same time that it approaches knowledge and science from a critical, yet pragmatically oriented, perspective. I hope that my study has made a positive contribution toward the theoretical articulation and practical application of this perspective.

ABBREVIATIONS

The following abbreviations have been used to refer to frequently cited sources. Full bibliographical information is available in the notes and bibliography. Unless I have referred to the English translation of a work, all translations from the Spanish are my own.

AC   Zea, *América como conciencia*

AD   Zea, *Apogeo y decadencia del positivismo en México*

AL   Zea, ed., *América Latina en sus ideas*

ALFL   Salazar Bondy, et al., *América Latina: filosofía y liberación*

CPM   Zea, *Conciencia y posibilidad del mexicano*

DM   Mariátegui, *Defensa del marxismo*

EF   Salazar Bondy, *¿Existe una filosofía de nuestra América?*

FEL   Dussel, *Filosofía ética latinoamericana, 6/III*

FH   Zea, *Filosofía de la historia americana*

FLL   Cerutti Guldberg, *Filosofía de la liberación latinoamericana*

IFL   Dussel, *Introducción a la filosofía de la liberación*

PH   Ramos, *El perfil del hombre y la cultura en México*

PL   Dussel, *Philosophy of Liberation*

PM   Zea, *Positivism in Mexico*

PO   Freire, *Pedagogy of the Oppressed*

SE   Mariátegui, *Siete ensayos de interpretación de la realidad peruana*

SIE   Mariátegui, *Seven Interpretive Essays on Peruvian Reality*

SL   Boff and Boff, *Salvation and Liberation*

TC   Roig, *Teoría y crítica del pensamiento latinoamericano*

TL   Gutiérrez, *A Theology of Liberation*

NOTES

Introduction

1. See Jorge J. E. Gracia, ed., *Latin American Philosophy in the Twentieth Century: Man, Values, and the Search for Philosophical Identity* (Buffalo: Prometheus Books, 1986), pp. 13–39. See also Leopoldo Zea, *The Latin American Mind*, trans. James H. Abbott and Lowell Dunham (Norman: University of Oklahoma Press, 1963).

2. For example, having discussed the work of Mariátegui at some length, I move on to an analysis of several other theories that are not Marxist rather than attempt to cover the history of Latin American Marxism up to the present time.

3. The leading work in the field has been done by Jorge Gracia, whose publications include, as author, "Importance of the History of Ideas in Latin America," *Journal of the History of Ideas* 36 (1975): 177–84; "Philosophical Analysis in Latin America," *History of Philosophy Quarterly* 1 (1984): 111–22; as coauthor, with Iván Jaksić, "The Problem of Philosophical Identity in Latin America," *Inter-American Review of Bibliography* 34 (1984): 53–71; as editor, *Latin American Philosophy in the Twentieth Century*, op. cit.; as chief editor, *Philosophical Analysis in Latin America* (Dordrecht: Reidel, 1984); as guest editor and contributor, a special double issue on "Latin American Philosophy Today," *The Philosophical Forum* 20 (1988–89); as coeditor, with Mireya Camurati, and contributor, *Philosophy and Literature in Latin America: A Critical Assessment of the Current Situation* (Albany: State University of New York Press, 1989). Gracia's work, which also shows the results of a fruitful collaboration with the Argentine philosopher Risieri Frondisi (1920–83), has helped to make possible the study of Latin American philosophy in the United States.

The study of Latin American philosophy in North America has often been conducted from an interdisciplinary perspective, e.g., Iván Jaksić, *Academic Rebels in Chile: The Role of Philosophy in Higher Education and Politics* (Albany: State University of New York Press, 1989), and Solomon Lipp, *Leopoldo Zea: From Mexicanidad to a Philosophy of History* (Waterloo, Ont.: Wilfrid Laurier University Press, 1980). Other publications of special relevance to the present study include Ofelia Schutte, "Origins and Tendencies of the Philosophy of Liberation in Latin American Thought: A Critique of Dussel's Ethics," *The Philosophical Forum* 22 (1991): 270–95; "The Master-Slave Dialectic in Latin America: The Social

Criticism of Zea, Freire, and Roig," *The Owl of Minerva* 22 (1990): 5–18; "Philosophy and Feminism in Latin America: Perspectives on Gender Identity and Culture," *The Philosophical Forum* 20 (1988–89): 62–84; "Nietzsche, Mariátegui, and Socialism: A Case of 'Nietzschean Marxism' in Peru?" *Social Theory and Practice* 14 (1988): 71–85; and "Toward an Understanding of Latin American Philosophy: Reflections on the Formation of a Cultural Identity," *Philosophy Today* 31 (1987): 21–34. In the United States, the Society for Iberian and Latin American Thought (SILAT), founded in 1977, has promoted the study of Latin American philosophy and the history of philosophical ideas.

The study of social and political philosophy in Latin America and the Caribbean has also engaged the interest of other North American philosophical societies. For example, the Society for the Philosophical Study of Marxism and, more recently, the Radical Philosophers' Association have sponsored meetings with philosophers in Cuba since the early 1980s. Selections from a 1985 conference appear in *Ideology & Independence in the Americas,* ed. April Ane Knutson (Minneapolis: Marxist Educational Press, 1989). Recent meetings cosponsored by the University of Havana and the Cuban Society for Philosophical Investigations (1990, 1991) have proven to be of a more pluralistic nature. The Society for Women in Philosophy has cosponsored meetings on philosophical feminism with sister societies in Mexico (1988) and Argentina (1989). These meetings are based on the special interests of the participants and do not necessarily address the topic of a Latin American philosophy as such.

Chapter 1. Social Liberation, Identity, and the Recovery of Early Marxist Thought

1. See José Martí, *Our America: Writings on Latin America and the Struggle for Cuban Independence,* ed. Philip S. Foner (New York: Monthly Review Press, 1977), and José Vasconcelos, *La raza cósmica* (Mexico: Espasa Calpe Mexicana, 1948). See also Jorge J. E. Gracia and Iván Jaksić, eds., *Filosofía e identidad cultural en América Latina* (Caracas: Monte Avila Editores, 1983).

2. At the First International Meeting on Latin American Philosophy, held in Ciudad Juárez, Mexico, in May 1990, there were no sessions on the subject of feminist philosophy or the issue of women in society. Still, there was an effort to include women in the program. Two papers from U.S. participants incorporated a feminist perspective, including a presentation by Amy Oliver on the subject of Leopoldo Zea, marginality, and feminism. The recent special issue of *The Philosophical Forum* on "Latin American Philosophy Today," edited by Jorge Gracia, also includes an article on feminism (see introduction, note 3).

3. The Juárez conference mentioned in note 2 featured a dialogue between the Mexican thinker Leopoldo Zea and the Peruvian theologian Gustavo Gutiérrez. The influence of the theology of liberation on liberation philosophy has been widely known but seldom studied as such. On this subject, see Horacio Cerutti Guldberg, *Filosofía de la liberación latinoamericana* (Mexico: Fondo de Cultura Económica, 1983), pp. 113–54.

4. Sheldon B. Liss, *Marxist Thought in Latin America* (Berkeley: University of California Press, 1984), p. 129.

5. Michael Löwy, ed., *El marxismo en América Latina*, translated from the French by O. Barahona and U. Doyhamboure (Mexico: Ediciones Era, 1982), p. 19. In this and subsequent notes, all translations from the Spanish are my own unless an English language edition is cited.

6. José Aricó, ed., *Mariátegui y los orígenes del marxismo latinoamericano* (2d ed.; Mexico: Ediciones Pasado y Presente, 1980), p. xix.

7. Mercedes Santos Moray, ed., *Marxistas de América: Julio Antonio Mella, José Carlos Mariátegui, Aníbal Ponce, Juan Marinello* (Havana: Editorial Arte y Literatura, 1985), p. 8.

8. For biographical information on Mariátegui, see Jesús Chavarría, *José Carlos Mariátegui and the Rise of Modern Peru, 1890–1930* (Albuquerque: University of New Mexico Press, 1979), and the introduction by Jorge Basadre to the English-language edition of the *Siete Ensayos*, *Seven Interpretive Essays on Peruvian Reality*, by José Carlos Mariátegui, trans. Marjory Urquidi (Austin: University of Texas Press, 1971), pp. vii–xxxii. Of special interest is Estuardo Nuñez, *La experiencia europea de Mariátegui y otros ensayos* (Lima: Empresa Editora Amauta, 1978).

9. See José Carlos Mariátegui and Ricardo Martínez de la Torre, eds., *Amauta: revista mundial de doctrina, literatura, arte, polémica*, facsimile edition in six volumes (32 issues, September 1926–March 1930; Lima: Empresa Editora Amauta, 1976).

10. The collected edition of Mariátegui's works is *Obras completas de José Carlos Mariátegui* (20 vols.; Lima: Empresa Editora Amauta, 1957–70). For Mariátegui's texts in Spanish, I have relied primarily on the following editions: José Carlos Mariátegui, *Siete ensayos de interpretación de la realidad peruana* (Mexico: Ediciones Era, 1979); José Carlos Mariátegui, *Obra política*, ed. Rubén Jiménez Ricárdez (Mexico: Ediciones Era, 1979); José Carlos Mariátegui, *Obras*, ed. Francisco Baeza (2 vols.; Havana: Casa de las Américas, 1982); and the journal *Amauta*, op. cit.

11. Mariátegui, SIE, p. xxxiv.

12. Mariátegui probably saw Gramsci at the Congress of Livorno in

1921, when the Italian Communist party was founded. He attended the congress as a journalist for the Peruvian newspaper *El Tiempo*. For various hypotheses regarding the Gramscian influence on Mariátegui, see Aníbal Quijano, *Introducción a Mariátegui* (Mexico: Ediciones Era, 1982), pp. 42–44, 72–77; Antonio Melis, "Mariátegui, el primer marxista de América," in Aricó, ed., *Mariátegui*, pp. 205–10 and 213; Robert Paris, "El marxismo de Mariátegui," in Aricó, pp. 140–44; and Nuñez, *La experiencia europea de Mariátegui*, pp. 26–29. One point in common between Mariátegui and Gramsci is their reading of Marx from a perspective influenced by Italian idealism, in particular that of Croce.

13. Mariátegui, SIE, p. 32.

14. Ibid., p. 33.

15. See Harry E. Vanden, *National Marxism in Latin America: José Carlos Mariátegui's Thought and Politics* (Boulder: Lynne Rienner Publishers, 1986), pp. 62–63.

16. For Mariátegui's controversy with the APRA, see Quijano, pp. 87–112, and the section "Mariátegui, ¿Aprista o marxista?" in Aricó, ed., *Mariátegui*, pp. 1–51. For a different view, see Abelardo Villegas, *Reformismo y revolución en el pensamiento latinoamericano* (5th ed.; Mexico: Siglo XXI, 1980), pp. 141–80. Villegas states that the Alianza Popular Revolucionaria Americana or APRA party was founded by Haya de la Torre in 1924. Haya also founded the Partido Aprista Peruano (PAP) in 1931 (p. 173).

17. "Punto de vista antiimperialista," in José Carlos Mariátegui, *Obra política*, p. 276. An English translation has been published: "The Anti-Imperialist Perspective," *New Left Review* 70 (1971): 67–72.

18. Alberto Flores Galindo, *La agonía de Mariátegui: la polémica con la Komintern* (Lima: DESCO, 1980), p. 21.

19. Ibid., p. 24.

20. Ibid., p. 133.

21. Ibid., p. 50.

22. Aricó, ed., *Mariátegui*, p. liv.

23. Quijano, pp. 110–11; Aricó, ed., *Mariátegui*, pp. xxxiv–xl.

24. The reference is to Nietzsche, *The Wanderer and His Shadow*, § 121. See *The Complete Works of Friedrich Nietzsche*, ed. Oscar Levy (18 vols., 1909–11; reprint, New York: Russell and Russell, 1964), 7:255.

25. Mariátegui, SIE, p. xxxiii.

26. Friedrich Nietzsche, *Thus Spoke Zarathustra*, trans. Walter Kaufmann (New York: Viking Press, 1966), p. 152.

27. Mariátegui, SIE, pp. 3–4.

28. Luce Irigaray, *This Sex Which Is Not One*, trans. Catherine Porter with Carolyn Burke (Ithaca, N.Y.: Cornell University Press, 1985). Postmodern feminism attempts to reevaluate woman's body and certain aspects of the unconscious from a standpoint prior to the imposition of the Law of the Father on the unconscious. For a discussion of some affinities between Nietzsche and Mariátegui, see chapter 2.

29. Mariátegui, SIE, pp. 161–62.

30. Ibid., p. 161.

31. Ibid.

32. Ibid., p. 162.

33. Ibid., pp. 164–65.

34. Citations to *Defensa del marxismo* will be to the collection *Obras*, 1:121–203. (See chap. 1, n. 10.) *Defensa del Marxismo* first appeared as a series of articles published intermittently in Mariátegui's journal *Amauta* in 1928–29. (See chap. 1, n. 9.) Mariátegui's references to Benedetto Croce are taken from Croce's *Materialismo storico ed economia marxista*. The fourth edition of this work (Bari: Guiseppe Laterza, 1921) is listed in Harry Vanden's inventory of Mariátegui's library collection (Vanden, *National Marxism*, p. 131).

35. Mariátegui, DM, *Obras*, 1:139; first published in *Amauta* 18 (1928).

36. Mariátegui, SIE, p. 151.

37. Mariátegui, DM, *Obras*, 1:139.

38. Ibid., p. 142.

39. Ibid., p. 139.

40. Ibid.

41. Mariátegui, *Obras*, 1:449.

Chapter 2. Mariátegui's Socialist Anthropology

1. This edition was arranged according to a design left by Mariátegui before his death. See *El alma matinal y otras estaciones del hombre*

de hoy (2d ed.; Lima: Empresa Editora Amauta, 1959), editorial note, p. 5. The four articles reviewed in the first part of this chapter were first published in the Lima newspaper *Mundial* during 1925.

2. José Carlos Mariátegui, *Seven Interpretive Essays on Peruvian Reality*, trans. Marjorie Urquidi, with an introduction by Jorge Basadre (Austin: University of Texas Press, 1971). For the Spanish text I have used the Mexican edition *Siete ensayos de interpretación de la realidad peruana* (Mexico: Ediciones Era, 1979). References to *Defensa del marxismo* are to José Carlos Mariátegui, *Obras*, ed. Francisco Baeza (2 vols.; Havana: Casa de las Américas, 1982). The original essays constituting DM first appeared in Mariátegui's journal *Amauta* in the years 1928–29. They can be found in José Carlos Mariátegui and Ricardo Martínez de la Torre, eds., *Amauta: Revista mensual de doctrina, literatura, arte, polémica* (facsimile edition in 6 vols.; Lima: Empresa Editora Amauta, 1976).

3. The references here are not to Nietzsche—another writer who often used "dawn" and "twilight" metaphors in his work—but to the Spanish writer Ramón Gómez de la Serna, whose book *El alba y otras cosas* was published in Madrid in 1923.

4. See Mariátegui, "El alma matinal," *Obras*, 1:403–404.

5. Ibid., p. 405.

6. Ibid., p. 407.

7. The philosopher cited is Nietzsche. See *Die fröhliche Wissenschaft* (*The Joyful Wisdom*), § 283.

8. Mariátegui, *Obras*, 1:407.

9. Ibid., p. 410.

10. Mariátegui cites an author by the name of Luis Bello as the source of this quotation, whose full version is, "It is useful to correct Descartes: 'I struggle, therefore I exist'" (*Obras*, 1:411).

11. Mariátegui, *Obras*, 1:411.

12. Jack J. Roth, *The Cult of Violence: Sorel and the Sorelians* (Berkeley: University of California Press, 1980).

13. Ibid., p. 216.

14. See also Robert Paris, "El marxismo de Mariátegui," in Aricó, ed., *Mariátegui*, pp. 119–44.

15. George Sorel, *Reflections on Violence*, trans. T. E. Hulme and J. Roth (New York: Collier Books, 1961), pp. 142–43.

16. Ibid., pp. 122–23.

17. In *Reflections on Violence* Sorel argues that there are only two options within socialism—orthodox Marxism, which he finds unacceptable, and his own views.

18. Mariátegui, *Obras*, 1:412.

19. Ibid.

20. Ibid., p. 413.

21. Ibid.

22. Ibid., p. 415.

23. Ibid., pp. 415–16.

24. Ofelia Schutte, *Beyond Nihilism: Nietzsche without Masks* (Chicago: University of Chicago Press, 1984), pp. 11–37.

25. R. Hinton Thomas, *Nietzsche in German Politics and Society, 1890–1918* (La Salle, Ill.: Open Court, 1983).

26. Mariátegui, *Obras*, 1:416.

27. Ibid., p. 417.

28. Ibid., pp. 417–18.

29. Ibid., p. 420.

30. Ibid., p. 424.

31. Of course, there have been other exceptions, including the views of Hume, Nietzsche, and contemporary deconstructive thought on the self. But these are still often regarded as exceptions to mainstream Western humanism.

32. Some examples that come to mind are Marx's critique of alienation in the 1844 *Manuscripts* and Ernesto "Che" Guevara's idea of the new human being as stated in his well-known essay, "Socialism and Man in Cuba" (1965).

33. Mariátegui, DM, *Obras*, 1:149.

34. Ibid., pp. 149–50.

35. Ibid., p. 151. See Benedetto Croce, *Historical Materialism and the Economics of Karl Marx*, trans. C. M. Meredith (New York: Macmillan, 1924). Cf. chapter 1, n. 34.

36. Mariátegui, DM, *Obras*, 1:151.

37. Ibid.

38. Ibid., pp. 153–54.

39. Ibid., p. 156.

40. Ibid., p. 157.

41. See Adolfo Sánchez Vázquez, "Marxism in Latin America," *The Philosophical Forum* 20, nos. 1–2 (1988–89): 114–28.

42. Mariátegui, DM, *Obras,* 1:160.

43. Ibid., pp. 160–61.

44. Ibid., p. 160.

45. See chapter 5.

46. Mariátegui, SIE, p. 152.

47. Ibid., p. 151.

48. Mariátegui, DM, *Obras,* 1:161.

49. Ibid., p. 162.

50. From the author's note to the *Seven Interpretive Essays.* I have modified Urquidi's translation ("and I believe the only salvation for Indo-America lies in European and Western science and thought" [SIE, p. xxxiv]), since Mariátegui's actual statement is: "Y creo que no hay salvación para Indo-América sin la ciencia y el pensamiento europeos u occidentales" (SE, p. 14).

51. See Carlos Daniel Valcárcel, *Rebeliones coloniales sudamericanas* (Mexico: Fondo de Cultura Económica, 1982).

52. Manuel González Prada, *Páginas libres, Horas de lucha,* ed. Luis Alberto Sánchez (Caracas: Biblioteca Ayacucho, 1976), p. 44. In an important 1904 essay, "Nuestros Indios," González Prada undertakes a critique of the Indians' oppression and again makes a passing reference to their apathy during the War of the Pacific (ibid., p. 342).

53. See Braulio Muñoz, *Sons of the Wind: The Search for Identity in Spanish American Indian Literature* (New Brunswick: Rutgers University Press, 1982), pp. 65–71 and Sheldon Liss, *Marxist Thought in Latin America* (Berkeley: University of California Press, 1984), pp. 127–28.

54. González Prada, p. 242.

55. Mariátegui, SIE, p. 171.

56. Antonio Melis, "Mariátegui, el primer marxista de América," in Aricó, ed., *Mariátegui,* p. 204.

57. Mariátegui, SIE, p. 22.

58. Ibid., p. 70.

59. Mariátegui, SE, p. 88.

60. Mariátegui, "Freudismo y Marxismo," DM, *Obras*, 1:166–68.

61. Mariátegui, SIE, p. 30.

62. Ibid.

63. Ibid.

64. Mariátegui, SE, addendum to chap. 2, p. 41.

65. Ibid., p. 42.

66. Ibid., pp. 42–43.

67. Mariátegui, SIE, pp. 34–35.

68. Ibid., pp. 35, 36.

69. Ibid., p. 36; see also pp. 55–61.

70. Ibid., p. 58.

71. For a study of Mariátegui's life and thought in the context of the political evolution of Peru, see Jesús Chavarría, *José Carlos Mariátegui and the Rise of Modern Peru, 1890–1930* (Albuquerque: University of New Mexico Press, 1979).

72. Much has been made of the fact that Mariátegui placed Sorel's name here next to Marx's, rather than using the name of Engels. This is an indication of his debt to Sorelism.

73. Mariátegui, SIE, p. 74.

74. Ibid., p. 78.

75. Ibid., pp. 157–58.

76. Mariátegui, DM, *Obras*, 1:199.

77. Ibid., p. 198.

78. Ibid., p. 158.

79. See chapter 1.

80. Quoted by Jorge Basadre in the Introduction to the North American edition of the *Seven Interpretive Essays*, p. xiv. The reference is to an interview with Mariátegui published in the Lima journal *Variedades* on 23 March 1923.

81. Mariátegui, *Obras*, 2:250.

82. Ibid.

Chapter 3. Philosophy and the Problem of Cultural Identity

1. See Domingo Faustino Sarmiento, *Facundo* (published in 1845 as *Civilización y barbarie*) (Buenos Aires: Ediciones Estrada, 1940); Juan Bautista Alberdi, *Bases y puntos de partida para la organización política de la República Argentina* (1st ed., 1853; Buenos Aires, Ediciones Estrada, 1943), and Leopoldo Zea, *Filosofía de la historia americana* (Mexico: Fondo de Cultura Económica, 1978).

2. Cf. José Martí, *Política de nuestra América*, prologue by Roberto Fernández Retamar (2d. ed.; Mexico: Siglo XXI, 1979) and Enrique José Rodó, *La América nuestra* (Havana: Casa de las Américas, 1977).

3. See Abelardo Villegas, *Autognosis: el pensamiento mexicano en el siglo XX* (Mexico: Instituto Panamericano de Geografía e Historia, 1985).

4. Samuel Ramos, *El perfil del hombre y la cultura en México* (Mexico: Espasa-Calpe Mexicana, 1984), p. 81. All subsequent references will be to this edition. The translations from the Spanish are my own. Ramos's work is also available in English. See *Profile of Man and Culture in Mexico*, trans. Peter G. Earle (Austin: University of Texas Press, 1962).

5. Ramos, PH, p. 82.

6. Ramos, PH, p. 31. For the reference to Nietzsche, see *The Will to Power*, § 1041, and *Beyond Good and Evil*, § 39.

7. Ramos, PH, pp. 11–13.

8. Ibid., p. 13.

9. Ibid., p. 14.

10. Ibid.

11. Ibid., p. 15.

12. Ibid., p. 16.

13. Ibid., p. 26.

14. Samuel Ramos, *Hacia un nuevo humanismo* (first published in 1940; Mexico: Fondo de Cultura Económica, 1962). For selections from this work in English translation see *Latin American Philosophy in the Twentieth Century*, ed. Jorge J. E. Gracia (Buffalo, prometheus Books, 1986), pp. 69–77.

15. Ramos, PH, p. 18.

16. Ibid.

17. Ibid., p. 39.

18. Ibid., p. 40.

19. Ibid., p. 34.

20. Ibid., pp. 90, 92.

21. Ibid., p. 63.

22. Ibid., p. 65.

23. Ibid., p. 38.

24. Ibid., p. 39.

25. Ibid., p. 61.

26. Ibid., p. 57.

27. Ibid., pp. 55–56.

28. Ibid., p. 65.

29. Ibid., p. 76.

30. Ibid., p. 93.

31. Ibid., p. 87.

32. Ramos distances himself from an indigenist perspective, while he is explicit about the need to establish a Mexican identity vis-à-vis the European. For example, in *Historia de la filosofía en México* he writes: "We want to see this world, discovered by European philosophy, but [we want to see it] with [Latin] American eyes, and to determine our own destinies in relation to the whole of this world." Cited in Villegas, *Autognosis*, p. 117.

33. See Villegas, *Autognosis*, p. 115.

34. Ibid., p. 114. See also José Ortega y Gasset, *Meditations on Quixote*, trans. Evelyn Rugg and Diego Marín (New York: W. W. Norton, 1961), p. 45.

35. Zea's predecessors Samuel Ramos and José Gaos had also written on the history of philosophy in Mexico. Gaos was a strong promoter of research on Mexican philosophy and its historical evolution.

36. Leopoldo Zea, *Positivism in Mexico*, trans. Josephine H. Schulte (Austin: University of Texas Press, 1974), preface to the English translation,

pp. xiii–xxiii. See also Zea, *Apogeo y decadencia del positivismo en México* (a sequel to *El positivismo en México*) (Mexico: El Colegio de Mexico, 1944).

37. Zea, PM, p. 79.

38. Ibid., p. 16.

39. For a different and more sympathetic view of Mexican positivism, the liberal tradition, and the role of *La Libertad* in this period of Mexican history, see Charles Hale, *The Transformation of Liberalism in Nineteenth-Century Mexico* (Princeton: Princeton University Press, 1989). Hale makes extensive use of European sources, primarily French and English documentation, in his assessment of the characteristics and development of positivism in Mexico.

40. Zea, AD, p. 84.

41. Ibid., p. 85.

42. Ibid., p. 87.

43. Ibid.

44. See chapter 4. Such a consciousness is exemplified by the tradition of Martí's "nuestra América," Vasconcelos's "raza cósmica," and so on.

45. Leopoldo Zea, *Conciencia y posibilidad del mexicano,* with *El occidente y la conciencia en México* and *Dos ensayos sobre México y lo mexicano* (reprints of 1952 and 1953 eds.; Mexico: Editorial Porrúa, 1982), pp. 5–6.

46. Ibid., p. 6.

47. Leopoldo Zea, *América como conciencia* (2d ed.; Mexico: UNAM, 1983), p. 20. First published in 1953.

48. Ibid., pp. 21–22.

49. Ibid., p. 26.

50. Ibid.

51. Ibid., p. 41.

52. Ibid., p. 126.

53. Ibid.

54. Ibid., p. 30.

55. Ibid., pp. 27–28.

56. Salazar Bondy uses José Martí's expression *"nuestra América,"* which refers to Latin America and affirms the independence of the

region's cultural values from its northern neighbor, the United States. He also narrows the limits of his study to what he calls "Hispanic Indo-America" (*la América Hispanoindia*). By this he means to exclude Brazil and the Caribbean from the focus of his work, although he notes that there are historical and cultural similarities among all the countries of the region.

57. Some related positions are found in aspects of the works of Frantz Fanon and Enrique Dussel.

58. Augusto Salazar Bondy, "Prólogo," *Para una filosofía del valor* (Santiago de Chile: Editorial Universitaria, 1971), pp. 11–14.

59. That Salazar Bondy's conception of philosophy is analytically inspired has led to an initially favorable reception of his work in the United States. The reception of his work in this country, however, is oriented toward the first part of his argument, the thesis that thus far there is no genuine Latin American philosophy. Salazar Bondy's important critique of imperialism as the cause of this deficiency remains relatively unknown.

60. Augusto Salazar Bondy, *¿Existe una filosofía de nuestra América?* (Mexico: Siglo XXI, 1968), p. 112.

61. Ibid., p. 113.

62. Augusto Salazar Bondy, et al., *América Latina: filosofía y liberación* (Buenos Aires: Editorial Bonum, 1974), pp. 40–41.

63. Salazar Bondy, EF, p. 113.

64. Ibid., p. 116.

65. Salazar Bondy, *Sentido y problema del pensamiento filosófico hispano-americano*, with English translation and comments by Arthur Berndtson and Fernando Salmerón (Lawrence: University of Kansas Center for Latin American Studies, Occasional Publications no. 16, September 1969), pp. 17–18 and 21–27. Cf. EF, pp. 112–33.

66. Salazar Bondy argues for an alternative to a capitalist theory of development in "La alternativa del Tercer Mundo," in Jorge Bravo Bresani, et al., *El reto del Perú en la perspectiva del tercer mundo* (Lima: Moncloa-Campodónico, 1972), pp. 97–118.

67. Salazar Bondy, EF, p. 100.

68. Ibid.

69. Ibid., p. 101.

70. Selections from this essay are also published in Jorge J. E. Gracia, ed., *Latin American Philosophy in the Twentieth Century* (Buffalo: Prometheus Books, 1986), pp. 233–44.

71. See the comments by Arthur Berndtson and Francisco Salmerón in *Sentido y problema del pensamiento filosófico hispano-americano,* pp. 22–29 (English version) and 28–34 (Spanish version).

72. Augusto Salazar Bondy, *La filosofía en el Perú* (Washington: Unión Panamericana, 1954); the text includes an English translation. See also Augusto Salazar Bondy, *Historia de las ideas en el Perú contemporáneo* (2 vols.; Lima: Francisco Moncloa, 1965).

73. Salazar Bondy, *Historia de las ideas en el Perú contemporáneo,* 2:458–59.

74. See Salazar Bondy, "La alternativa del Tercer mundo," in *Reto,* pp. 97–118.

75. See Paulo Freire and Augusto Salazar Bondy, *¿Qué es y cómo funciona la concientización?* (Lima: Editorial Causachun, 1975). Salazar Bondy's contribution on pp. 83–89 can be read in the context of the rest of the book, authored by Freire.

76. Salazar Bondy, ALFL, pp. 50–51.

77. Notice the analogy with the theology of liberation's option for the oppressed.

78. Salazar Bondy, ALFL, p. 47.

79. In addition to Leopoldo Zea and Augusto Salazar Bondy, the main speakers at this symposium held at the Universidad del Salvador in 1973 were Julio César Terán Dutari, an Ecuadorian theologian, and the Chilean philosopher Félix Schwartzmann, who argued that the original value of a philosophical work is a result of its universal human value. A companion volume to this symposium collection, with essays by a diverse group of Argentine philosophers (including Osvaldo Ardiles, Hugo Assmann, Horacio Cerutti, and Enrique Dussel) on the theme of liberation philosophy in Latin America was published under the title *Hacia una filosofía de la liberación latinoamericana* (Buenos Aires: Bonum, 1973). For an analysis of liberation philosophy in Argentina, see chapter 6.

80. Leopoldo Zea, *La filosofía americana como filosofía sin más* (Mexico: Siglo XXI, 1969), p. 31.

81. In addition to the University of Kansas lecture comments already mentioned, see, for example, works by Horacio Cerutti, Jorge Gracia, Francisco Miró Quesada, and Pablo Guadarrama.

82. Salazar Bondy, EF, p. 121; Gracia, ed., *Latin American Philosophy in the Twentieth Century,* p. 241.

83. Salazar Bondy is referring here to Mariátegui's article, "¿Existe un pensamiento hispano-americano?" published in the newspaper *Mun-*

dial, Lima, 1 May 1925. The article can be found in *Marxistas de América,* ed. Mercedes Santos Moray (Havana: Editorial Arte y Literatura, 1985), pp. 116–19.

84. Salazar Bondy, ALFL, pp. 42–43. Salazar Bondy studied for two years in Mexico under José Gaos at the Colegio de México during his distinguished career in Latin American philosophy. See Salazar Bondy, *La filosofía en el Perú,* p. 9.

85. Salazar Bondy, ALFL, p. 43.

86. Friedrich Nietzsche, *Thus Spoke Zarathustra,* "On Redemption."

87. Cf. Zea, *La filosofía americana como filosofía sin más,* pp. 150–60.

88. Ibid., pp. 157–60.

Chapter 4. The Humanity of *Mestizaje* and the Search for Freedom

1. Leopoldo Zea, *Filosofía de la historia americana* (Mexico: Fondo de Cultura Económica, 1978).

2. See G. W. F. Hegel, *Lectures on the Philosophy of World History,* trans. H. B. Nisbet (Cambridge: Cambridge University Press, 1975).

3. G. W. F. Hegel, *The Phenomenology of Mind,* trans. J. B. Baillie (New York: Harper Torchbooks, 1967), pp. 228–40.

4. See Leopoldo Zea, *The Latin American Mind,* trans. James H. Abbott and Lowel Dunham (Norman: University of Oklahoma Press, 1963), pp. 11–15.

5. Zea, FH, p. 26.

6. Cf. Lourdes Arizpe, "El 'Indio': Mito, Profecía, Prisión," in *América Latina en sus ideas,* ed. Leopoldo Zea (Mexico and Paris: Siglo XXI and UNESCO, 1986), pp. 333–44.

7. Zea, "Introducción," AL, p. 17.

8. Zea, FH, p. 165.

9. Cf. Octavio Paz, *The Labyrinth of Solitude: Life and Thought in Mexico,* trans. Lysander Kemp (New York: Grove Press, 1961).

10. Zea, FH, p. 167.

11. Cf. Frantz Fanon, *Black Skin, White Masks,* trans. Charles Lam Markmann (New York: Grove Press, 1967).

12. Zea, FH, pp. 168–70, 269ff.

13. Ibid., p. 169.

14. The passages cited by Zea are from Juan Ginés de Sepúlveda, *Tratado sobre las justas causas de la guerra contra los indios* (Mexico: Fondo de Cultura Económica, 1941), and Bartolomé de las Casas, *Del único modo de atraer a todos los pueblos a la verdadera religión* (Mexico: Fondo de Cultura Económica, 1942).

15. Zea, FH, p. 118.

16. Ibid., p. 117.

17. Ibid.

18. Ibid., p. 123; the reference is to Sepúlveda, p. 133.

19. Zea, FH, p. 125.

20. Ibid., p. 130; the reference is to Las Casas, p. 3.

21. See María Teresa Berruezo León, *La lucha de Hispanoamérica por su independencia en Inglaterra, 1800–1830* (Madrid: Ediciones de Cultura Hispánica, 1989), pp. 92–95.

22. Ibid., pp. 41–42.

23. For an analysis of the highly complex political and economic aspects of the Hispanic American postindependence period, see Leslie Bethell, ed., *Spanish America after Independence, c. 1820–c. 1870* (Cambridge: Cambridge University Press, 1987).

24. Zea, FH, p. 188.

25. Ibid., p. 202.

26. Ibid.; from Bolívar's letter to General Juan José Flores, 9 November 1830.

27. Zea, FH, pp. 211–60.

28. Ibid., pp. 231–43.

29. Ibid., p. 247.

30. Ibid., pp. 203–10.

31. Ibid., pp. 250–57.

32. Zea refers to his book, *El positivismo en México* (Mexico: Fondo de Cultura Económica, 1968). See chap. 3, n. 36 for information on the English translation.

33. FH, p. 258; the reference is to Domingo Faustino Sarmiento, *Argirópolis* (Buenos Aires: Editorial Universitaria de Buenos Aires, 1968). Cf. Sarmiento, *Conflicto y armonía de las razas en América* (Buenos Aires: Editorial Intermundo, 1946) and *Facundo* (published in 1845 as *Civilización y barbarie*) (Buenos Aires: Ediciones Estrada, 1940).

34. Zea, FH, pp. 261–68.

35. Ibid., p. 264.

36. Ibid.

37. Ibid., p. 265; the reference is to Juan Bautista Alberdi, *Bases y puntos de partida para la organización política de la República Argentina* (Buenos Aires: Ediciones Estrada, 1943), p. 48.

38. José Martí, "Nuestra América," in *Política de nuestra América*, prologue by Roberto Fernández Retamar (2d. ed.; Mexico: Siglo XXI, 1979), pp. 35–44. All references to Martí's essay will be to this edition. In those cases where Zea refers to Martí, additional information will be given. Martí's essay was published originally in *La Revista Ilustrada de Nueva York*, 10 January 1891 and in *El Partido Liberal*, Mexico, 30 January 1891.

39. Martí, "Nuestra América," pp. 43–44.

40. Martí, "Carta de despedida (A Manuel Mercado)," *Política de nuestra América*, p. 322. The letter is dated 18 May 1895.

41. Martí, "Nuestra América," p. 41; cited by Zea, FH, p. 291.

42. Ibid., p. 42; cited by Zea, FH, p. 291.

43. Ibid., p. 39; cited by Zea, FH, p. 290.

44. Ibid., p. 40; cited by Zea, FH, p. 292.

45. Martí, "Nuestra América," p. 40

46. On 18 May 1895, hours before dying in battle, Martí wrote to his Mexican friend Manuel Mercado: "Every day I am in danger of giving my life for my country and for my duty...of stopping in time, with the independence of Cuba, the United States' expansion through the Antilles and their falling, with an even greater force, upon our lands of [Latin] America. Everything I have done until today, and will go on doing, will be for this [purpose]." From Martí, "Carta de Despedida," in *Politica de nuestra América*, p. 321.

47. Arturo Ardao has written a number of books on the history of ideas in Uruguay, among them, *Espiritualismo y positivismo en el Uruguay* (Mexico, 1950), *La filosofía en el Uruguay en el siglo XX* (Mexico,

1956), *Racionalismo y liberalismo en el Uruguay* (Montevideo, 1962), and *Etapas de la inteligencia uruguaya* (Montevideo, 1971). Francisco Miró Quesada has authored works on logic, philosophy of mathematics, and philosophy of law as well as *Apuntes para una teoría de la razón* (Lima, 1969), *Humanismo y revolución* (Lima, 1969), *Despertar y proyecto del filosofar latinoamericano* (Mexico: FCE, 1974), and *Proyecto y realización del filosofar latinoamericano* (Mexico: FCE, 1981). Arturo Andrés Roig is the author of several works including *Los krausistas argentinos* (Puebla, 1969), *Platón o la filosofía como libertad y expectativa* (Mendoza, 1971), *El espiritualismo argentino entre 1850 y 1900* (Puebla, 1972), *Teoría y crítica del pensamiento latinoamericano* (Mexico: FCE, 1981), and *Filosofía, universidad y filósofos en América Latina* (Mexico: UNAM, 1981). Abelardo Villegas is the author of many works on Mexican philosophy and Latin American social thought, including *La filosofía de lo mexicano* (Mexico, 1966), *Panorama de la filosofía iberoamericana actual* (Buenos Aires, 1963), *Positivismo y porfirismo* (Mexico, 1972), *Reformismo y revolución en el pensamiento latinoamericano* (Mexico: Siglo XXI, 1972), *Cultura y política en América Latina* (Mexico, 1977), and *Autognosis: el pensamiento mexicano en el siglo XX* (Mexico: Instituto Panamericano de Geografía e Historia, 1985).

48. See chap. 4, n. 6.

49. Zea, AL, p. 14.

50. Leopoldo Zea, "The Actual Function of Philosophy in Latin America," trans. Iván Jaksić, in *Latin American Philosophy in the Twentieth Century*, ed. Gracia, p. 229.

51. See Ofelia Schutte, "The Master-Slave Dialectic in Latin America: The Social Criticism of Zea, Freire, and Roig," *The Owl of Minerva* 22 (1990): 5–18.

52. Arturo Andrés Roig, *Teoría y crítica del pensamiento latinoamericano* (Mexico: Fondo de Cultura Económica, 1981). See also Roig, "The Actual Function of Philosophy in Latin America," in *Latin American Philosophy in the Twentieth Century*, ed. Gracia, pp. 247–59.

53. Roig, TC, p. 11. By "anthropological a priori" Roig means the condition for the possibility of a type of philosophical knowledge rooted in a historico-temporal, as opposed to a transcendental, subjectivity. He claims such knowledge is life-oriented and its possibility owes much to Hegel (TC, p. 13).

54. Ibid., pp. 44–75.

55. In particular, see Roberto Fernández Retamar, *Calibán. Apuntes sobre la cultura de nuestra América* (2d ed.; Mexico: Diógenes, 1974), cited by Roig, p. 51.

56. Roig, TC, p. 51.

57. See Horacio Cerutti Guldberg, *Filosofía de la liberación latinoamericana* (Mexico: Fondo de Cultura Económica, 1983), pp. 59–65.

58. Roig, TC, p. 51.

59. Ibid., pp. 100–114.

60. Francisco Miró Quesada, "Ciencia y Técnica: Ideas o Mitoides," AL, pp. 72–94.

61. Ibid., p. 72.

62. Ibid., pp. 91–97.

63. Ibid., p. 85. In this part of the essay the term "myth" is used to include the sense of "mythlike beliefs."

64. Ibid., p. 93.

65. Ibid.

66. Ibid., p. 94.

67. Ibid., pp. 93–94.

68. Francisco Miró Quesada, "Man Without Theory," trans. William Cooper, in *Latin American Philosophy in the Twentieth Century*, ed. Gracia, pp. 137–48.

69. Ibid., p. 141.

70. Ibid., p. 147.

71. Leopoldo Zea, *La filosofía americana como filosofía sin más* (México: Siglo XXI, 1969), p. 157.

72. Roig, TC, p. 113.

73. Ibid., pp. 113–14.

Chapter 5. Consciousness on the Side of the Oppressed

1. Paulo Freire, *Pedagogy of the Oppressed*, trans. Myra Bergman Ramos (New York: Seabury Press, 1970), p. 93.

2. Ibid., p. 56.

3. Ibid., p. 76.

4. Ibid., p. 77.

5. Ibid., p. 67.

6. Ibid., p. 69.

7. Ibid.

8. Ibid., pp. 71–72.

9. Paulo Freire, *Acción cultural para la libertad* (Mexico: Casa Unida de Publicaciones, 1983), p. 93.

10. For example, an unusual image of Ernesto "Che" Guevara is offered. Freire states that Guevara comes close to using "evangelical language" when describing his feelings for Cuban peasants (PO, p. 171).

11. Cf. PO, p. 84.

12. Ibid., p. 64.

13. Ibid., p. 73.

14. Ibid., pp. 47–48.

15. Ibid., p. 135.

16. Ibid., pp. 135–36.

17. Mass mobilizations may be needed to reduce illiteracy or to take care of other urgent matters. But even in these cases, the role of teacher would fall primarily to the people themselves, not to the leaders. For example, following the Cuban Revolution, an extraordinary literacy campaign took place in the 1960s. Its success was due to the generous participation of the Cuban people. Yet in *Pedagogy*, Freire fails to mention the Cuban project or to give credit to ordinary citizens, many of them students themselves, who contributed to this campaign. Instead, when he speaks about Cuba, he focuses on what leaders such as Fidel Castro or Che Guevara say *about* the people. This erasure of popular action on behalf of education calls into question the consistency with which he applies his own views to particular cases in which people have responded actively to government initiatives to eliminate illiteracy in rural areas.

18. Cf. Freire, PO, p. 79.

19. Ibid., p. 170.

20. Freire, *Acción cultural para la libertad*, p. 84.

21. Ibid., p. 87.

22. Deane William Fern, *Third World Liberation Theologies: An Introductory Survey* (Maryknoll, N.Y.: Orbis Books, 1986), p. 11.

23. Leonardo Boff and Clodovis Boff, *Salvation and Liberation*, trans. Robert R. Barr (Maryknoll, N.Y.: Orbis Books, 1984), p. 20.

24. Ibid., pp. 35–36.

25. Ibid., p. 36.

26. Gustavo Gutiérrez, *A Theology of Liberation: History, Politics, and Salvation*, trans. Sister Caridad Inda and John Eagleson (Maryknoll, N.Y.: Orbis Books, 1973). All citations are to this edition unless otherwise specified. A revised edition of this work with a new introduction by Gutiérrez was published in 1988 by Orbis Press. The revised edition makes an effort to move toward nonspecific uses of language with respect to gender, therefore showing a sensitivity to the issue of women's marginalization through uses of language. There is also a change in one section, formerly entitled "Christian Brotherhood and Class Struggle" (1973 ed., pp. 272–85). This section is replaced by another entitled "Faith and Social Conflict" (1988 ed., pp. 156–61). The revision of this section does not affect the present interpretation of Gutiérrez's work.

27. This interpretation is based on Gutiérrez's major study, originally published in 1971. See also "Teología y ciencias sociales," *Páginas* (Lima) 9, nos. 63–64 (1984), and "Entre las calandrias," *Páginas* no. 100, December 1989. An English translation of "Teología" appears in Gustavo Gutiérrrez, *The Truth Shall Make You Free*, trans. Matthew J. O'Connell (Maryknoll, N.Y.: Orbis Books, 1990), pp. 53–81.

28. Gutiérrez, TL, p. ix.

29. Ibid., p. 15.

30. Ibid., p. 12.

31. Ibid., p. 13.

32. Ibid., p. 15.

33. Ibid., p. 14.

34. Ibid., p. 15.

35. Ibid., p. 89.

36. Ibid., pp. 36–37.

37. Ibid., p. 24.

38. Ibid., pp. 24–25.

39. Ibid., p. 84.

40. Ibid., chapter 6, and pp. 111–13.

41. Ibid., p. 87.

42. Ibid.

43. Ibid.

44. Ibid., p. 90.

45. Ibid., pp. 296–97.

46. Ibid., p. 301.

47. Ibid., p. 300.

48. Ibid., p. 301.

49. Ibid.

50. Gutiérrez's discussion of poverty and its three distinct meanings is an elaboration of similar distinctions found in the Medellín document "The Poverty of the Church." The latter's language appears to be politically neutral when compared to Gutiérrez's interpretation. See TL, pp. 305–6.

51. Gutiérrez, TL, pp. 139–40.

52. See José Martí, "Versos Sencillos," in *José Martí: Major Poems*, ed. Philip S. Foner, trans. Elinor Randall (New York: Holmes and Meier, 1982), pp. 66–67.

53. Camilo Torres, "Los 'No Alineados,'" in Horacio Bojorge et al., *Retrato de Camilo Torres* (Mexico: Grijalbo, 1969), pp. 154–56.

54. Camilo Torres, "Mensaje a los cristianos," in *Retrato*, p. 153.

55. Ibid., pp. 152–53.

56. Camilo Torres, "Proclama al Pueblo Colombiano," in *Retrato*, pp. 156–57.

57. In 1984 Gutiérrez reflects on the significance of the Eucharist in the context of a Christian community as follows: "To be a Christian is to be a witness of the Resurrection, to proclaim the kingdom of life. This is the life we celebrate in the Eucharist, the first task of the ecclesial community. In the breaking of the bread we commemorate the love and fidelity which took Jesus to his death, and [we commemorate] the confirmation of his mission, on behalf of all and especially on behalf of the poor, through his Resurrection. The breaking of the bread is, simultaneously, the point of departure and the point of arrival of the Christian community" ("Teología y las ciencias sociales," *Páginas* 9, nos. 63–64 [1984]: 15). See chap. 5, n. 27.

58. Gutiérrez, TL, p. 137. A clarification that may apply to these remarks is given in the revised edition to *A Theology of Liberation* (1988): "The fact that there are oppositions among members of the Christian com-

munity does not negate the principle of the church's essential unity, but they are indeed an obstacle on the church's historical journey toward this unity, an obstacle that must be overcome with lucidity and courage" (p. 161). Gutiérrez also states that the call to unity among Christians extends beyond the boundaries of the Catholic Church.

59. Gutiérrez, TL, p. 138.

60. Writing in 1979, Leonardo Boff states: "Today, for example, we perceive that the Christian ideal is closer to socialism than to capitalism. It is not a matter of creating a Christian socialism. It is a matter of being able to say that the socialist system, when actually carried out in reality, enables Christians better to live the humanitarian and divine ideals of their faith. These ideals can also be realized in the capitalist system, as we see from centuries of Christianity lived by a capitalist society. But the capitalist system is attended by many contradictions that could be overcome in another system—which for its part will present other contradictions, but lesser ones" (*Salvation and Liberation*, pp. 10–11).

61. Gutiérrez, TL, pp. 26–27.

62. Ibid., p. 30.

63. Ibid., pp. 111–13.

64. Ibid., p. 111.

65. Ibid., p. 202.

66. Ibid.

67. TL, p. 112. The citation is to *El presente de Chile y el Evangelio*, mimeo (Santiago de Chile, 1970). Cf. TL, rev. ed., p. 66.

68. Gutiérrez, TL, p. 112.

69. Ibid., p. 113. Cited in *El Mercurio*, 17 April 1971.

70. Gutiérrez, TL, pp. 113–14.

71. Ibid., p. 113.

72. On the Nicaraguan process, see Richard Harris and Carlos M. Vilas, eds., *La revolución en Nicaragua: liberación nacional, democracia popular y transformación económica* (Mexico: Ediciones Era, 1985) and Donald C. Hodges, *Intellectual Foundations of the Nicaraguan Revolution* (Austin: University of Texas Press, 1986); on religion in socialist Cuba, see Raúl Vidales, ed., *II Encuentro internacional de teólogos y científicos sociales* [Cuba, 1983] (Mexico: Conferencia Cristiana por la Paz de Latinoamérica y el Caribe [1983?]). In Cuba the policies affecting religious belief improved significantly after the publication of *Fidel y la religión:*

Conversaciones con Frei Betto (Havana: Oficina de Publicaciones del Consejo de Estado, 1985).

73. For an analysis of conservative arguments against liberation theology and defenses against them, see Anselm Kyongsuk Min, *Dialectic of Salvation: Issues in Theology of Liberation* (Albany: State University of New York Press, 1989).

Chapter 6. The Philosophy of Liberation in Critical Perspective

1. Hugo E. Biagini, *Filosofía americana e identidad: el conflictivo caso argentino* (Buenos Aires: Editorial Universitaria, 1989), p. 309.

2. Ibid.

3. Susan Calvert and Peter Calvert, *Argentina: Political Culture and Instability* (Pittsburgh: University of Pittsburgh Press, 1989), pp. 157–58.

4. Biagini, p. 310. Biagini makes a similar point in "Contemporary Argentinian Philosophy," in *Philosophy and Literature in Latin America*, ed. Jorge J. E. Gracia and Mireya Camurati (Albany: State University of New York Press, 1989), pp. 10–11.

5. In a note to the English language edition of *Philosophy of Liberation*, Dussel mentions that eighteen professors were expelled from the faculty of philosophy at the Universidad Nacional de Cuyo in Mendoza, Argentina, and that similar things took place all over the country. He states that books published by the editorial house Siglo XXI were shredded and that half of the students in the philosophy department at UNC–Mendoza were expelled and not allowed to enroll in any other Argentine university. See Enrique Dussel, *Philosophy of Liberation*, trans. Aquilina Martinez and Christine Morkovsky (Maryknoll, N.Y.: Orbis Books, 1985), p. 200.

6. See Arturo A. Roig, "Un proceso de cambio en la universidad argentina actual (1966–1973)," *Revista de filosofía latinoamericana* 1 (1975): 101–24.

7. Horacio Cerutti Guldberg, *Filosofía de la liberación latinoamericana* (Mexico: Fondo de Cultura Económica, 1983). See also Horacio Cerutti Guldberg, "Actual Situation and Perspectives of Latin American Philosophy for Liberation," *The Philosophical Forum* 20, nos. 1–2 (1988–89): 43–61. For Cerutti's first (and highly interesting) critique of the philosophy of liberation, see "Ubicación política de los orígenes y el desarrollo de la Filosofía de la Liberación latinoamericana," *Cuadernos salmantinos de filosofía* [Salamanca, Spain] 3 (1976): 351–60. Other related publica-

tions by Cerutti include: "Posibilidades y límites de una filosofía después de la 'Filosofía de la Liberación,'" *Anales de la Universidad de Cuenca* [Ecuador] 33 (1978): 9–17; the foreword to a special edition of *Nuestra América* [Mexico] 11 (1984), on the subject of the philosophy of liberation, with contributions by Enrique Dussel, Abelardo Villegas, Arturo Roig, Edgar Montiel, María Luisa Rivara de Tuesta, Ofelia Schutte, Gregor Sauerwald, and Manuel Velázquez; and "Revolución francesa y filosofía para la liberación," *Cuadernos americanos: nueva época* 6 (1989): 70–77.

8. See Ofelia Schutte, "Origins and Tendencies of the Philosophy of Liberation in Latin American Thought: A Critique of Dussel's Ethics," *The Philosophical Forum* 22:3 (1991): 270–95. A forthcoming issue is expected to include Dussel's response.

9. Cerutti, FLL, p. 314.

10. Ibid., p. 315.

11. See Cerutti in FLL, p. 31 and Enrique Dussel, *Introducción a la filosofía de la liberación* (2d ed.; Bogota: Editorial Nueva América, 1982), p. 20. (First published in 1977, this book was reedited in 1979 with an extensive biographical introduction.) The names of Rodolfo Kusch and Carlos Cullen are mentioned by Juan Carlos Scannone, S.J., in "Religión del pueblo, sabiduría popular y filosofía inculturada," in *III Congreso internacional de filosofía latinomericana* (Bogota: Universidad Santo Tomás, 1985), pp. 200 and 205.

12. Cerutti, FLL, p. 83.

13. See Oscar Terán, *En busca de la ideología argentina* (Buenos Aires: Catálogos, 1986), pp. 195–253.

14. Dussel, "La filosofía de la liberación en Argentina: Irrupción de una nueva generación filosófica," in *La filosofía actual en América Latina* (Mexico: Grijalbo, 1976), pp. 55–62; cited in Cerutti, FLL, p. 31.

15. See Mark C. Taylor, ed., *Altarity* (Chicago: University of Chicago Press, 1987), p. xxvii.

16. See the concluding remarks to chapter 4.

17. Dussel, IFL, p. 16.

18. Dussel, *La producción teórica de Marx: un comentario a los Grundrisse* (Mexico: Siglo XXI, 1985), p. 11. Dussel's recent work on Marx includes *Hacia un Marx desconocido* (Mexico: Siglo XXI, 1988), and a third volume is forthcoming. The idea of reconstructing Marx's theory from the standpoint of Dussel's philosophy of liberation was a product of the "Mexican stage" of Dussel's thought. He states that now that he is sit-

uated in Mexico, his philosophical "interlocutors" will be different from those he had in Argentina: "Here, the interlocutors of a national, popular Latin American [position]…are [Anglo-American analytic] philosophical logic…and North-Atlantic [Western] Marxism" (IFL, pp. 28–29).

19. Dussel, IFL, p. 20.

20. Enrique Dussel, "Para una fundación dialéctica de la liberación latinoamericana," *Stromata* 30:1–2 (1974): 84 and 89, respectively. Cited in Cerutti, FLL, p. 255.

21. Enrique Dussel, *Para una ética de la liberación latinoamericana* (2 vols.; Buenos Aires: Siglo XXI, 1973). Three other volumes followed: *Filosofía ética latinoamericana 6/III* (Mexico: Edicol, 1977), *Filosofía ética latinoamericana IV* (Bogota: Universidad Santo Tomás, 1979), and *Filosofía ética latinoamericana V* (Bogota: Universidad Santo Tomás, 1980). A summary of his position appeared as *Filosofía de la liberación* (Mexico: Edicol, 1977). It was reprinted with corrections and published under the same title by the Universidad Santo Tomás, Bogota, 1980. The English translation, *Philosophy of Liberation*, op. cit., is from the Bogota edition.

22. See chap. 6, nn. 18, 21.

23. See Jorge J. E. Gracia and Iván Jaksić, "The Problem of Philosophical Identity in Latin America," *Inter-American Review of Bibliography* 34 (1984): 53–71 and Jorge J. E. Gracia, ed., *Latin American Philosophy in the Twentieth Century*, pp. 209–16. Other discussions of this topic include: Pablo Guadarrama, *Valoraciones sobre el pensamiento filosófico cubano y latinoamericano* (Havana: Editora Política, 1985); Raúl Fornet Betancourt, *Problemas actuales de la filosofía en Hispanoamérica* (Buenos Aires: Ediciones FEPAI, 1985); and Alejandro Serrano Caldera, *Filosofía y crisis: en torno a la posibilidad de la filosofía latinoamericana* (Mexico: UNAM, 1987).

24. This discussion will not cover the articles by Mario Casalla and Daniel Guillot.

25. Roig, "Un proceso de cambio en la universidad argentina actual."

26. Arturo Roig, "Cuatro tomas de posición a esta altura de los tiempos," *Nuestra América* 11 (1984): 58.

27. Osvaldo Ardiles, "Líneas básicas para un proyecto de filosofar latinoamericano," *Revista de filosofía latinoamericana* 1 (1975): 5–15.

28. Ibid., p. 6.

29. Ibid., p. 7.

30. Ibid.

31. Ibid., pp. 6–7.

32. Ibid., p. 8.

33. Ibid., p. 9.

34. Ibid., p. 12.

35. Ibid.

36. Ibid., p. 13.

37. Ibid., p. 9.

38. Among the best-known Argentine philosophers whose thought has been influential in this century are Alexandro Korn (1860–1936), José Ingenieros (1877–1925), Francisco Romero (1891–1962), Carlos Astrada (1886–1970), and Risieri Frondizi (1910–83).

39. See Schutte, "Origins and Tendencies of the Philosophy of Liberation in Latin American Thought: A Critique of Dussel's Ethics."

40. Enrique Dussel, "Elementos para una filosofía politica latinoamericana," *Revista de filosofía latinoamericana* 1 (1975): 61.

41. Ibid., p. 70.

42. Ibid., pp. 73–74.

43. Ibid., p. 74.

44. Ibid., p. 78.

45. Ibid., p. 80.

46. See Dussel, PL, pp. 156–60.

47. See Emmanuel Levinas, *Totality and Infinity: An Essay on Exteriority*, trans. Alphonso Lingis (The Hague: Martinus Nijhoff, 1979). Originally published as *Totalité et infini: essai sur l'exteriorité* (The Hague: Martinus Nijhoff, 1961). Dussel had studied with Levinas in Paris.

48. Dussel, PL, pp. 84–85.

49. Ibid., p. 166.

50. "The 'system' pretends to be the only pedagogical means [adequate to] fulfill its finality.... In the same way, for example, the 'educational system' assumes that the child [el niño] is completely ignorant, a *tabula rasa*,...an orphan, [someone] without culture (because *popular culture* is devalued as inexistent). The 'school' thus takes upon itself the sublime duty to offer the whole of culture to the child.... What is true is that

in this way it eliminates the educational subsystems, for in the past it has been the family, the old man of the neighborhood or barrio, the priest or the [child's] aunt who educated the children" (Dussel, FEL, p. 162). The situation in real life, however, is that the school environment, while ideological, is no more or less ideologically charged than the environment of the barrio, where informal 'schooling' might be conducted by the old man, the priest, or the aunt named in the example. None of these systems or 'subsystems' is a totality unto itself. The barrio and the school are interacting networks of information at times coexisting, at times clashing with each other. Oversimplifying the matter will not solve the problems of oppression/liberation depicted by this example.

51. Dussel, FEL, p. 146.

52. Ibid., p. 151.

53. Dussel, PL, p. 25.

54. Rodolfo Kusch, "Una reflexión filosófica en torno al trabajo de campo," *Revista de filosofía latinoamericana* 1 (1975): 90–100. Also published as "Filosofía del trabajo de campo" in R. Kusch, *Geocultura del hombre americano* (Buenos Aires: Fernando García Cambeiro, 1976), pp. 123–35.

55. Kusch, "Una reflexión filosófica," p. 90

56. Ibid., pp. 90–91.

57. Ibid., p. 91.

58. Ibid.

59. Ibid., p. 92.

60. Ibid., p. 96.

61. Ibid., p. 98.

62. Ibid.

63. Ibid., p. 99.

64. Ibid.

65. Ibid., p. 100.

66. Ibid.

67. Horacio Cerutti, "Propuesta para una filosofía política latinoamericana," *Revista de filosofía latinoamericana* 1 (1975): 51–59.

68. Ibid., p. 53.

69. Ibid.

70. Ibid., pp. 54–55.

71. Ibid., p. 56.

72. Ibid., p. 58.

73. See chapter 4, and Ofelia Schutte, "The Master-Slave Dialectic in Latin America: The Social Criticism of Zea, Freire, and Roig," *The Owl of Minerva* 22 (1990): 5–18.

74. Cerutti, "Propuesta...," p. 59.

75. Ibid.

76. Cerutti has maintained this line of thought until the present time. He continues to pursue a philosophy "for" liberation, insisting that such a philosophy should not collapse into what he has designated in various publications as a "populist" philosophy "of liberation." As early as 1976 his critique of positions held by Dussel, Scannone, Casalla, and Kusch appeared in Spain. Although he warns that each of these authors takes a different stand on liberation, he sketches some political and epistemological traits characterizing this group, insofar as their views may be contrasted with those of a "dissident" sector, critical of populism: "Populism postulates the need for a first philosophy that is ethical and political and that is foundational for scientific discourse and political praxis.... Those of us who were dissidents indicated that to postulate a first philosophy, no matter how well 'dressed up' with adjectives such as 'ethical,' 'political,' or 'of liberation,' was nothing more than to reiterate the...logos of a philosophy modeled upon Aristotelianism [whose character of 'first philosophy' is] to be overcome" ("Ubicación...," p. 358). Cerutti also charges the group supporting populism with using censorship against the dissident sector of the philosophy of liberation, of which he was a member (ibid., p. 355). For other relevant publications by Cerutti, see chap. 6, n. 7.

77. Terán, *En busca de la ideología argentina*, pp. 195–253.

78. See Biagini, *Filosofía americana e identidad*, op. cit.

79. A notable exception to the conservative reading of Heidegger is the case of Carlos Astrada (1894–1970), who had studied with Heidegger in Freiburg in the late 1920s and later became a well-known Argentine Heideggerian until about the end of the Second World War, when he developed a strong interest in Western Marxism. (See Gracia, ed., *Latin American Philosophy in the Twentieth Century*, pp. 117–33.) Astrada's way of relating Marxism and Heideggerian phenomenology differs sharply from that of the liberation philosophers. Whereas Astrada uses Marxism to criticize a conservative approach to the interpretation of Heidegger's

thought, the populist wing of liberation philosophy would use Heidegger's critique of modernity and scientific-technological thinking to criticize Marxism. Astrada died in 1970, before the philosophy of liberation movement took shape in Argentina.

80. Ardiles, "Líneas...," pp. 10–11.

81. Ibid., p. 14.

82. Ibid., p.10.

83. Ibid.

84. Mario Casalla, "Husserl, Europa, y la justificación ontológica del imperialismo," *Revista latinoamericana de filosofía* 1 (1975): 35.

85. In the section on "Economics" in PL, Dussel does not offer any hints except that an "economics of liberation" would be one of "service to the other as other" and that "it is worship offered to the Absolute" (pp. 151–52).

86. Dussel argues against the dissolubility of marriage (FEL, p. 196), the infertile couple (p. 106), "feminist homosexuality" (p. 117), and sexual pleasure disconnected from procreation, which he calls "homosexualizing" (p. 120; cf. pp. 85–97). See also "Filicide," in PL, pp. 90–95, and "Erotics," PL, pp. 78–87.

87. The intention to revise his past position on abortion and homosexuality was made known during a presentation at the First International Meeting of Latin American Philosophy, Ciudad Juárez, Mexico, 21 May 1990. Dussel stated that the basic principle guiding his position is that "the person is not a means but only an end."

88. Terán, *En busca de la ideología argentina,* pp. 247–49.

89. Dussel, FEL, pp. 88–97.

90. Ibid., p. 117.

91. Ibid., p. 120; cf. pp. 85–97.

92. Dussel, PL, pp. 87–88. See also FEL, p. 121.

93. Cf. Dussel, PL, pp. 158–59.

Chapter 7. Cultural Identity, Liberation, and Feminist Theory

1. Carlos Vaz Ferreira, *Sobre feminismo,* in *Obras de Carlos Vaz Ferreira* (Montevideo: Impresora Uruguaya, 1957), 9:37–38ff.

2. See Silvia Rodríguez Villamil, "Los 'feminismos' de comienzos de siglo en Uruguay," in *Nuestra memoria, nuestro futuro: mujeres e historia*, ed. María del Carmen Feijoo (Santiago, Chile: Isis Internacional, 1988), pp. 67–78. Rodríguez Villamil notes that in Uruguay, the order of appearance of various feminist positions was as follows: anarchist, socialist, "Batllist," and communist. She also notes that socialist women called themselves both "socialist" and "feminist" without viewing this as contradictory. For an analysis of the reformist-revolutionary characteristics of Batllismo, see Abelardo Villegas, *Reformismo y revolución en el pensamiento latinoamericano* (5th ed.; Mexico: Siglo XXI, 1980), pp. 117–40. For a historical background on women's political movements in Latin America, including the feminist movements of the early and late parts of the twentieth century, see Luis Vitale, *La mitad invisible de la historia latinoamericana: el protagonismo social de la mujer* (Buenos Aires: Sudamericana/Planeta, 1987).

3. Graciela Hierro, ed., *La naturaleza femenina* (Mexico: UNAM, 1985).

4. See Anna Macías, *Against All Odds: The Feminist Movement in Mexico to 1940* (Westport, Conn.: Greenwood Press, 1982), pp. 4–5.

5. Angel Flores and Kate Flores, eds., *Poesía feminista del mundo hispano* (Mexico: Siglo XXI, 1984), p. 60.

6. Sor Juana Inés de la Cruz, *Respuesta a Sor Filotea de la Cruz* (Mexico: Distribuciones Hispánicas, 1986), p. 19.

7. Gloria Ardaya, "Mujeres en las rebeliones indígenas de 1780–1781," in *Nuestra memoria, nuestro futuro*, ed. Feijoo, pp. 33–42.

8. The 1987 meeting, hosted by Mexico, included the participation of approximately fifteen hundred women and offered more than one hundred workshops on such topics as feminism and religion, health care, lesbian mothers, and a dialogue with members of the Federation of Cuban Women. See Rosa Ma. Rodríguez and Isabel Barranco, "Miscelánea 'mi luchita,'" *fem* 11, no. 60 (1987): 5–9. The 1990 meeting, held in Argentina, was attended by nearly double the number of women who attended the previous Encuentro.

9. Some papers from the Argentine conference have appeared in AAMEF's publication *Hiparquia* 3 (1990) and 4 (1991).

10. Graciela Hierro, *Ética y feminismo* (Mexico: UNAM, 1985). See also Graciela Hierro, *De la domesticación a la educación de las mexicanas* (Mexico: Editorial Fuego Nuevo, 1989).

11. "Bibliografía básica feminista," *fem* 2, no. 5 (1977): 91–93.

12. Examples of this genre include the novel *Hasta no verte, Jesús*

mío (Mexico: Ediciones Era, 1969) by the Mexican Elena Poniatowska, and the testimonial narratives of the Bolivian Domitila Barrios and the Guatemalan Rigoberta Menchú. See Moema Viezzer, *"Si me permiten hablar..." Testimonio de Domitila* (2d ed.; Mexico: Siglo XXI, 1978), and Elizabeth Burgos, *Me llamo Rigoberta y así me nació la conciencia* (Mexico: Siglo XXI, 1985).

13. See the special issue on "Las mujeres: la mayoría marginada," in *Nueva sociedad* [Caracas], 78 (July/August 1985): 40–135. Essays include: Carmen Lugo, "Machismo y violencia"; Ana Vázquez, "Feminismo: dudas y contradicciones"; Julieta Kirkwood, "Feministas y políticas"; Virginia Olivo de Celli, "Igualdad y autonomía"; and Haydée Birgin, "Cuando del poder se trata: la mujer en el tercer mundo." A collection of twenty-two feminist essays, including most of the essays mentioned, is *Y hasta cuándo esperaremos mandan-dirun-dirun-dán: mujer y poder en América Latina*, ed. Alberto Koschützke (Caracas: Editorial Nueva Sociedad, 1989).

14. Hierro, "La moralidad vigente y la condición femenina," in *La naturaleza femenina*, ed. Hierro, p. 111.

15. Navarro, "Ideología patriarcal," in *La naturaleza femenina*, ed. Hierro, pp. 97–98.

16. Ibid., pp. 101–2.

17. Mirta Henault, "Argentina: mujeres en la resistencia I," *fem* 8, no. 37 (1984–85): 47–49. Special issue of *fem* on "Women and violence."

18. Ximena Bunster-Burotto, "Surviving Beyond Fear: *Women and Torture in Latin America*" in June Nash and Helen Safa, eds., *Women and Change in Latin America* (South Hadley, Mass.: Bergin and Garvey, 1986), pp. 297–325.

19. Carmen González, "Violencia en las instituciones jurídicas," in *La mujer y la violencia invisible*, ed. Eva Giberti and Ana María Fernández (Buenos Aires: Editorial Sudamericana and Fundación Banco Patricios, 1989), p. 181.

20. Under Marianella García-Villas's leadership, the Comisión de Derechos Humanos of El Salvador was able to document the following cases of violations against human rights in that country between October 1979 and December 1982: 43,337 murders, 3,200 disappeared persons, and more than 700 political prisoners. Numerous human rights leaders and Archbishop Oscar Romero (murdered in 1980 by right-wing forces) were among the many victims. Between 1980 and 1983 the Salvadoran nongovernmental commission headed by Marianella García-Villas received the Dutch Jaap Van Praaf award, the Spanish Isabel la Católica medal, and a Swedish prize for its journalistic work in defense of human

rights. García-Villas also served as vice-president of the International Federation for Human Rights, a United Nations consultant organization ("Marianella García-Villas, víctima de la represión en El Salvador," *fem* 7, no. 28 [1983]: 42).

21. Ibid. Several issues of *fem* carry articles on the kidnapping and disappearance of Alaide Foppa.

22. Judith Astelarra, "La violencia doméstica," *fem* 8, no. 37 (1984–85): 7–9 and Ana Valdemoro, "Crimen contra las mujeres," *fem* 1, no. 4 (1977): 22–25. See also María Norma Mogrovejo Aquise, "La violación en el Perú: realidad y tratamiento jurídico," in *Y hasta cuándo esperaremos*, ed. Koschützke, pp. 241–51.

23. Carmen Lugo addresses the issue of "heterosexist hegemonic domination" in Mexican society in "Machismo y violencia," in *Y hasta cuándo esperaremos*, ed. Koschützke, pp. 219–30. First published in *Nueva sociedad* 78 (1985). The issue of violence against women is placed in the context of violence against ethnic minorities, handicapped people, prostitutes, and gays by a system of finance capital contributing to unemployment, welfare cutbacks, the increase of infant mortality and infant malnutrition, ill-health, and so on.

24. Due to the clandestine nature of illegal abortion, it is difficult to calculate the exact number of women's deaths. In 1985, Carmen Lugo cites a figure of possibly 80,000 deaths per year in Mexico (Lugo, "Machismo y violencia," in Koschützke, p. 229). Some have suggested the figures could be higher; but whether the number is in the hundreds or thousands, the problem cannot be erased (M. Acosta, "Fantasías y realidades sobre el aborto en México," *fem* 8, no. 31 (1983–84): 37. In Argentina, where a similar situation makes it difficult to give actual figures, a recent article suggests a rough estimate of one woman dying every two days from a clandestine abortion (Carmen González, "Violencia en las instituciones jurídicas," in *La mujer y la violencia invisible*, ed. Giberti and Fernández, p. 180).

25. Mary Garcia Castro, "Controle da natalidade, legalização do aborto e feminismo," *Revista civilização brasileira*, no. 26 (1980): 223–31.

26. Lourdes Arizpe, "¿Beneficia el desarrollo económico a la mujer?" *fem* 1, no. 1 (1976): 27–34.

27. Ibid., p. 29.

28. Ibid., p. 34.

29. Lourdes Benería and Martha Roldán, *The Crossroads of Class and Gender: Industrial Homework, Subcontracting, and Household Dynamics in Mexico City* (Chicago: University of Chicago Press, 1987), p. 6. See also Helen Safa, "Female Employment in the Puerto Rican Working

Class" and Marianne Schmink, "Women and Industrial Development in Brazil," in *Women and Change in Latin America,* ed. Nash et al., pp. 84–105, 136–64.

30. Jorge Carrillo, "Transformaciones en la industria maquiladora de exportación," in *Las maquiladoras: ajuste estructural y desarrollo regional* (Tijuana, Mexico: El Colegio de la Frontera del Norte and Fundación Friedrich Ebert, 1989), p. 42.

31. Ibid., p. 49.

32. Carrillo notes other factors as responsible for the gradual masculinization of the work force, namely, the growth of the auto parts industry, automation, and the scarcity of a female work force in some of the border cities (p. 49). It should be noted, however, that the group within which hiring takes place is one of young, single women willing to sign up for temporary job contracts.

33. María Patricia Fernández Kelly, "Tecnología y empleo femenino en la frontera México-Estados Unidos," in *Fuerza de trabajo femenino urbano en México: participación económica y política,* ed. Jennifer Cooper et al. (2 vols.: Mexico: UNAM and Grupo Editorial Miguel Angel Porrúa, 1989), 2:382–83. See also Rubi Jiménez Betancourt, "Participación femenina en la industria maquiladora, cambios recientes," in the same collection, 2:393–424.

34. Guillermina Valdés-Villalba, "Aprendizaje para la producción y transferencia de tecnología en la industria de maquila de exportación," in *Reestructuración industrial: maquiladoras en la frontera México-Estados Unidos,* ed. Jorge Carrillo (Mexico: Consejo Nacional de Fomento Educativo, 1989), p. 376.

35. Estela Suárez, "La fuerza de trabajo femenina en el sector servicios," in *Fuerza de trabajo femenina,* ed. Cooper et al., 2:501.

36. *Five Studies on the Situation of Women in Latin America* (Santiago, Chile: United Nations [Estudios e Informes de la CEPAL], 1983), p. 187.

37. For the first time in the last hundred years, domestic work took second place in terms of the proportion of female representation. The first place was held by the health sector, where women made up 86 percent of the work force. Yet health only takes up 7.1 percent of the service sector in contrast to 35 percent represented by domestic work. See Estela Suárez, "La fuerza de trabajo femenina en el sector servicios," *Fuerza de trabajo femenina,* ed. Cooper and Barbieri, 2:541–16, 532, 534.

38. *Mujer y trabajo doméstico* (Bogota: Servicio Colombiano de Comunicación Social, Serie "Mujer y Sociedad," 1981), 58 pages. See also Mary Garcia Castro, "A questão da mulher na reprodução da força de trabalho," *Revista civilizão brasileira,* no. 26 (1980): 157–71.

39. See Elizabeth Stone, ed., *Women and the Cuban Revolution* (New York: Pathfinder Press, 1981), pp. 16–18.

40. For excerpts from the Family Code and other official documents concerning women in Cuba, see Elizabeth Stone, ed., *Women and the Cuban Revolution*, pp. 133–51. For the complete text of the Family Code and other important documents, see *La mujer en Cuba socialista*, an official publication of the Cuban Ministry of Justice (Havana: Editorial Orbe, 1977). For a journalistic account of women's rights in Cuba, see Ana María Radselli, "Por la plena igualdad de la mujer," *Cuba internacional* (July 1985): 36–43. For women in Nicaragua, see Elizabeth Maier, *Nicaragua: la mujer en revolución* (Mexico: Ediciones de Cultura Popular, 1980) and *Las sandinistas* (Mexico: Ediciones de Cultura Popular, 1985). See also Aida Redondo Lubo, "La mujer en la construcción de la nueva sociedad," in *La revolución en Nicaragua*, ed. Richard Harris and Carlos M. Vilas (Mexico: Ediciones Era, 1985), pp. 239–57. Redondo Lubo's essay was left out of the English-language edition of this work.

41. See Orlandina de Oliveira, ed., *Trabajo, poder y sexualidad* (Mexico: El Colegio de México, 1989), pp. 53–58. Five essays on domestic work from a wide variety of perspectives are included in this collection.

42. Yolanda Corona Caraveo, "Conceptualización y valoración del trabajo doméstico: el punto de vista de los niños," in *Trabajo, poder y sexualidad*, ed. Oliveira, pp. 81–101.

43. Noemí Ehrenfeld Lenkiewicz, "El ser mujer: identidad, sexualidad y reproducción," in *Trabajo, Poder y Sexualidad*, ed. Oliveira, p. 392.

44. Elizabeth Jelin, ed., *Ciudadanía y participación: las mujeres en los movimientos sociales latino-americanos*, foreword by Lourdes Arizpe (Geneva: United Nations Research Institute for Social Development, 1987), p. 322.

45. Jelin, ed., *Ciudadanía y participación*, p. 5.

46. Ibid., p. xvi. From the foreword, "Democracy for a Small Bigeneric Planet," by Lourdes Arizpe.

47. Ibid., p. xviii.

48. Isabel Larguía and John Dumoulin, *Hacia una concepción científica de la emancipación de la mujer* (Havana: Editorial Ciencias Sociales, 1983). Reissued with an additional final chapter as *La mujer nueva: teoría y práctica de su emancipación* (Buenos Aires: Centro Editor de América Latina, 1988).

49. Larguía and Dumoulin, *Hacia una concepción*, pp. 13–14.

50. Ibid., p. 20.

51. Ibid., p. 26.

BIBLIOGRAPHY

Abril, Xavier, et al. *Mariátegui y la literatura*. Lima: Empresa Editora Amauta, 1980.

Alberdi, Juan Bautista. *Bases y puntos de partida para la organización política de la República Argentina*. Buenos Aires: Ediciones Estrada, 1943.

Aman, Kenneth. "Marxism(s) in Liberation Theology." *Crosscurrents* 34 (1984–85): 427–38.

Ardiles, Osvaldo. "Líneas básicas para un proyecto de filosofar latinoamericano." *Revista de filosofía latinoamericana* 1 (1975): 5–15.

Ardiles, Osvaldo, Hugo Assmann, et al. *Hacia una filosofía de la liberación latinoamericana*. Buenos Aires: Editorial Bonum, 1973.

Aricó, José. *Marx y América Latina*. 2d ed. Mexico: Alianza Editorial Mexicana, 1982.

———, ed. *Mariátegui y los orígenes del marxismo latinoamericano*. 2d ed. Mexico: Ediciones Pasado y Presente, 1980.

Arizpe, Lourdes. "¿Beneficia el desarrollo económico a la mujer?" *fem* 1, no. 1 (1976): 27–34.

———. "Democracia para un pequeño planeta bigenérico." Foreword to *Ciudadanía y participación: las mujeres en los movimientos sociales latino-americanos*, edited by Elizabeth Jelin. Geneva: UNRISD, 1987.

———. "El 'indio': mito, profecía, prisión." In *América Latina en sus ideas*, edited by Leopoldo Zea. Mexico and Paris: Siglo XXI and UNESCO, 1986.

Benería, Lourdes, and Martha Roldán. *The Crossroads of Class and Gender: Industrial Homework, Subcontracting, and Household Dynamics in Mexico City*. Chicago: University of Chicago Press, 1987.

Bergson, Henri. *Creative Evolution*. Translated by A. Mitchell. New York: Henry Holt and Co., 1913.

Berruezo León, María Teresa. *La lucha de Hispanoamérica por su independencia en Inglaterra. 1800–1830*. Madrid: Ediciones de Cultura Hispánica, 1989.

Bethell, Leslie, ed. *Spanish America after Independence c. 1820–c. 1870.* Cambridge: Cambridge University Press, 1987.

Biagini, Hugo E. "Contemporary Argentinian Philosophy." In *Philosophy and Literature in Latin America,* edited by Jorge J. E. Gracia and Mireya Camurati. Albany: State University of New York Press, 1989.

————. *Filosofía americana e identidad: el conflictivo caso argentino.* Buenos Aires: Editorial Universitaria, 1989.

Boff, Leonardo, and Clodovis Boff. *Salvation and Liberation: In Search of a Balance between Faith and Politics.* Translated by Robert R. Barr. Maryknoll, N.Y.: Orbis Books, 1984.

Bojorge, Horacio, et al. *Retrato de Camilo Torres.* Mexico: Grijalbo, 1969.

Calvert, Susan and Peter Calvert. *Argentina: Political Culture and Instability.* Pittsburgh: University of Pittsburgh Press, 1989.

Carrillo, Jorge. "Transformaciones en la industria maquiladora de exportación." In *Las maquiladoras: ajuste estructural y desarrollo regional,* edited by Bernardo González Aréchiga and Rocío Barajas Escamilla. Tijuana, Mexico: El Colegio de la Frontera del Norte and Fundación Friedrich Ebert, 1989.

Casas, Bartolomé de las. *Del único modo de atraer a todos los pueblos a la verdadera religión.* Mexico: Fondo de Cultura Económica, 1942.

Caso, Antonio. *El problema de México y la ideología nacional.* Mexico: Libro-Mex, 1955.

Castro, Mary Garcia. "A questão da mulher na reproduçao da força de trabalho." *Revista civilizão brasileira,* no. 26 (1980): 157–71.

————. "Controle da natalidade, legalização do aborto e feminismo." *Revista civilização brasileira,* no. 26 (1980): 223–31.

Cerutti Guldberg, Horacio. "Actual Situation and Perspectives of Latin American Philosophy for Liberation." *The Philosophical Forum* 20 (1988–89): 43–61.

————. *Filosofía de la liberación latinoamericana.* Mexico: Fondo de Cultura Económica, 1983.

————. *Hacia una metodología de la historia de las ideas (filosóficas) en América Latina.* Guadalajara, Mexico: Universidad de Guadalajara, 1987.

————. "Posibilidades y límites de una filosofía después de la 'Filosofía de la Liberación.'" *Anales de la Universidad de Cuenca* [Ecuador] 33 (1978): 9–17.

———. "Propuesta para una filosofía política latinoamericana." *Revista de filosofía latinoamericana* 1 (1975): 51–59.

———. "Revolución francesa y filosofía para la liberación." *Cuadernos americanos: nueva época* 6 (1989): 70–77.

———. "Ubicación política de los orígenes y el desarrollo de la Filosofía de la Liberación latinoamericana." *Cuadernos salmantinos de filosofía* [Salamanca, Spain] 3 (1976): 351–60.

Chaney, Elsa M., and Mary Garcia Castro, eds. *Muchachas No More: Household Workers in Latin America and the Caribbean*. Philadelphia: Temple University Press, 1989.

Chavarría, Jesús. *José Carlos Mariátegui and the Rise of Modern Peru, 1890–1930*. Albuquerque: University of New Mexico Press, 1979.

Christian Peace Conference. *Christians in the Struggle for Liberation*. Translated by Stephanie Lindsey. Prague: Christian Peace Conference, 1985.

Cooper, Jennifer, Teresita de Barbieri, et al. *Fuerza de trabajo femenino urbano en México: participación económica y política*. 2 vols. Mexico: UNAM and Grupo Editorial Miguel Angel Porrúa, 1989.

Croce, Benedetto. *Historical Materialism and the Economics of Karl Marx*. Translated by C. M. Meredith. New York: Macmillan, 1924.

Crocker, David A. "Insiders and Outsiders in International Development Ethics." *Ethics and International Affairs* 5 (1991): 149–73.

Cruz, Sor Juana Inés de la. *Respuesta a Sor Filotea de la Cruz*. Mexico: Distribuciones Hispánicas, 1986.

Cueva, Mario de la, et al. *Estudios de la historia de la filosofía en México*. Mexico: UNAM, 1963.

Davis, Harold Eugene. *Latin American Thought: A Historical Introduction*. New York: The Free Press, 1972.

Dussel, Enrique. "Elementos para una filosofía política latinoamericana." *Revista de filosofía latinoamericana* 1 (1975): 60–80.

———. *Filosofía de la liberación*. Bogota: Universidad Santo Tomás, 1980.

———. *Filosofía ética latinoamericana V*. Bogota: Universidad Santo Tomás, 1980.

———. *Filosofía ética latinoamericana IV*. Bogota: Universidad Santo Tomás, 1979.

———. *Filosofía ética latinoamericana 6/III*. Mexico: Edicol, 1977.

———. *Hacia un Marx desconocido*. Mexico: Siglo XXI, 1988.

———. *Introducción a la filosofía de la liberación*. 2d ed. Bogota: Editorial Nueva América, 1982.

———. *Para una ética de la liberación latinoamericana*. 2 vols. Buenos Aires: Siglo XXI, 1973.

———. *Philosophy of Liberation*. Translated by Aquilina Martinez and Christine Morkovsky. Maryknoll, N.Y.: Orbis Books, 1985.

———. *La producción teórica de Marx: un comentario a los Grundrisse*. Mexico: Siglo XXI, 1985.

Easton, Loyd D., and Kurt H. Guddat, eds. *Writings of the Young Marx on Philosophy and Society*. Garden City, N.Y.: Doubleday Anchor Books, 1967.

Fanon, Frantz. *Black Skins, White Masks*. Translated by Charles Lam Markmann. New York: Grove Press, 1967.

———. *The Wretched of the Earth*. Translated by Constance Farrington. New York: Grove Press, 1963.

Feijoo, María del Carmen, ed. *Nuestra memoria, nuestro futuro: mujeres e historia*. Santiago, Chile: Isis Internacional, 1988.

Fern, Deane William. *Third World Liberation Theologies: An Introductory Survey*. Maryknoll, N.Y.: Orbis Books, 1986.

Fernández Retamar, Roberto. *Calibán. Apuntes sobre la cultura de nuestra América*. 2d ed. Mexico: Diógenes, 1974.

———. *Caliban and Other Essays*. Translated by Edward Baker. Minneapolis: University of Minnesota Press, 1989.

———. "Our America and the West." *Social Text* 15 (1986): 1–25.

Five Studies on the Situation of Women in Latin America. Estudios e Informes de la CEPAL. Santiago, Chile: United Nations, 1983.

Flores, Angel, and Kate Flores. *Poesía feminista del mundo hispano*. Mexico: Siglo XXI, 1984.

Flores Galindo, Alberto. *La agonía de Mariátegui: la polémica con la Komintern*. Lima: DESCO, 1980.

Fornet Betancourt, Raúl. *Problemas actuales de la filosofía en Hispanoamérica*. Buenos Aires: Ediciones FEPAI, 1985.

Freire, Paulo. *Acción cultural para la libertad*. Mexico: Casa Unida de Publicaciones, 1983.

———. *Pedagogy of the Oppressed.* Translated by Myra Bergman Ramos. New York: Seabury Press, 1970.

Freire, Paulo, and Augusto Salazar Bondy. *¿Qué es y cómo funciona la concientización?* Lima: Editorial Causachun, 1975.

Gaos, José. *En torno a la filosofía mexicana.* Mexico: Porrúa y Obregón, Editores, 1955.

———. *Filosofía mexicana de nuestros días.* Mexico: UNAM, 1954.

García Salvatecci, Hugo. *Sorel y Mariátegui.* Lima: Enrique Delgado Valenzuela, 1979[?].

Giberti, Eva, and Ana María Fernández, eds. *La mujer y la violencia invisible.* Buenos Aires: Editorial Sudamericana and Fundación Banco Patricios, 1989.

Goloboff, Gerardo Mario. "Ideas estéticas y literarias de José Carlos Mariátegui." *Cuadernos Hispanoamericanos* [Madrid], no. 395 (1983):1–10.

Gómez-Martínez, José Luis. "Consideraciones epistemológicas para una filosofía de la liberación." *Cuadernos americanos: nueva época* 4, no. 22 (1990): 106–19.

González Prada, Manuel. *Páginas libres, Horas de lucha.* Preface and notes by Luis Alberto Sánchez. Caracas: Biblioteca Ayacucho, 1976.

Gracia, Jorge J. E. "Importance of the History of Ideas in Latin America." *Journal of the History of Ideas* 36 (1975): 177–84.

———. "Philosophical Analysis in Latin America." *History of Philosophy Quarterly* 1 (1984): 111–22.

———, ed. *Latin American Philosophy in the Twentieth Century: Man, Values, and the Search for Philosophical Identity.* Buffalo: Prometheus Books, 1986.

Gracia, Jorge J. E., and Iván Jaksić. "The Problem of Philosophical Identity in Latin America." *Inter-American Review of Bibliography* 34 (1984): 53–71.

Gracia, Jorge J. E., and Mireya Camurati, eds. *Philosophy and Literature in Latin America: A Critical Assessment of the Current Situation.* Albany: State University of New York Press, 1989.

Gracia, Jorge J. E., and Iván Jaksić, eds. *Filosofía e identidad cultural en América Latina.* Caracas: Monte Avila Editores, 1983.

Gracia, Jorge J. E., Eduardo Rabossi, Enrique Villanueva, and Marcelo Dascal, eds. *Philosophical Analysis in Latin America.* Dordrecht: Reidel, 1984.

Guadarrama, Pablo. *Valoraciones sobre el pensamiento filosófico cubano y latinoamericano.* Havana: Editora Política, 1985.

Guadarrama, Pablo, and Edel Tussel Oropeza. *El pensamiento filosófico de Enrique José Varona.* Havana: Editorial Ciencias Sociales, 1986.

Guevara, Ernesto "Che." *Man and Socialism in Cuba.* Havana: Book Institute, 1967.

———. "El socialismo y el hombre en Cuba." In *Obra revolucionaria*, edited by Roberto Fernández Retamar. Mexico: Ediciones Era, 1967.

Gutiérrez, Gustavo. *A Theology of Liberation: History, Politics, and Salvation.* Translated and edited by Sister Caridad Inda and John Eagleson. Maryknoll, N.Y.: Orbis Books, 1973.

———. *A Theology of Liberation: History, Politics, and Salvation.* Translated and edited by Sister Caridad Inda and John Eagleson. 2d. ed., rev. Maryknoll, N.Y.: Orbis Books, 1988.

———. *The Truth Shall Make You Free: Confrontations.* Translated by Matthew J. O'Connell. Maryknoll, N.Y.: Orbis Books, 1990.

Hale, Charles. *The Transformation of Liberalism in Late Nineteenth-Century Mexico.* Princeton: Princeton University Press, 1989.

Harris, Richard, and Carlos M. Vilas, eds. *La revolución en Nicaragua: liberación nacional, democracia popular y transformación económica.* Mexico: Ediciones Era, 1985.

Hegel, G. W. F. *Lectures on the Philosophy of World History.* Translated by H. B. Nisbet. Cambridge: Cambridge University Press, 1975.

———. *The Phenomenology of Mind.* Translated by J. B. Baillie. New York: Harper Torchbooks, 1967.

Heidegger, Martin. "Letter on Humanism." In *Martin Heidegger: Basic Writings*, edited by David Farrell Krell. New York: Harper and Row, 1977.

Hierro, Graciela. *De la domesticación a la educación de las mexicanas.* Mexico: Editorial Fuego Nuevo, 1989.

———. *Ética y feminismo.* Mexico: UNAM, 1985.

———, ed. *La naturaleza femenina.* Mexico: UNAM, 1985.

Hodges, Donald C. *Intellectual Foundations of the Nicaraguan Revolution.* Austin: University of Texas Press, 1986.

Irigaray, Luce. *This Sex Which Is Not One.* Translated by Catherine Porter, with Carolyn Burke. Ithaca, N.Y.: Cornell University Press, 1985.

Jaksić, Iván. *Academic Rebels in Chile: The Role of Philosophy in Higher Education and Politics*. Albany: State University of New York Press, 1989.

James, William. *Essays in Pragmatism*. New York: Hafner Press, 1948.

Jelin, Elizabeth, ed. *Ciudadanía y participación: las mujeres en los movimientos sociales latino-americanos*. Foreword by Lourdes Arizpe. Geneva: United Nations Research Institute for Social Development, 1987.

———, ed. *Women and Social Change in Latin America*. Foreword by Lourdes Arizpe. Translated by J. Ann Zammit and Marilyn Thomson. Geneva: United Nations Research Institute for Social Development; London: Zed Books, 1990.

Knutson, April Ane, ed. *Ideology & Independence in the Americas*. Minneapolis: Marxist Educational Press, 1989.

Koschützke, Alberto, ed. *Y hasta cuándo esperaremos mandan-dirun-dirun-dán: mujer y poder en América Latina*. Caracas: Editorial Nueva Sociedad, 1989.

Kusch, Rodolfo. *Geocultura del hombre americano*. Buenos Aires: Fernando García Cambeiro, 1978.

———. "Una reflexión filosófica en torno al trabajo de campo." *Revista de filosofía latinoamericana* 1 (1975): 90–100.

Larguía, Isabel, and John Dumoulin. *Hacia una concepción científica de la emancipación de la mujer*. Havana: Editorial Ciencias Sociales, 1983.

———. *La mujer nueva: teoría y práctica de su emancipación*. Buenos Aires: Centro Editor de América Latina, 1988.

Lavrin, Asunción, ed. *Latin American Women: Historical Perspectives*. Westport, Conn.: Greenwood Press, 1978.

Levinas, Emmanuel. *Totality and Infinity: An Essay on Exteriority*. Translated by Alphonso Lingis. The Hague: Martinus Nijhoff, 1979.

Lipp, Solomon. *Leopoldo Zea: From Mexicanidad to a Philosophy of History*. Waterloo, Ont.: Wilfrid Laurier University Press, 1980.

———. *Three Argentine Thinkers*. New York: Philosophical Library, 1969.

———. *Three Chilean Thinkers*. Waterloo, Ont.: Wilfrid Laurier University Press, 1975.

Liss, Sheldon B. *Marxist Thought in Latin America*. Berkeley: University of California Press, 1984.

Löwy, Michael, ed. *El marxismo en América Latina (de 1909 a nuestros días)*. Translated by Oscar Barahona and U. Doyhamboure. Mexico: Ediciones Era, 1982.

Macías, Anna. *Against All Odds: The Feminist Movement in Mexico to 1940*. Westport, Conn.: Greenwood Press, 1982.

Maier, Elizabeth. *Nicaragua: la mujer en revolución*. Mexico: Ediciones de Cultura Popular, 1980.

————. *Las sandinistas*. Mexico: Ediciones de Cultura Popular, 1985.

"Marianella García-Villas, víctima de la represión en El Salvador." *fem* 7, no. 28 (1983): 42.

Mariátegui, José Carlos. *El alma matinal y otras estaciones del hombre de hoy*. 2d ed. Lima: Empresa Editora Amauta, 1959.

————. "The Anti-Imperialist Perspective." *New Left Review* 70 (1971): 67–72.

————. *Defensa del marxismo*. In *Obras,* edited by Francisco Baeza. 2 vols. Havana: Casa de las Américas, 1982.

————. *Obra política*. Edited by Rubén Jiménez Ricárdez. Mexico: Ediciones Era, 1979.

————. *Obras*. Edited by Francisco Baeza. 2 vols. Havana: Casa de las Américas, 1982.

————. *Obras completas de José Carlos Mariátegui*. 20 vols. Lima: Empresa Editora Amauta, 1957–70.

————. *Siete ensayos de interpretación de la realidad peruana*. Mexico: Ediciones Era, 1979.

————. *Seven Interpretive Essays on Peruvian Reality*. Translated by Marjory Urquidi. With an introduction by Jorge Basadre. Austin: University of Texas Press, 1971.

Mariátegui, José Carlos, and Ricardo Martínez de la Torre, eds. *Amauta: Revista mensual de doctrina, literatura, arte, polémica*. Facsimile edition in 6 vols. Lima: Empresa Editora Amauta, 1976.

Martí, José. *José Martí: Major Poems*. Edited by Philip S. Foner. Translated by Elinor Randall. New York: Holmes and Meier, 1982.

————. *Our America: Writings on Latin America and the Struggle for Cuban Independence*. Edited by Philip S. Foner. Translated by Elinor Randall et al. New York: Monthly Review Press, 1977.

————. *Política de nuestra América*. Edited by José Aricó. Prologue by Roberto Fernández Retamar. 2d. ed. Mexico: Siglo XXI, 1979.

Marx, Karl. *Capital: A Critique of Political Economy.* Edited by Frederick Engels. Translated by Samuel Moore and Edward Aveling. 3 vols. New York: International Publishers, 1967.

Min, Anselm Kyongsuk. *Dialectic of Salvation: Issues in Theology of Liberation.* Albany: State University of New York Press, 1989.

Miró Quesada, Francisco. "Ciencia y Técnica: Ideas o Mitoides." In *América Latina en sus ideas*, edited by Leopoldo Zea. Mexico and Paris: Siglo XXI and UNESCO, 1986.

———. *Despertar y proyecto del filosofar latinoamericano.* Mexico: Fondo de Cultura Económica, 1974.

———. "Man Without Theory." In *Latin American Philosophy in the Twentieth Century*, edited by Jorge J. E. Gracia. Buffalo: Prometheus Books, 1986.

———. *Proyecto y realización del filosofar latinoamericano.* Mexico: Fondo de Cultura Económica, 1981.

La mujer en Cuba socialista. Havana: Editorial Orbe, 1977.

Muñoz, Braulio. *Sons of the Wind: The Search for Identity in Spanish American Indian Literature.* New Brunswick: Rutgers University Press, 1982.

Nash, June, and Helen Safa, eds. *Sex and Class in Latin America.* New York: Praeger, 1976.

———, eds. *Women and Change in Latin America.* South Hadley, Mass.: Bergin and Garvey, 1986.

Nietzsche, Friedrich. *The Complete Works of Friedrich Nietzsche.* Edited by Oscar Levy. 18 vols. 1909–11. New York: Russell and Russell, 1964.

———. *Thus Spoke Zarathustra.* Translated by Walter Kaufmann. New York: Viking Press, 1966.

Nueva Sociedad [Caracas] 78 (1985): 40–135. Special issue: "Las mujeres: la mayoría marginada."

Nuñez, Estuardo. *La experiencia europea de Mariátegui y otros ensayos.* Lima: Empresa Editora Amauta, 1978.

Oliveira, Orlandina de, ed. *Trabajo, poder y sexualidad.* Mexico: El Colegio de México, 1989.

Oliver, Amy A. "Sobre algunas relaciones entre la filosofía de la historia y el feminismo." *Cuadernos americanos: nueva época* 22 (1990): 154–64.

Ortega y Gasset, José. *Meditations on Quixote.* Translated by Evelyn Rugg and Diego Marín. Prologue by Julián Marías. New York: W. W. Norton, 1961.

Paris, Robert, et al. *El marxismo latinoamericano de Mariátegui.* Buenos Aires: Ediciones de Crisis, 1973.

Paz, Octavio. *The Labyrinth of Solitude: Life and Thought in Mexico.* Translated by Lysander Kemp. New York: Grove Press, 1961.

Pérez-Stable, Marifeli. "Cuban Women and the Struggle for 'Conciencia.'" *Cuban Studies* 17 (1987): 51–72.

Pescatello, Ann, ed. *Female and Male in Latin America.* Pittsburgh: University of Pittsburgh Press, 1973.

Quijano, Aníbal. *Introducción a Mariátegui.* Mexico: Ediciones Era, 1982.

Ramos, Samuel. *Hacia un nuevo humanismo.* Mexico: Fondo de Cultura Económica, 1962.

———. *Historia de la filosofía en México.* Mexico: UNAM, 1943.

———. *El perfil del hombre y la cultura en México.* Mexico: Espasa-Calpe Mexicana, 1984.

———. *Profile of Man and Culture in Mexico.* Translated by Peter G. Earle. Austin: University of Texas Press, 1962.

Rodó, José Enrique. *La América nuestra.* Prologue by Arturo Ardao. Havana: Casa de las Américas, 1977.

———. *Ariel.* Madrid: Espasa-Calpe, 1948.

———. *Ariel.* Translated by Margaret Sayers Peden. Foreword by James W. Symington. Prologue by Carlos Fuentes. Austin: University of Texas Press, 1988.

Roig, Arturo Andrés. "The Actual Function of Philosophy in Latin America." In *Latin American Philosophy in the Twentieth Century,* edited by Jorge J. E. Gracia. Buffalo: Prometheus Books, 1986.

———. "Cuatro tomas de posición a esta altura de los tiempos." *Nuestra América* 11 (1984): 55–59.

———. *Filosofía, universidad y filósofos en América Latina.* Mexico: UNAM, 1981.

———. "Un proceso de cambio en la universidad argentina actual (1966–1973)." *Revista de filosofía latinoamericana* 1 (1975): 101–24.

———. *Teoría y crítica del pensamiento latinoamericano.* Mexico: Fondo de Cultura Económica, 1983.

Roth, Jack J. *The Cult of Violence: Sorel and the Sorelians*. Berkeley: University of California Press, 1980.

Safa, Helen Icken. "Women's Social Movements in Latin America." *Gender and Society* 4 (1990): 354–69.

Salazar Bondy, Augusto. "La alternativa del Tercer Mundo." In Jorge Bravo Bresani et al., *El reto del Perú en la perspectiva del tercer mundo*, pp. 97–118. Lima: Moncloa-Campodónico, 1972.

———. *¿Existe una filosofía de nuestra América?* Mexico: Siglo XXI, 1968.

———. *La filosofía en el Perú*. Bilingual edition. Washington: Unión Panamericana, 1954.

———. *Historia de las ideas en el Perú contemporáneo*. 2 vols. Lima: Francisco Moncloa, 1965.

———. "The Meaning and Problem of Hispanic American Thought." In *Latin American Philosophy in the Twentieth Century*, edited by Jorge J. E. Gracia. Buffalo: Prometheus Books, 1986.

———. *Para una filosofía del valor*. Santiago de Chile: Editorial Universitaria, 1971.

———. "El proceso de la instrucción pública." In Luis E. Valcárcel, *El problema del indio*, with Augusto Tamayo Vargas, "El proceso de la literatura," pp. 35–51. Lima: Empresa Editora Amauta, 1976.

———. *Sentido y problema del pensamiento filosófico hispano-americano*. With English translation and comments by Arthur Berndtson and Fernando Salmerón. Occasional Publications, no. 16. Lawrence: University of Kansas Center for Latin American Studies, 1969.

Salazar Bondy, Augusto, Leopoldo Zea, et al. *América Latina: filosofía y liberación. Simposio de filosofía latinoamericana*. Buenos Aires: Editorial Bonum, 1974.

Sánchez Vázquez, Adolfo. "Marxism in Latin America." *The Philosophical Forum* 20 (1988–89): 114–28.

Santos Moray, Mercedes, ed. *Marxistas de América: Julio Antonio Mella, José Carlos Mariátegui, Aníbal Ponce, Juan Marinello*. Havana: Editorial Arte y Literatura, 1985.

Sarmiento, Domingo Faustino. *Argirópolis*. Buenos Aires: Editorial Universitaria, 1968.

———. *Conflicto y armonía de las razas en América*. Buenos Aires: Editorial Intermundo, 1946.

———. *Facundo*. Buenos Aires: Ediciones Estrada, 1940.

Scannone, Juan Carlos, S.J. "Religión del pueblo, sabiduría popular y filosofía inculturada." In *III Congreso internacional de filosofía latinoamericana*. Bogota: Universidad Santo Tomás, 1985.

Schutte, Ofelia. *Beyond Nihilism: Nietzsche without Masks*. Chicago: University of Chicago Press, 1984.

———. "The Master-Slave Dialectic in Latin America: The Social Criticism of Zea, Freire, and Roig." *The Owl of Minerva* 22 (1990): 5–18.

———. "Nietzsche, Mariátegui, and Socialism: A Case of 'Nietzschean Marxism' in Peru?" *Social Theory and Practice* 14 (1988): 71–85.

———. "Origins and Tendencies of the Philosophy of Liberation in Latin American Thought: A Critique of Dussel's Ethics." *The Philosophical Forum* 22 (1991): 270–95.

———. "Philosophy and Feminism in Latin America: Perspectives on Gender Identity and Culture." *The Philosophical Forum* 20 (1988–89): 62–84.

———. "Toward an Understanding of Latin American Philosophy: Reflections on the Formation of a Cultural Identity." *Philosophy Today* 31 (1987): 19–34.

Sepúlveda, Juan Ginés de. *Tratado sobre las justas causas de la guerra contra los indios*. Mexico: Fondo de Cultura Económica, 1941.

Serrano Caldera, Alejandro. *Filosofía y crisis: en torno a la posibilidad de la filosofía latinoamericana*. Mexico: UNAM, 1987.

Sorel, George. *The Illusions of Progress*. Translated by John Stanley and Charlotte Stanley. Berkeley: University of California Press, 1969.

———. *Reflections on Violence*. Translated by T. E. Hulme and J. Roth. New York: Collier Books, 1961.

Stabb, Martin S. *In Quest of Identity*. Chapel Hill: University of North Carolina Press, 1967.

Stanley, John. *The Sociology of Virtue: The Political and Social Theories of George Sorel*. Berkeley: University of California Press, 1981.

Stein, William W. "An Anthropological Appreciation of José Carlos Mariátegui." *Revolutionary World* 49/50 (1982): 69–96.

———. "Images of the Peruvian Indian Peasant in the Work of José Carlos Mariátegui." *Historical Reflections/Réflexions Historiques* 11 (1984): 1–35.

Stone, Elizabeth, ed. *Women and the Cuban Revolution*. New York: Pathfinder Press, 1981.

Taylor, Mark C., ed. *Altarity*. Chicago: University of Chicago Press, 1987.

Terán, Oscar. *Aníbal Ponce: ¿El marxismo sin nación?* Mexico: Ediciones Pasado y Presente, 1983.

———. *En busca de la ideología argentina*. Buenos Aires: Catálogos, 1986.

Thomas, R. Hinton. *Nietzsche in German Politics and Society, 1890–1918*. La Salle, Ill.: Open Court, 1983.

Valcárcel, Carlos Daniel. *Rebeliones coloniales sudamericanas*. Mexico: Fondo de Cultura Económica, 1982.

Valcárcel, Luis. *Tempestad en los Andes*. Preface by José Carlos Mariátegui. Lima: Biblioteca Amauta, Editorial Minerva, 1927.

Valdés-Villalba, Guillermina. "Aprendizaje para la producción y transferencia de tecnología en la industria de maquila de exportación." In *Reestructuración industrial: maquiladoras en la frontera México-Estados Unidos*, edited by Jorge Carrillo. Mexico: Consejo Nacional de Fomento Educativo, 1989.

Vanden, Harry E. *Mariátegui: influencias en su formación ideológica*. Translated by José María Quimper. Lima: Empresa Editora Amauta, 1975.

———. *National Marxism in Latin America: José Carlos Mariátegui's Thought and Politics*. Boulder: Lynne Rienner Publishers, 1986.

Vasconcelos, José. *La raza cósmica*. Mexico: Espasa-Calpe Mexicana, 1948.

———. *Obras completas*. 4 vols. Mexico: Libreros Mexicanos Unidos, 1957–61.

Vaz Ferreira, Carlos. *Obras de Carlos Vaz Ferreira*. 25 vols. Montevideo: Cámara de Representantes de la República Oriental del Uruguay, 1957–63.

———. *Sobre feminismo*. Montevideo: Impresora Uruguaya, 1957.

Vidales, Raúl, ed. *II Encuentro internacional de teólogos y científicos sociales* [Cuba, 1983]. Mexico: Conferencia Cristiana por la Paz de Latinoamérica y el Caribe [1983?].

Villegas, Abelardo. *Autognosis: el pensamiento mexicano en el siglo XX*. Mexico: Instituto Panamericano de Geografía e Historia, 1985.

———. *Reformismo y revolución en el pensamiento latinoamericano*. 5th ed. Mexico: Siglo XXI, 1980.

Vitale, Luis. *La mitad invisible de la historia latinoamericana: el protagonismo social de la mujer*. Buenos Aires: Sudamericana/Planeta, 1987.

Zea, Leopoldo. "The Actual Function of Philosophy in Latin America." In *Latin American Philosophy in the Twentieth Century*, edited by Jorge J. E. Gracia. Buffalo: Prometheus Books, 1986.

———. *América como conciencia*. 1953. 2d ed. Mexico: UNAM, 1983.

———. *América en la historia*. Mexico: Fondo de Cultura Económica, 1957.

———. *Apogeo y decadencia del positivismo en México*. Mexico: El Colegio de México, 1944.

———. *Conciencia y posibilidad del mexicano*. With *El occidente y la conciencia de México* and *Dos ensayos sobre México y lo mexicano*. 1952 and 1953. Reprint. Mexico: Editorial Porrúa, 1982.

———. *Descubrimiento e identidad latinoamericana*. Mexico: UNAM, 1990.

———. *La filosofía americana como filosofía sin más*. Mexico: Siglo XXI, 1969.

———. *Filosofía de la historia americana*. Mexico: Fondo de Cultura Económica, 1978.

———. "Identity: A Latin American Philosophical Problem." *The Philosophical Forum* 20 (1988–89): 33–42.

———. *The Latin American Mind*. Translated by James H. Abbott and Lowell Dunham. Norman: University of Oklahoma Press, 1963.

———. *Latinoamérica Tercer Mundo*. Mexico: Extemporáneos, 1977.

———. *Positivism in Mexico*. Translated by Josephine Schulte. Austin: University of Texas Press, 1974.

———. *El positivismo en México*. Mexico: Fondo de Cultura Económica, 1968.

———. *The Role of the Americas in History*. Edited by Amy Oliver. Translated by Sonja Karsen. Savage, Md.: Rowman and Littlefield, 1992.

———, ed. *América Latina en sus ideas*. Mexico and Paris: Siglo XXI and UNESCO, 1986.

INDEX

Abortion, 203; and control over women's bodies, 214; legal aspects of, 217–18, 224, 226, 230; moral aspects of, 217–18

Absolutism: choice between, and critique, 199–200. *See also* Alterity, as ground for new absolute, in Dussel

Acción cultural para la libertad, 143, 148

African cultures: and Afro-Latin heritage, 12, 83–84; and *mestizaje,* 241

Alberdi, Juan Bautista, 121

Alienation: capitalism, socialism, and, 106; and dogmatism, 51; and feminine sexuality, 226–28; Freire on, 146; Gutiérrez on, 153; Marxist analysis of, 156; Ramos on, 81–82, 102; Salazar on, 101, 106; and self-consciousness, 130

Allende, Salvador, 166, 178

Alma matinal, El, 35, 36–39, 41–47, 48, 50

Alterity: dual use of, by Dussel, 188–89; and erasure or rejection of difference, 203–5; as ground for new absolute, in Dussel, 178–79, 180, 186–87, 190, 199–201; Kusch on, 191–93; as ground for sexual morality, in Dussel, 202–3; Roig on, 138–39; and service to the Other, 199–201

Amauta, 20, 27, 31, 33, 49, 59, 71

America: in Hegel's thought, 109–11; Mariátegui on Indo-Hispanic, 57–58, 60–64, 67–68, 70–71; Zea on meaning of, 90–91. *See also* Conquest; Conquest of America; Martí, José, and notion of *nuestra América*

América como conciencia, 87, 90–94

América Latina en sus ideas, 124

American, the: ontology of. *See* Kusch, Rodolfo

Analectics. *See* Dialectics

Anti-imperialism. *See* Imperialism

Apogeo y decadencia del positivismo en México, 87–88

APRA (Alianza Popular Revolucionaria Americana), 23, 62

Ardao, Arturo, 124

Ardiles, Osvaldo, 176, 177, 193, 195, 199; on Latin American philosophy, 197–98; on modernity and imperialism, 185–86, 197; on national project, 183, 184–86; and rejection of Argentine philosophy, 186

Argentina. *See* Alberdi, Juan Bautista; Ardiles, Osvaldo; Aricó, José; Cerutti, Horacio; Dussel, Enrique; Human rights; Kusch, Rodolfo; Madres de la Plaza de Mayo; Participatory models of feminist social change; Peronism; Philosophy of liberation, origins of; Roig, Arturo; Sarmiento, Domingo; Women's Studies

Argentine Anti-Communist Alliance, 175

Aricó, José, 19, 25

Ariel, 129